HUSTLER:
THE
CLINTON
LEGACY

by Joe Sobran

selected and edited by
Tom McPherren

Griffin Communications
Vienna, Virginia

The following essays are reprinted with permission from *The Wanderer:* "The Devil's Own"; "Legacy"; "The Sad Bomber"; "Balkan Bill"; "Chinese Shadows"; "Idle Thoughts"; "The Dysfunctional Clintons"; "Endgame"; "The Moral Mafia"; and "Clinton the Klutz."

The following essays are reprinted with permission from *SOBRAN'S: The Real News of the Month:* "Clinton without Sex"; "Majority Rule"; "The Well-Adjusted President"; "Clinton's America"; "True Colors"; "Bill of the Balkans"; "The Bombs of August"; "Two Liars"; "Billy Con"; "The Flying Clintons"; "The Secret Settlement"; "The Clinton Scandals"; "Near-Victims"; "The X-Rated Presidency"; "The Trash Team"; "Entrippment"; "Impeachment Politics"; "The Framers versus Clinton"; "Raising McCain"; and "Where Did the Left Go?"

"Power and Betrayal: The Clinton Legacy" is reprinted with permission of The Vere Company.

All other essays are reprinted with permission of Universal Press Syndicate.

Griffin Communications
P.O. Box 1383
Vienna, Virginia 22183

Library of Congress
Catalog Card Number: 00–134950

To the woman who knows him best:
Jane Doe

TABLE OF CONTENTS

CHAPTER 4 ▪ THE POLITICAL HOUDINI

CHAPTER 5 ▪ MR. AND MRS.

CHAPTER 6 ▪ CLINTON AND PAULA JONES

Editor's Appreciation

As a history-minded man of strong opinions, I sometimes read books about historical figures whom I respect written by historians whom I don't. That experience always has the iron flavor of duty. It was just the opposite with friend Joe's book on the man Clinton. Editing this book, though a professional undertaking and not a reading for pleasure, turned out to be a pleasure all the same.

True, it was one of those horrible pleasures, like reading Suetonius on the twelve Caesars. And let me say it plain: in this book, Joe emerges as our Suetonius, even though he had only one Caesar to write about. (One was plenty.) Though Bill Clinton hasn't yet emulated his Roman predecessors by turning into a god — the ravings of his courtiers notwithstanding — he is fast turning into a historical figure. We all owe thanks to Joe, our man of respect, for turning himself into a historian of the unrespectable.

I'm grateful to Joe's publisher, Fran Griffin of Griffin Communications, for recruiting me as editor. It was an honor I'll cherish forever. It was quite an experience, too. Though reading Joe on Clinton was a pleasure, putting together any book is, well, *work.* Fran started building the book before I even arrived on the construction site, and she stayed right there to help with the heavy lifting. Both of us now have — how shall I put this? — a far richer and more profound understanding of what's involved in putting a major book together than we had when we started.

Our understanding would be richer still had Ronald Neff, master proofreader, not been there to protect us from ourselves, so thanks be to Neff, him of the eagle eye, and honored practitioner of a precious art that is going the way of stone carving as our culture of literacy fades away.

Readers know how useful a good index is, but they may not know just how daunting a task indexing is. For that matter, lassoing a talented, trustworthy indexer can itself be daunting. Susan A. Neff, intrepid indexer, saved Fran and me from all manner of dauntishness. Thanks, Sue.

We also owe a tip of the hat to St. Martin De Porres Print Shop, of New Hope, Kentucky, our loyal and patient typesetter.

Finally, I thank Ann Coulter, herself a courageous dissident and honored chronicler of the Clinton Time, for putting Joe's perspective into perspective in her perspicacious Foreword.

Tom McPherren
June 2000

Foreword

I've been putting off writing this foreword more than I usually put off writing (which is quite a bit, now that I'm making my living as a writer) because I can't bear the idea of my prose next to the prose of Joe Sobran. He is the master. Especially on Bill Clinton. I hear he's good on Shakespeare, but really Clinton is his muse. Every once in a while, I think I'm a reasonably competent writer. And then I read a Sobran column.

Mere hours after the breaking of the "cigar story" (as we delicately refer to it), talk-radio hosts everywhere were quoting Sobran's observation, "I thought President Clinton was trying to *discourage* young people from using tobacco products." Joe has mused that the only question about indicting the president is whether he can be tried as an adult. He remarked that if Ted Kennedy had been Clinton, Mary Jo Kopechne would be a stalker. Around the time *Hustler* publisher Larry Flynt sprang into action in behalf of the president, Joe called me to say, "When you're being defended by the likes of Alan Dershowitz, Larry Flynt, and Geraldo Rivera, a conviction is really superfluous."

Sobran is the only writer whose columns consistently leave me thinking to myself, *Why didn't I say that?* Sometimes I did say it. He had so many excellent one-liners on Clinton, he could afford to give me a few, gratis. (If you read it closely, you'll notice that Joe is the only person I cite in my book *High Crimes and Misdemeanors* for a turn of phrase, rather than for some factual point.)

Clinton was breathtakingly, symphonically perfect for Joe. To paraphrase Joe (speaking of Jay Leno), it almost makes you wonder whether he put Clinton up to it. On the one hand, Clinton has become the crucible for every significant cultural battle since the end of the Cold War. But on the other hand, he's just a horny hick. Perfect.

The end-of-impeachment news stories all included the surreal premise that the Clinton scandal was limited to Clinton. We'd all get back to the work of the American people, Clinton would serve out his term, and that was that. I rather doubt it. Clinton isn't going away any more than did the Alger Hiss–Whittaker Chambers dispute, the McCarthy hearings, the Vietnam War, or — though this may be too recent to be sure about — the Bork nomination battle.

As a cultural prism, Clinton is, most obviously, the avatar of the sexual revolution. He's "good on women's issues" because he is for abortion, while he treats actual women like dogs.

In the battle of the generations, Clinton represents the self-righteous, hubristic, war-protesting baby boomers. In this generational battle, however, it was not Bob Dole's World War II generation manning the phalanxes on the other side, but the Generation X-ers. We had learned from our elders. Using civil rights law, constitutional law, and the Internet — and a healthy lack of respect for "authority" — Paula Jones, her attorneys, and Matt Drudge are the ones who exposed this lip-biting pervert for what he was. It wasn't Bob Dole impotently crooning, "Where's the outrage!"

Still, somehow the media has taken to suggesting that the "Vast Right-Wing Conspiracy" is composed of the likes of Pat Robertson, Newt Gingrich, and Jerry Falwell. I'm sure those fellows are very good at what they do, and I wish them well, but I don't recall their drafting legal pleadings, taking any depositions, or hitting the "send" button on breaking Internet reports.

It was a Small, Intricately Knit Right-Wing Conspiracy, anyway. And all we needed were courts of law and computers. Frankly, we were getting a little tired of hearing about the "greatest generation" or whatever those self-congratulatory boomers had anointed themselves.

Clinton even embodies the long-standing law-school brawl over whether the law is an engine of equality or a weapon. If the law were an abstract set of principles before which all people are equal, the feminists should have been tickled pink to have caught a live one in their sexual-harassment net. Alas, they were not.

Suddenly the female accusers were all trailer-park trash who were probably asking for it. It seems that sometimes women do make these things up, the feminists now admitted. More than that, though. Sometimes — the feminists now instructed us — whole armies of women would lyingly accuse the same man.

They should have thought of that before writing the rules.

Legal inquiries into consensual workplace affairs — inquiries that had always been allowed in sexual-harassment cases — were now deemed dangerous and unprecedented witch-hunts. As Joe has summarized the new state of the law: when a Republican stands accused, it's "sexual harassment"; when a Democrat stands accused, it's a "witch-hunt."

"Barbara Battalino!" became the battle cry for conservatives, but not because she was admirable. Quite the opposite. Battalino had performed "a certain type of sex" (as Paula Jones called it) on a client and then perjured herself about it. But she went to prison. The point was, if that's what happens to little powerless people such as Barbara Battalino who perjure themselves "just about sex," then that's what is supposed to happen to the most powerful man in the country when he perjures himself about sex. That's what the rule of law means.

The Independent Counsel law has also gone the way of perjury and sexual harassment. It was one thing when low-level officials in Republican administrations were being investigated by independent counsels with unlimited time, resources, and authority. When the law was used to catch a Democrat, well, that was different.

The funny thing is, Clinton is the precise reason you want to have an Independent Counsel statute. Not because he's a Democrat, but because: (1) he's president, and (2) he's a criminal. The whole idea behind the law was that the attorney general could not be relied upon to perform a credible criminal investigation of her boss, the president. Everyone forgets that, and the reason is, the law was written so broadly and was so easily triggered that it quickly came to resemble nothing so much as a way to harass low-level presidential appointees. Catching criminals in high places was the putative reason it was written. But when it came to Clinton, the putative reason became the pretend reason.

A lot of conservatives had long opposed the law for constitutional reasons — reasons a liberal couldn't explain if his life depended on it. They still oppose it. But Democrats might as well join with the feminists in admitting that when they voted for the law, what they meant was that it was supposed to be used only as a weapon against *Republicans.*

If only Clinton were caught using the "N-word," we'd find out they were joking about that, too. Then there would be no taboos left at all.

Who would have thought the twentieth century's cultural prism would end up being some Elmer Gantry who cares about no one and nothing so much as getting laid? What luck! From the moment the Monica Lewinsky scandal broke, Joe and I couldn't decide whether we wanted the man impeached and removed immediately, or given a third term.

It took the Senate acquittal to turn me into a deeply, pathetically despondent mess. The day of the acquittal was the one day I remember being the most depressed about the country since the scandal broke. For the next few weeks, Joe would call every couple of days claiming he thought he might have located a silver lining, but always recommending that I call back quickly before he forgot what it was.

Well, now I have it — here it is; this is the silver lining. The country may not care about honor, the "rule of law" is a joke, and the only removable offense is being a Republican, but at least we got Joe's book out of it.

Ann Coulter

Introduction

A s Bill Clinton's impeachment trial drew toward an end, the word "closure" was often and hopefully invoked. Most Americans hoped the result would be at least some kind of resolution of the bitter controversy.

Expressing vague contrition (again) after his acquittal — an outcome he owed to the bitter and obdurate partisanship of the Democrats, to the timidity of the Republicans, and to his own rancorous smear campaign against his opponents — Clinton himself spoke of "forgiveness" and "reconciliation." Then he set about with a flurry of activity to bury the memory of his scandals: reforming Social Security, visiting Mexico, threatening to bomb Kosovo, promoting the idea of his wife's running for a New York Senate seat.

But scandal wouldn't go away. The lurking story of his alleged rape of an Arkansas woman in 1978, when he was state attorney general, burst onto the front pages. While Clinton's defenders took the skeptical attitude they usually adopt when an accusation surfaces, the woman offered a telling detail. In 1991, she said, Clinton approached her and tried to mollify her with the words: "Can you ever forgive me? I'm not the same man I used to be." She said she replied: "You just go to hell."

Simulated remorse has been a constant in the Clinton scandals: whenever he can't deny the facts, he feigns repentance and reformation. This worked for him in 1992, when he nebulously admitted he'd "caused pain in my marriage," to 1998, when he nebulously retracted his seven-month lie about "that woman, Miss Lewinsky" in the name of defending and repairing "my family life." Whether lying or pretending to repent, Clinton has made a point of exhibiting piety and dedication to his family.

Juanita Broaddrick, the woman who said Clinton had raped her, presented a touching contrast to Clinton's brazenness. When NBC's Lisa Myers asked why she had never before gone public with her story, the rather dowdy middle-aged woman tearfully explained that she had held it back for more than twenty years because she feared that "nobody in the world would believe me." The interview was punctuated with brief clips of a young Bill Clinton, his curly hair falling over his ears in the style of the late Seventies, already jaunty in his confidence that the world would believe anything he said. For some, the truth is painful to speak; for others, lies come all too easily.

As usual, Clinton had his defenders, ever ready to question the veracity of women telling their dark stories: Geraldo Rivera, Jerry Spence, Alan Dershowitz, Eleanor Smeal, Eleanor Clift. But Mrs. Broaddrick was describing the same man we had come to know from earlier stories: the cocky sexual aggressor who relied on the power of his office both to serve his appetites and to conceal his crimes, and who could also adopt the pose of remorse, when necessary, with smooth facility.

Even Clinton's defenders didn't argue that rape was beneath his character. Instead, they vaguely suggested that Mrs. Broaddrick's delay in making the charge meant that any woman could dredge up old stories for the purpose of discrediting him. But it's not as if we might believe such stories if they were told of anyone but Clinton; no other president has been both impeached and accused of rape. If any previous president had been charged with sexual assault, the story would have been deemed too bizarre to merit coverage; in Clinton's case, the charge was only too plausible.

Questioned about Mrs. Broaddrick's charge, Clinton's own vice president, Al Gore, far from doubting its truth, merely said Clinton should be forgiven for "mistakes in his personal life." It was perhaps the most revealing remark about Clinton to emanate from the closed circle of his sycophants.

In a short, the American public was meeting the very man the feminists had denounced for years: the powerful and respectable-seeming sexual predator — a white male, of course — who took ruthless advantage of vulnerable women. The catch was that this particular predator was a man who had won the hearts of feminists by being "good on women's issues," chiefly abortion, while his prey weren't always the kind of victims the feminists had in mind. So, in a crazy role-reversal, feminists defended Clinton against the women who accused him, expressing skepticism about the accusers themselves. Hillary Clinton herself, who had praised Anita Hill for charging Clarence Thomas with no more than vulgar language, resolutely stood by her man.

It was a situation only Bill Clinton could have created. He had told too many glib and audacious lies. He had broken too many rules — and laws. He had abused his offices in too many ways, of which procuring and exploiting women was only one. He had acted as if he could talk and maneuver his way out of any jam he got himself into. And in doing these things, he had made too many enemies, of whom the deadliest proved to be a simple woman named Paula Jones.

The twentieth century has been the age of equal opportunity, chiefly in politics. With the general abolition of hereditary monarchy and the rise of popular government, power has been available to anyone with the ambition and skill to seize it. Never before have so many rulers seemed to rise from nowhere: Lenin, Trotsky, Mussolini, Stalin, Hitler, Mao, Juan Peron, Fidel Castro, Ho Chi Minh, Pol Pot, and other unpedigreed men of the people (many of whom were known by adopted names) who had in common only the hunger for power and a brilliance in improvising.

William Jefferson Clinton (born William Jefferson Blythe), an almost comical American version of the type, is far from the worst. He has no taste for mass murder, though certain inconvenient individuals in his life have suffered convenient accidents. He hasn't wrought anything approaching the damage Franklin Roosevelt inflicted on the Constitution, not to mention world war. He has been considerably less destructive than Lyndon Johnson.

Clinton's chief accomplishment has been to bring a new level of degeneracy to the presidency. In forcing his party to defend him against removal from office, he has also exposed the cynicism of Washington and much of the country beyond the Beltway. American politics is no longer a debate about principles; it's a quarrel about booty. The struggle over abortion, likewise, is not a debate about embryology; some people really don't object to the taking of innocent life, regardless of whether it is "fully human." Those who aren't disturbed by abortion — even the cruelest late-term abortion, requiring the extraction of the child's brain in the birth canal — are beyond any moral appeal, and Clinton's adamant support for abortion under all circumstances (while saying it should be "safe, legal — and rare") is the chief reason feminists and liberals continue to defend him.

Barring some unforeseeable calamity, this will be Clinton's legacy: cynicism, in the sense of sheer indifference to evil — to lying, corruption, and cruelty. A president's "legacy" is usually thought of as a permanent cost imposed on the country: if not a war, then a legislative "program" that becomes an irremovable feature of every annual budget. The Clintons tried to pass such a program in the form of national health care, but failed, even when the Democrats controlled both houses of Congress. We should note that the word "program" appears nowhere in the Constitution, and federal entitlement programs are all unconstitutional; but of course nobody, including conservative Republicans, raised this objection during the debate. The Clintons' pet proposal was defeated anyway.

Of course Bill Clinton has never thought of himself as cynical. Like most politicians who, with vicarious generosity, take credit for benefits paid for by others' taxes, he thinks of himself as a benefactor. The necessary role of force and extortion in government-provided benefits, which inevitably require some people to support others, never troubles him. As far as he is concerned, his own good will is the source of those benefits, and a "legacy" would mean his being honored by history for having arranged them. But he has proved a failure when it comes to ambitious legislation, and with his enemies controlling Congress for the remainder of his presidency he is likely to remain so.

Instead, he will be remembered for things he never meant to happen. As a result of a magazine article about his use of Arkansas state troopers to procure women for him, he was sued by Paula Jones over an incident he thought he had concealed; the Supreme Court ruled that Mrs. Jones could prosecute her suit during his presidency; her lawyers learned that he was conducting an affair with a White House intern; he denied it under oath, and encouraged the intern to lie too; the story broke into the media; he lied repeatedly for seven months, involving everyone around him in the lie; and he was impeached for perjury and obstruction.

Clinton could and should have been removed from office just for the measures he took to conceal the acts for which he was formally impeached. He not only lied to the public; through his surrogates he spread slanders against the special prosecutor and Republican members of the House Judiciary Committee. But in all this his fellow Democrats in Congress acted as his accomplices, and they were determined to acquit him no matter what he had done. His success in turning opinion polls in his favor encouraged the Democrats to ignore and belittle his guilt, while affecting to deem his conduct "reprehensible."

In the end the Republicans were routed; Clinton said that the Constitution had been "re-ratified" by his acquittal. It was vintage Clinton: effrontery in the guise of modesty.

He is a fascinating, maddening, and perplexing character, forever adopting genial and earnest poses in public while seeming to have no inner life. Privately he is said to have a furious temper, carefully concealed from the public eye; we get intimations of his vindictive streak through such hatchet men as James Carville and Sidney Blumenthal. But though Clinton is the most voluble of men, with superficially appropriate words for every occasion, he has no eloquence, no words that seem to come from the "real" Clinton. Everything he says is measured solely for its effect on others; nothing he says is remembered, unless in irony. "I didn't inhale"; "I feel your pain"; "The era of big government is over"; "I did not have sexual relations with that woman."

It's not his lies alone that make Clinton so exasperating; it's the posturing — the lip-biting, the finger-wagging, the Bible-quoting — that accompanies them. No matter how often the lies are exposed, he is soon back at it, his voice cracking with sincerity, like a clever kid who thinks he can snow the grownups by laying it on good and thick. To observe him for any length of time is to have your intelligence insulted early and often. No matter how low your opinion of him, sooner or later you find you've overestimated him.

We now know that before he realized there was physical evidence (on the fatal cocktail dress) refuting his denial of sexual relations with "that woman," Clinton was secretly circulating the heartless lie that Monica Lewinsky was a "stalker" who had tried unsuccessfully to seduce him — this, after leading her to believe he might marry her after leaving office. Poor, deluded Monica, in the middle of her own troubles, was still trying to protect him while he was trying to destroy her in order to save himself, treacherously using the power of the presidency against her.

Never mind adultery, perjury, high crimes and misdemeanors: human behavior just doesn't get any more rotten than that. Move over, Iago.

I have studied Clinton as a character since the 1992 Democratic primaries, when he seemed oddly difficult to get a handle on. He was hailed as a "new Democrat," without the leftist thrust typical of the party since the McGovern era, but that label didn't really capture him; he was verbally agile, adroitly mixing liberal and conservative shibboleths to widen his appeal without defining himself.

At first, like most Beltway-based commentators, I paid little attention to the dark rumors emanating from Arkansas concerning drug smuggling and even murder. Such rumors are hard to evaluate, though they seem more plausible today than in 1992, when one still assumed that a sort of invisible hand would prevent a low criminal from approaching the White House. Even now my focus is on Clinton's character as it discloses itself in the less-disputed facts of his personal and public conduct.

The columns in this book trace the gradual unfolding of Clinton's character during his presidency, up to the moment of his acquittal. He has appeared successively as a rather bland enigma, a comic rogue, a sexual adventurer, and finally a sinister criminal of remarkable audacity. I'm still amazed that he hasn't tripped himself up along the way; that he has dared, time and again, to use one crime to conceal another; and that he has judged his public so well at every crucial step. Even with due credit to his resilience and tenacity, which have enabled him to recover from blunders no other man could have survived, his may be the most unedifying success story in American history.

Clinton has finally defined himself. By surviving the attempt to remove him from the office he has so filthily disgraced, he also defines our age. It says more about us than about him that he stands condoned.

Joe Sobran

Prologue

Power and Betrayal: The Clinton Legacy

This article was first presented as a lecture by Joe Sobran at the Third Anniversary Celebration of SOBRAN'S, *November 15, 1997. Its original title was "Two Types of Treason."*

My earliest memories date back to what is now called the McCarthy Era, though I didn't pay any attention to politics while it was going on. I don't even remember noticing McCarthy's death forty years ago, when I was eleven. I do remember my mother despising Richard Nixon for having said that Helen Gahagan Douglas was "soft on Communism." My secret reaction was to wonder whether Mrs. Douglas *was* soft on Communism, but I didn't dare ask.

In those days I had a single, simple idea of treason. It meant consciously betraying someone you owed loyalty to, especially your country. The spy, the turncoat, the foreign agent — Benedict Arnold was the model traitor, as I learned in school. He'd just plain lied about which side he was on. That was what I understood as the essence of treason.

Later I'd add the Rosenbergs and Alger Hiss to the list, as well as anyone who belonged to the Communist Party. Nobody I knew doubted that Communism was just plain evil. If they thought otherwise, I never had an inkling of it. Communism and treason were synonyms.

I couldn't imagine why anyone would commit treason or become a Communist. It didn't even occur to me to ask. The world was full of odd things and people: the giraffe, the platypus, the skunk, and the traitor. They were all part of the variety of creation, and they didn't seem to me to call for an explanation.

As I got older, I met more liberals, and by the Sixties, which began during my teens, liberalism was even fashionable. For a while I considered myself a liberal, though it went without saying that that didn't imply any sympathy with Communism. Being liberal meant being anti-Communist. So I thought.

But by then more and more liberals, for some reason, spoke of anti-Communism with derision. I couldn't understand this. It drove me nuts. They ridiculed anti-Communism without explaining why, and without being willing to commit themselves about Communism. They regarded McCarthyism as a terrible thing, but not Communism. It was worse than that. They implied that it was a mortal sin to *call* someone a Communist, but not such a serious sin to *be* a Communist. In fact their tone began to suggest that Communism was a sign of "idealism," and that the real victims of McCarthyism weren't the innocent liberals who were falsely accused of being Communists, but the actual Communists who had been identified as such.

To me that meant that McCarthy was essentially right. And probably Nixon too.

I never did meet many real Communists. As far as I know, none — I'm sure I'd have remembered! But I did meet countless liberals.

I don't think I'd have really minded an out-and-out Communist who admitted being one. But the liberals who equivocated about it, jeering at anti-Communism while never declaring themselves, affecting a superior irony to the most basic moral challenge of modern politics — them I despised.

Actually, I did see a flesh-and-blood Communist once. One evening in the early Eighties, when I lived in New Jersey, I was dining with my three kids in a popular diner on Nassau Street across from Princeton University. A few tables away I noticed a familiar face, that of a man sitting with a couple of other men. Where had I seen him before?

Suddenly I remembered! It was Gus Hall, head of the American Communist Party! He was speaking at Princeton that night! There were posters all over town, and I'd nearly forgotten.

I had to tell my kids. I'd raised them, of course, to understand that Communism was evil. But there was one problem. I was always pulling their little legs. By then they were used to my tall tales. If I even cracked a smile while I told them we were sitting near the top Communist in the United States, they'd think it was another of my jokes! After all, if he was a real Communist, it wouldn't be a laughing matter.

So it was absolutely imperative to tell them with a straight face. In a low voice I said: "Kids, don't look now, but that man over there is the head of the Communist Party in this country."

All three of them gave me a searching look. Was this a gag? The top Communist in the *whole United States*? The skepticism on their faces was too much for me. It destroyed my composure. I started giggling. "Oh, sure, Dad!" The harder I laughed, the surer they were that I was kidding again. I was the Dad Who Cried Wolf.

I finally stopped laughing and explained that the only reason I'd laughed was that I knew they wouldn't believe me. I kept my voice down so as not to offend Mr. Hall, even if he was still defending Stalin's good name after all those years. Finally they were willing to give me a chance to prove my case. So when we left the diner I showed them the posters. It was tough going, but I eventually succeeded in proving to their satisfaction that Gus Hall was a Communist. I began to understand what Joe McCarthy had gone through.

That night I even went to hear Hall speak. He drew an audience of about a hundred who fitted comfortably into a large classroom. The Princeton kids asked him tough questions and jeered at some of his answers, such as "A lot of the things Stalin did were necessary." I had to admire the nerve it took to say that. But for the most part, he was rather disappointing. Most of his talk sounded less like Lenin than like an op-ed piece in the *New York Times*. At the end of the evening the students gave him a thunderous ovation.

Anyway, that was my closest encounter with an actual Communist.

No doubt there are plenty of people who become traitors for the simplest of reasons: thirty pieces of silver will do. And there are others who find some foreign government to their liking and become its secret operatives. But these are unusual, extreme, and rather melodramatic cases.

In one sense, the liberals had a point about McCarthy: he trafficked in melodrama. He made Communism sound more lurid than it was. He reduced it to spies and intrigue. In a way he trivialized it, as some of the honest and truly anti-Communist liberals charged.

But McCarthy's real sin was a sin of omission. He fingered a lot of

Communist and pro-Communist small fry who had wormed into the government during the Roosevelt administration, but he never dared to finger the real villain: Franklin Roosevelt himself. That would have taken more guts than Joe McCarthy, or the entire U.S. Marine Corps, had.

I won't bore you by repeating a point I've made so many times in the past, but Franklin Roosevelt was the best friend Stalin and the Soviet Union ever had. When I think of him, I almost pity Alger Hiss for taking the rap. I suspect that in his own mind Hiss wasn't really a traitor. He was just doing what he thought the boss would have approved of, if he hadn't been under political constraints. Roosevelt had to worry about what the reactionaries would say; Hiss could discreetly ignore all that. But Hiss, like Roosevelt, saw the Soviets as the allies of the progressive forces in this country, and for both of them that was what really counted.

And Roosevelt? Was he a conscious traitor? I don't think so.

I think he felt it was his sovereign prerogative to redefine the nature of American society. Centralizing power, soaking the rich, interpreting the Constitution to suit himself — he saw nothing wrong with any of this. He was like his sometime friend Joe Kennedy, in a way: Kennedy didn't think he was betraying his wife and children with his constant adulteries. He even brought his mistress for Thanksgiving dinner with the family.

The most common kind of treason doesn't even think of itself as treason. Roosevelt lied a lot, but he could have done most of what he did without actually lying, in the crude sense of stating facts he knew to be false. He didn't actually have to break the law, either, though he did that too when he gave secret aid to the British and the Soviets. His actual lies and crimes were only conveniences. The real trouble went deeper.

As I say, the other kind of traitor is somewhat opaque: the man who consciously works for the defeat of the side he pretends to be on. It's hard for most of us to understand that guy. But I think we can understand Roosevelt's kind more easily. He's a common modern type.

As a Catholic, I've known many Catholics, including priests, who behave like the political liberals I described earlier. They adopt an undefined tone of derision toward the dogmatic and the traditional, but you can never really pin them down. In time you realize that they don't believe in anything. But they aren't honest enough to leave the Church. You can respect the overt atheist who says he just doesn't believe in this hocus-pocus. But the character who will neither affirm nor deny, yet insists on being regarded as a good Catholic and resents having his orthodoxy impeached even as he sneers at orthodoxy and works to destroy it — he's a problem. He's *the* problem.

That type of person is the problem for Catholics, for Protestants, for Jews. Maybe it's only my limited experience, but I can't imagine a Muslim or Eastern Orthodox version of the type; these faiths seem to be too rigid and vigorous to permit much in the way of devious ambiguity. But the Western religions are plagued by it. So is Western politics.

I don't know whether it's entirely fair to identify this style with liberalism. But people of this disposition usually find liberalism a convenient ideological cover for what they do. They have a deep aversion to simple definition. They are fond of rhetorical questions that begin: "Who is to say ...?" Who is to say what obscenity is? Who is to say when life begins? Who is to say what is "normal" in sexual behavior? (The word "normal" is always enclosed in quotation marks.)

One of the many reasons that I adore Shakespeare is that he shows us a world of norms. Even his villains usually realize they are abnormal, and they know that abnormal means evil. They are fully conscious of their own envy: envy was still recognized as a sin by all sides during the Reformation. Envy meant malice, spite, the hatred of the good.

Shakespeare knows that man is seriously flawed and that envy is a grave temptation for all of us. In our time we profess to believe that people are basically good and we no longer recognize envy as a capital sin, though we are dimly aware of it as a reality. We speak obsessively of "hate," but the hate we refer to is only a certain kind of social prejudice: hatred of racial minorities, and so forth. It seems to be a temptation chiefly for white Christian heterosexual males, and the remedy for it is to give the government more power to supervise everyone's associations and even motives.

Our moral map is actually much cruder than Shakespeare's. No subtlety escapes him. But *our* moral map leaves large areas of human motivation uncharted. We are constantly reminded of the hatred of whites for blacks, men for women, Christians for Jews, heterosexuals for homosexuals, majorities for minorities, natives for foreigners, believers for nonbelievers. We have a whole lexicon of cant words: racism, sexism, anti-Semitism, nativism, ethnocentrism, fundamentalism, McCarthyism, xenophobia, even homophobia. These words are like an array of artillery, all aimed in the same general direction.

While these hostilities are emphasized, exaggerated, and even legislated against, we never hear about hostilities in the other direction. Aren't they real too? Just as a matter of simple realism, you might expect a minority to feel a certain amount of spite toward a majority. After all, if a minority has been excluded, it's bound to feel a resentment that the majority never has any reason to feel. If the majority regards itself as morally, intellectually, and esthetically superior, even if this attitude is unconscious, the minority is likely to feel a certain humiliation, and nothing breeds more hatred than humiliation. Who has to think about height all the time? The six-footer or the dwarf?

Envy, being the hatred for the superior, is the sin of those who feel inferior. It's the sin of pride in defeat. And I don't suggest that it's somehow peculiar to social minorities. We all feel it in some situations. We all know humiliation. But our "moral map," as I call it, doesn't make room for this universal reality. And when a sin is unnamed, it goes unrecognized and uncontrolled.

A few years ago, when I noticed that words like "nativism" have no counterparts on the other side of the equation, I coined the word "alienism" to fill the gap. I wish I could think of a better one, but that one will still have to do. We have reached a point where alienation and envy have actually become normalized and idealized, especially when they occur among social minorities.

And notice what has happened to the word "minorities." It used to refer to pretty clearly distinct social groups who were less numerous than the dominant group. Now it has become a moral category of sorts. Homosexuals, for example, are no longer perverts or deviants; they are a "minority" in a morally positive sense. Whether their conduct is normal is a forbidden question. (Who is to say what is "normal"?) The only question permitted in public life is whether they are "discriminated against," and to ask this question is already to answer it. Of course they are! And the government should protect them!

Take Shakespeare again. His plays are full of alienated characters — and they are usually villains. Richard the hunchback, Shylock the Jew, Edmund the bastard, and Iago the officer who is passed over for promotion — they all have real grievances, and Shakespeare lets them speak their piece so eloquently that we sometimes sympathize with them. But their alienation, he leaves no doubt, is a threat to normal life, the good and healthy life as he conceives it, and as we all recognize it. Shakespeare doesn't quibble at natural law with rhetorical questions. But his villains do.

But notice that even when his villains want power, they don't really want to change society. They only want to rule. The recent production of *Richard III* that showed Richard as a fascist profoundly misunderstood the play, and in fact the world. Killing children doesn't make you a fascist. (Nowadays it makes you a feminist.) Richard, Macbeth, and Claudius, the usurpers, have no program to "build a new society." They represent a different kind of evil from the revolutionary — a much less harmful form of evil, in fact. They leave most of normal life untouched. They kill only those relatively few people above them and hurt a few others incidentally. Their alienation is limited.

But modern politics is geared to the alienated. The modern state has to police more and more of our lives, because it has set itself against the normal. It defines normal acquisition as greed, normal group preferences as bigotry, and normal morality as hate. Consequently it has to watch over us at all times to make sure we aren't too assertive about our normality, while it caters to our abnormalities.

Treason used to mean the subversion of the state. But the state itself now works the subversion of society. In other times, including Shakespeare's, it has been understood that the state's whole justification for existing is to support and protect normal life against the criminal, the savage, the perverse. Even tyrants never questioned this assumption.

But in our time the state itself is the seat of treason. What else can you call a state that treats abortion as a right, and assaults even small schoolchildren with propaganda that teaches them that sodomy is good? The public school has become the equivalent of a Communist reeducation camp, where moral reality is inverted.

Franklin Roosevelt only catered to the economic parasite. To that extent he was an enemy of the normal. But he never took it into his head to promote abortion and sodomy. Stalin himself never made homosexuality part of the Five-Year Plan.

I don't mean to suggest that the ultimate goal of the modern state is to turn us all into homosexuals. It's not that purposeful. But it is that normless.

The chief everyday business of the modern state is still theft — taking from some for the benefit of others in the name of "social justice." Bribery is always part of government, and in a democracy that includes bribing the voters. The free and spontaneous arrangements we want to make with our own wealth have to be condemned as unjust; President Clinton recently said it was "selfish" of Virginians to object to the state's car tax. This is the fundamental principle of statism: it equates compassion and generosity with the amount of wealth claimed by the state, while equating selfishness and greed with the amount the state can't get its claws into. At a minimum, the state panders to those who both resent other people's money and want it for themselves.

Shallow philosophers pose the question "Liberty or Equality?" as if it were a conundrum. As a practical matter, those who want power always favor equality. And by equality they don't mean equality in liberty, as Americans used to mean it; they mean equality at the expense of liberty. The state doesn't *recognize* people as equal; it professes to *make* them equal. That means it is hostile to any free society in which liberty produces the differences it inevitably produces.

After the 1994 elections that threw the Democrats out of power in Congress, President Clinton acknowledged that the people were alienated from the government. But the truth is that the government was alienated from the people. How can it profess to "represent" them when it is taking their earnings, policing all their activities, and trying to change their whole way of life? If a private individual did such things to you, you wouldn't say he "represented" you. You'd say he hated you.

More precisely, the government represents the alienated. Clinton himself is an odd case. He likes to present a moderate, even slightly conservative face to the electorate. He doesn't appear to be an especially alienated man. He seems right in his element, and happy to be there. It's his wife who seems to be the fanatic in the family.

And yet what do we make of his speaking last weekend to a gay and lesbian group, promising to see that their "rights" are secured? Was he just pandering again?

Maybe. I have no doubt he would turn against his gay supporters if he found it politically expedient. But that's what makes him interesting. Clinton has probably never committed treason in any legal sense. And yet absolutely nobody trusts him or takes his word for anything. He is the most notoriously slippery man ever to enter the White House, including any burglars who may have broken in. He has betrayed his wife and his old friends. In fact, betrayal has gotten him where he is today, and everyone knows it. His own party regards him as a treacherous man.

What a comment on democracy! I thought the original idea was that the people, allowed to choose their own leaders, would tend to elect the most honored and trusted men to the highest offices. We even saw this pathetic impulse, briefly, in the popular enthusiasm for Ross Perot and Colin Powell. Whether they deserved it is another question; but there's no doubt that millions of people were desperately eager to believe that a good man could be elected president. Americans really want to believe in their rulers.

But what kind of men do we keep getting? Roosevelt, Kennedy, Johnson, Nixon, and now Clinton. This is a problem that won't be corrected by statutory limits on campaign spending. There's something about our system that causes such men to rise to the top. We still have Jeffersons among us — men of quality and principle, even if they have their flaws — but they don't even go into politics now. What would they do there? What could they hope to achieve?

Betrayal isn't a rare phenomenon that occurs only at the margin of society. Often it happens right at the top. In fact this is where we should be most on our guard against it. The writings of the Founders, and their equally interesting opponents, are full of warnings about the dangers of power and tyranny. In plain terms, our rulers are our natural enemies. How many times do they have to prove it?

One of the most striking facts of the Clinton era is that the media have changed their posture toward government. During Republican administrations they prided themselves on being "adversarial" toward government, or at least toward the presidency. They were actually much less adversarial toward Congress, which was more liberal than the presidency in those days.

Now things are different. The media have become much less critical of the presidency and much more critical of Congress. The reason is obvious: they see the presidency as liberalism's last stronghold, while Congress has become relatively conservative.

Even more remarkable, the media have forsaken their posture of alienation and become patriotic. They accuse conservatives of being unpatriotic — the word they use is "anti-government." This is a little strange, since they used to describe the same conservatives as "superpatriotic."

The truth is that most conservatives used to support the government to a fault. They believe in certain functions of government, and they don't want it to exceed them. But now, of course, government not only usurps powers that don't belong to it, it fails in the functions most conservatives regard as legitimate. If they are alienated from the government, it's because the government has become the aggressive organ of the ideology I've called alienism.

Communism and all forms of utopian socialism have now failed economically. But this doesn't mean that the Left, including liberals, has accepted defeat. Far from it. In fact a genuine revolution is still under way.

The real revolution of our time isn't a socialist revolution. It's the sexual revolution. And Bill Clinton, for all his zigzagging on other issues, is a genuine sexual revolutionary.

He has consistently supported abortion, right up to the moment of birth. Since the media regard "partial-birth abortion" as a loaded term, let's call it birth-canal brain extraction. He is willing to fight for it. He has also supported the feminist agenda all the way. He had no objection to his former surgeon general, Joycelyn Elders's, call for teaching masturbation in school. He has been the first president to militate for gay rights. And in Catholic South America, his wife campaigned for contraception and abortion.

There has been a lot of talk about Clinton's "legacy," but I think everyone has missed his real legacy. He will be remembered as the Sex President. He is both advocate and exemplar of the sexual revolution that got into high gear during his formative years, the Sixties. He has lived it. I don't think it's wild speculation to surmise that he promotes it even now in large part as a way of justifying his own notoriously lecherous life.

Unlike John Kennedy, Clinton hasn't had to wait for posthumous revelations about his sex life. They have been front-page news since his candidacy in 1992. He appeared on *60 Minutes* with his wife to answer rumors about his adulteries. *The American Spectator* created a sensation with David Brock's report that he used state troopers to procure women. This gave rise to the sensational Paula Jones lawsuit. His former mistresses are now giving testimony about him. The press has even reported the alleged deformity of his private parts.

One unintended consequence of the sexual revolution is that Bill Clinton has lost — forfeited, really — the privacy and official dignity that all previous presidents have taken for granted. Nothing about him has been left to the imagination. The old taboos have fallen indeed! The old prudery, hangups, and Victorian inhibitions are gone! The First Amendment has triumphed — and it turns out to have some rather unexpected applications!

To say that the media favor Clinton is only part of the story.

When we say that, we mean the Ted Koppel–Tim Russert–David Brinkley issue-oriented media. We mustn't forget the pop culture sector of the media that isn't quite as interested in Bosnia, the Middle East peace process, and interest rates as in celebrity sex.

The panelists on *Washington Week in Review* may nod in solemn approval of the Clinton administration's policies. But in pop culture, Clinton has become nothing more than a hilarious butt, the horny hick who has somehow gotten into the the Oval Office. The presidency has become the Lincoln Bedroom farce.

Every night Jay Leno, David Letterman, and Conan O'Brien get their biggest laughs by joking about Clinton's sex life. If a sleazy night-club comic had ever joked about Eisenhower's sex life, he'd have been arrested. Lenny Bruce never dared make the kind of jokes that *Saturday Night Live* makes about Clinton. Welcome to the sexual revolution, Bill! Did we forget to mention that it includes dirty jokes about presidents who get caught playing around?

Last year, at a National Press Club dinner, Bill and Hillary had to sit in silence while the New York radio shock-jock Don Imus made a string of merciless jokes about Clinton's adulteries. It was all the worse because it wasn't funny. The audience's embarrassment was palpable. Henry VIII, no model husband himself, never had to go through that! But for all the subsequent controversy, the occasion was a net plus for Imus's career. He'd calculated correctly that he could get away with it, garnering a lot of publicity.

As far as I know, nobody has made the most obvious comment on all this: Clinton is, by far, beyond any comparison, the most humiliated public figure in American history. Clarence Thomas must sigh with relief that he's not Bill Clinton.

At a press conference, Carol Channing was once asked whether she remembered her most embarrassing moment. She answered: "Yes ... Next question?"

People don't forget humiliations. They may not talk about them, but they remember them. Given the power of pop culture nowadays, Clinton must realize — how can he help but realize? — that it's not his policy "achievements" that are defining his presidency, but his scandals, and especially his sexual scandals. People who couldn't find Bosnia with both hands know who Paula Jones is. The phrases "Arkansas state troopers" and "distinguishing characteristics" are to him what "expletive deleted" was to Nixon, only more so. *Much* more so.

He sought the presidency from boyhood, chasing women on the side, but he never bargained on this. He assumed that being president meant being respected by everyone. Isn't that pretty much the whole point? The pomp and dignity of the nation's highest office! Hail to the Chief! The successor to Washington, Jefferson, and Lincoln! He wasn't just going to be president — he was going to be a *great* president. Was there room for another face on Mount Rushmore?

It hasn't quite worked out that way. We already forget just how drastically Bill Clinton has changed the image of the presidency in just five years. Oh, how he has changed it — from Pennsylvania Avenue to Tobacco Road.

"Image" is a word from the Kennedy era. It suggests an aura of glamour that is notably lacking in the Clinton era. Even the dirt about Jack Kennedy links him to glamorous women, including Marilyn Monroe. Clinton is linked to the likes of Gennifer Flowers, and to a failed pass at Paula Jones which, by her account, says little for his savoir-faire.

At least Nixon could say, "I am not a crook" and complain that the press was "wallowing in Watergate." Poor Clinton can't even protest the treatment he's getting. He can't say, "I am not an adulterer." He can't afford to show that being the Dirty-Joke-in-Chief is bothering him. He just has to pretend he doesn't notice. He notices!

And he has brought it on himself. He can't turn back. There is no way out. I doubt that impeachment could rival the scalding humiliation he endures every day. It's almost unimaginable.

When Paula Jones filed suit, he couldn't admit he remembered her. He remembered! He hired the toughest lawyer in Washington and did everything he could to smear her. This isn't the way a president of the United States would respond to a lie by a little nobody. His attempts to settle out of court with a large cash payment and a statement attesting her good character, with typical Clintonian equivocation, don't exactly help refute her story.

Clinton has had his defenders in the press, but there is one defense none of them has dared to attempt: "Oh, he's not the type of man who would do a thing like that!" He's *exactly* the type. If a woman had accused Jimmy Carter of such a thing, nobody would have paid any attention. (If Carter had *admitted* doing it, we'd have had trouble believing him.)

So what does Clinton do? Does he discreetly steer away from sexual issues? No! He addresses a gay rights banquet and pledges his full support! He draws analogies between the gay rights movement and the abolitionist movement, the feminist movement, the civil rights movement. He talks about sodomy in the accents of Abraham Lincoln and Martin Luther King.

Why? Of course homosexuals are big donors to the Democratic Party now, but Clinton hardly needs the money. I think he has another motive. I think he feels he has to see the sexual revolution through to the bitter end. And I think he feels a deep empathy for his fellow deviants, even if his tastes differ somewhat from theirs. When he's among gays and lesbians, he's among people who don't laugh at him or look down on him. To them he's not just a risible white-trash parody of Jack Kennedy's secret life, the Arkansas cousin of Larry Flynt and Jimmy Swaggart. He's a moral leader! They admire him without irony! They make him feel the way he always thought a president would always feel!

Moral squalor, like misery, loves company. If Clinton can help to normalize even sexual perversion, if he can drag the whole country down to his own level, maybe, he reasons, his own conduct won't look so bad in retrospect. Like Fidel Castro, he may feel that history will absolve him. He envisions a future America, fully "liberated" about sex, in which his ordeal will be recalled with indulgence. He will be honored as a hero and martyr of the sexual revolution — the president who made it official that sexual freedom is a human right!

Is this Clinton's hidden agenda? I think so. Under the lofty rhetoric of "rights" we often find less edifying concerns.

Consider another pillar of the sexual revolution: Alfred Kinsey, author of the famed *Kinsey Report*. Kinsey taught educated Americans that all sorts of sexual practices — of which homosexuality was only one — were actually far more widespread than anyone had suspected. He said this in dry prose, backed up by a mountain of impressive statistics, complete with decimal points. In matters of sex, Kinsey was the very voice of disinterested science. And the result of his "findings" was to change American attitudes toward sexual morality, even though there is no logical connection between how people behave and how they ought to behave. His work provided the intellectual underpinning of the sexual revolution.

But recent studies of Kinsey himself, including a huge new biography, tell a different story. Kinsey was an utter fraud — but one of the most successful in the history of science. His methods were not only shoddy but profoundly dishonest. His samplings were deliberately skewed. His statistics were fake. His "findings" have been refuted by subsequent studies by more honest inquirers — though his "findings" are still cited as gospel, especially his "finding" that about 10 per cent of the population is homosexual. His use of children in his studies should have landed him in prison, assuming he was telling the truth about it (a large assumption). But it was excused as "science," and no law-enforcement official ever moved to prosecute him. And his work was financed and protected by the Rockefeller Foundation.

But he had his reasons. Kinsey himself was a promiscuous bisexual and masochist. Privately he both practiced and fostered perversion. He encouraged his wife — the mother of his four children — to have sexual intercourse with other men, which she often did. He held that pedophilia was harmless and that pedophiles were unjustly persecuted by law. A new biography describes his personal conduct in graphic detail. Suffice it to say that he makes Bill Clinton seem wholesome by comparison.

Kinsey's agenda was to bring the whole country down to his own level, and in fact nobody did more to advance the sexual revolution. Raised in a strict Protestant home, he betrayed his heritage — in the name of neutral-sounding "science." What an act! He had the remarkable faculty of writing about sex as if he took a purely clinical interest in it, like a Martian observing the curious biology of earthlings.

A horrifying man. Yet a *New York Times* reviewer of his biography, without disputing the facts, considers Kinsey's lies and sins redeemed by the results. After all, Kinsey helped give us sexual freedom! And the curious thing is that his behavior horrifies us less than it might because of the power of his own influence. Thanks to his work, his perversion isn't quite as shocking as it once would have been. If he had done a similar study of the prevalence of lying, maybe his mendacity wouldn't be so shocking either.

Bill Clinton may think he too will finally be redeemed by the results. It would be one thing if he were an honest advocate of sexual license. But he matches Kinsey in hypocrisy. He's the sort of man who can sing hymns in church with a tear trickling down his cheek (at least if a camera is aimed at him), and no president has quoted the Bible so often. He still wants Christians to think of him as their fellow Christian. Even Clinton can quote Scripture for his purpose.

In a sense, Kinsey is partly responsible for Clinton's election. This is now the kind of country in which, verily, any boy can grow up to be president, no matter what he does along the way. As the columnist Paul Greenberg observed the other day, Clinton falls somewhere between the con men of Mark Twain and the degenerates of William Faulkner.

I'm beginning to think democracy is the cruelest form of government, because it gives people exactly the kind of leaders they deserve. We finally have one who is so transparent that we can hardly complain we've been betrayed.

CHAPTER 1

THE REGIME

The Infernal Presidency

MAY 22, 1997

Americans are traditionally taught that any boy can grow up to be president, and nobody has taken that idea to heart like William Jefferson Clinton. Dreaming of greatness, he didn't foresee that his presidency would be consumed by such questions as: Just how bad is this president? Will he be impeached? Will his wife go to jail?

The first O. J. Simpson trial may be the fitting emblem for the Clinton years. Bill Clinton is his own Dream Team, artfully suppressing evidence, changing the subject, and getting himself off one hook after another, even when he's obviously guilty.

Any boy can be president, alas.

The historian Paul Johnson writes in *Esquire* that "there can be no doubt that Clinton has already seriously damaged the office [of the presidency]." He goes on: "Clinton's general moral standards are low or nonexistent. He seems to lie easily and fluently when cornered, and he seems to have had no scruples about using his office to enrich himself and his friends.... He is not so much consciously wicked as merely amoral, a man unaware of sharp distinctions between right and wrong."

What saves this president from ruin, Mr. Johnson observes, is partly the confusing multiplicity of his scandals; the public can barely focus on one before another distracts attention from it. With O. J. Simpson there were two corpses, but the proceedings still got tangled up in side issues. With Bill Clinton there never seems to be a central issue — just a kaleidoscopic serial scandal, which the public regards with weary cynicism. Just when you get up to speed on Vince

Foster, Susan McDougal, Paula Jones, and Craig Livingstone, out pop John Huang and his friends.

Meanwhile, the *Wall Street Journal* is conducting a running discussion on its editorial and correspondence pages as to whether Mr. Clinton is a "sociopath." A pair of psychiatrists from Arizona write: "Sociopaths are wonderful blamers. They are always ready to identify fault elsewhere." They can also be facile charmers, highly persuasive and seemingly compassionate to others while caring only for themselves.

Maybe, maybe. But is it just Bill Clinton? Doesn't the concept of a "sociopath" sound uncomfortably like a recipe for a successful career in modern mass politics?

Who but a ruthlessly ambitious though outwardly charming man is likely to rise to the top in a fluid system of unlimited opportunity, even if we call it "democracy"? The old idea of self-government was that communities would tend to choose their best men as their rulers and representatives. That may be possible in a small community, where people know each other and can judge each other's character.

But how can it happen in a mass society, where we may never hear of a candidate until he already has a powerful organization behind him? And in those circumstances what we hear of him is likely to be the result of a professionally engineered "image" rather than anyone's considered personal judgment.

This century's most disastrous rulers have been upstarts, almost unknown until they took power. Looking back over the fraud and carnage, you have to wonder if there isn't something to be said for pedigrees, blue blood, and snobbery, and even hereditary rule.

Samuel Johnson, a monarchist, opposed popular elections on grounds that the choice of a "rabble" was no more reliable than blind chance. You can go further. The choice of a rabble (that is to say, We the People) is likely to be an ambitious man who has positioned himself to be elected before the rabble knows he exists.

At least we know that a hereditary monarch didn't seek the job and didn't need a sociopath's skills to get it. If power must be given to someone, maybe it's wisest to impose it on someone who has no choice about it. The perks of monarchy are pretty good and should console him for the burdens. Besides, if he really hates the job, he can always abdicate.

Bill Clinton isn't our worst president, just the most degraded — the first occupant of the Oval Office to inspire zipper jokes and speculation about possible sociopathic tendencies. Somewhere, George III is having a good laugh.

An interesting detail is that many of those unpedigreed men of the people — Lenin, Trotsky, Stalin, Tito — took power under assumed names, rather than the ones they were born with. Bill Clinton was born William Jefferson Blythe.

Clinton without Sex

FEBRUARY 1998

C esare Borgia found icy appreciation of his political genius in Machiavelli's scandalous classic, *The Prince.* In its own time and long afterward, *The Prince,* was the most reviled book in Europe. Shakespeare and others used *Machiavel* as a byword for political wickedness.

Some modern scholars have suspected that Machiavelli's praise of Borgia's lies and cruelty was actually meant ironically or even satirically; my old friend and mentor James Burnham, on the other hand, believed Machiavelli should be seen as a champion of liberty. For Burnham, Machiavelli was the first to strip power politics of its pious cant and lay bare its inner logic; he was the supreme enemy of the illusions that tyranny employs.

The master of democratic politics

Burnham himself brought a scientific mind to politics: He was capable of admiring the skill of his enemies. He was not only a profound anti-Communist, but a sort of connoisseur of Communism. He realized that Lenin and Stalin and their heirs understood power without sentimentality.

The key to Burnham's Machiavellism was simple: everything in politics has to be evaluated not in terms of truth, but in terms of power. When a politician talks of civil rights, peace, defense, abortion, or anything else, we always have to ask what his words do to the field of power. Whether he is honest, sincere, or right is a separate question, and Burnham never denied this. But he still insisted on asking what the power-value of a given utterance was.

For Burnham the test of a politician, strictly as a politician, was simply whether he knew what he was doing. That was how he put it. He once said witheringly of Dwight McDonald, then a professing Trotskyite, that "the difference between Trotsky and McDonald is that Trotsky knows what he is doing." He meant that McDonald made the blunder of taking Trotsky's words at face value; and that Trotsky himself didn't.

For some time now I've thought that Bill Clinton deserves his own Machiavelli, or at least his own Burnham. No American public figure in our time has shown so complete a mastery of the logic of democratic politics. Not that he's infallible; he's made some awful blunders, and the ineptitude of his first two years in the White House cost the Democrats their immemorial control of Congress. But since the disastrous 1994 off-year elections, Clinton has recovered his balance, winning his own reelection and frustrating the Republicans at every turn.

How does he do it? Well, he was always a cheerful cynic; he had the makings of a superb politician from the start. But it's only fairly recently that Clinton has achieved the absolute focus that marks the maturation of genius. Virtually everything he says and does in public is calculated to enhance his own power. Nothing distracts him from this purpose.

More clearly than anyone else, Clinton understands that money is the key to modern politics. He denounces "greed" only for the purpose of embarrassing his enemies; he's not the least bit inhibited by his own moral strictures on the subject.

Money has always been important in politics, but never quite all-important. Lately, though, its role has been magnified by the sheer size of the American polity. Consider the analogy of baseball, where the dynamics of the game have been changed by free agency. Even today's mediocre players are far richer than Babe Ruth ever was, and because they can now switch teams at will, there is really hardly such a thing as a "home team" anymore. The composition of the teams changes phantasmagorically. The game on the field is at the mercy of the owners' bidding game. Whether this is good or bad depends on your point of view; but either way, you can't understand baseball without understanding how money has changed its logic.

As a vulnerable incumbent facing the 1996 election, Clinton saw with unusual clarity that raising huge sums of money was a must. This had previously been to the Republicans' advantage. He overcame it by going to foreign governments to finance his campaign, using ingenious methods that were either barely legal or illegal but not detectable (or, what amounts to the same thing, not detectable until it was too late to matter).

Meg Greenfield has put her finger on the nub: "tribute." In all ages, rulers have sold protection to those wealthy enough to afford it, and this has almost always been considered (as it still is in the Orient) a normal and ineradicable part of politics. Politics is by nature a marketplace of power, and tribute is of the essence. When reformers try to root it out, it simply comes back in new guises and euphemisms. Orientals consider the democratic West bafflingly hypocritical on the subject — inscrutable, you might say. But Clinton, the wily Occidental, understands them, and he has made himself understandable — and available — to them.

Of course it was a risky strategy, but the stakes were high and Clinton was in danger of defeat. It nearly backfired just before the 1996 election, when the first campaign financing scandals broke. Many of his Asian friends ran for cover, took the Fifth, fled the country. Meanwhile, the full extent of his venality showed up in revelations about White House coffees and the rental of the Lincoln Bedroom. Clinton is a man who understands symbols; more precisely, he understands that what are sacred symbols to others can be sources of cash for him.

As such stories continued to break for months after the election, the Republicans thought they'd finally caught him; they even began talking of impeaching him. They demanded that his attorney general appoint a special prosecutor.

Result? Clinton is soaring. His approval ratings are high. There is no special prosecutor or likelihood thereof. He is acting expansive and aggressive, getting his way with the Republican Congress, which is afraid to oppose most of his initiatives and afraid to press for the tax cuts its own constituencies crave.

Moreover, Clinton has brilliantly turned the Oriental issue around. He charged that his Republican accusers were "anti-Asian," then named the controversial Asian-American Bill Lann Lee assistant attorney general for civil rights, daring the Republicans to fight. This has turned many Asian-Americans against the Republicans, who used to take their support for granted.

Clinton understands with perfect lucidity that "civil rights" has become nothing more than a group spoils system, and he's cutting Asians, along with blacks, Jews, and Hispanics (not to mention women and homosexuals), into the game. With racial minorities growing steadily in numbers, he needs to keep the support of only a minority of whites. This is what he means when he repeats his mantra that "diversity" is "our greatest strength," while sponsoring a vapid "national dialogue on race."

Clinton simply never misses a trick. He has given up on trying to please everyone, but he still knows how to please everyone who doesn't already loathe him. If any vote is lying around unclaimed, including those of cat-lovers and dog-lovers, he snatches it.

When Lady Diana was killed, he immediately praised her work for "people with AIDS," instantly turning even that occasion to advantage with the gay crowd. Even his spontaneous emotions are transparently political; it doesn't bother him at all that most intelligent people see through him. He isn't trying to be a symbol of anything, and he's not too proud to win ugly. He just wants to win. And he wins.

Clinton is by no means a great master of power like Franklin Roosevelt, who built a lasting coalition and permanently changed the rules of the game. He has no grand strategy or vision. His only goal is to outsmart his opponents in the short run, and he is more than capable at that.

In some ways his lack of conviction and principle is a handicap. His attempts to sound inspirational, unlike Ronald Reagan's, fall flat. He doesn't even expect people to trust him. His private vices are so ill-concealed that he arouses disgust even among his supporters.

But he is a perfect mirror of the time. This is a post-Kennedy generation of disillusionment, in which utopian political rhetoric is still used, *faute de mieux,* without being taken seriously.

Americans have been taught to expect their presidents to be great men: men of substance, courage, eloquence, and dignity. Clinton has none of these qualities and hardly pretends to have them. He has no smack of the hero or man of destiny. On the contrary. He is nothing but a skilled political specialist, a charmingly unscrupulous improviser, possessing all the currently necessary arts of raising money, wooing important power blocs, and getting elected. He has no existence outside today's small political arena.

All this makes him an embarrassment to those who still believe in America's political mythology, but we've brought him on ourselves. We've turned politics into a game without rules — a game in which the winner gets to write the rules for the next round. It's a game no man of stature would want to play. But Bill Clinton, our picaresque president, revels in it.

♦ ♦ ♦

It would be interesting to know how many of those who defend Clinton in the opinion polls get income from the government.

♦ ♦ ♦

The "nonjudgmental" Democrats feel — or feign — violent moral indignation toward conservatives who uphold traditional standards. How relativists can get so mad is one of life's mysteries, but it's a fact. And they get far madder at Robert Bork and Clarence Thomas than they do at Bill Clinton. They affect to disapprove of Clinton's behavior, but they profess to forgive it. The truth is that they don't forgive it, because they really don't disapprove of it. He's their favorite church-going hypocrite. They love the hypocrites who profess Christianity while making war on Christian morality.

Chelsea and the Decision-Making Process

JANUARY 7, 1993

W hen the Clintons announced that they were sending Chelsea to an expensive and exclusive private school, their press secretary George Stephanopolous assured the public that "Chelsea was deeply involved in the decision-making process."

Ah, Washington talk. In the nation's capital, even a twelve-year-old doesn't just express her wishes: No, she's deeply involved in the decision-making process.

The school Chelsea and her parents chose is the Sidwell Friends School, where tuition runs $10,700 a year, hot lunches included. But in Washington that's what you pay for the very best.

Sidwell Friends' pupils are only 17 per cent black, and most of them well-to-do. In a city whose public schools are 89 per cent black, that's the functional equivalent of an all-white enclave. A posh, quota-free Caucasian refuge, as it were, with just enough blacks to ward off prosecution.

The Clintons' political support for the public schools, as against private schools, is orthodox liberal, in deference to the will of the puissant teachers' unions. But they didn't visit even one of Washington's public schools during the decision-making process.

Like so many liberals, they are eager to exercise a right they are less eager to extend to other parents. Well, why not? After all, liberalism is basically a set of guidelines for others, which is why the government exempts itself from so many of its own rules.

Liberal reaction to the Chelsea decision is interestingly mixed. On the one hand, there are those — even teachers' union officials — who purr their sympathy for the Clintons' desire to "do what is best for their daughter." On the other hand, there are those — such as the oracles who write editorials in the *New York Times* — who snarl that we must now "question the president-elect's commitment" to public education.

Unlike his sex life, it seems the president-elect's school choice for his daughter is not a private matter. We are well on the way to abolishing private life. And Mr. Clinton is in no position to complain, given his own "commitment," reaffirmed in his nomination acceptance speech, to privileged treatment for public schools. If our personal decisions about our children's schools are the government's business, then the rulers should expect to be scrutinized and criticized for their personal decisions.

In recent interviews, Mrs. Clinton has said that one goal of the Clinton administration will be "changing people's lives." Jeepers. That's a pretty expansive view of government. I not only don't recall seeing it in the preamble to the Constitution, I don't recall hearing it brought up as an issue in the recent campaign. But some people, if you give them even 43 per cent of the vote, will run with it. Mrs. Clinton seems more confident of a mandate than Mr. Clinton does — a mandate to change our lives, no less.

When she gets going — with her husband sitting unprotesting at her side — Mrs. Clinton sometimes exposes a fearfully raised consciousness. She flings out mysterious words and phrases like "generational" and "global" and "creating a culture within the government" and "redefining ourselves." Such is the Clintons' pillow-talk. Sort of New Age stuff, minus astrology.

It's inadequate to say the Clintons believe in big government. "Big" government suggests heavy, solid, bulky machinery, like one of Stalin's five-year plans to industrialize Russia. What the Clintons believe in is something more all-pervasive, like a gas. To them politics is a dimension of everything, offering the answer to every problem, the salve for every discontent.

They can't conceive of the state as a specific institution, one among many, serving narrow functions like paving streets and arresting criminals. No, for them it's central to society, to human existence. Its members and organs must be infused with a "culture," which will guide it in "changing people's lives."

But not Chelsea's. That's different. The Chelsea issue brings the Clintons back to earth. It's rather reassuring that they are still normal enough not to want to entrust her to the tender mercies of Washington's public schools.

Now if we can only get it through to them that the rest of us have our Chelseas too ...

Stalin, for some reason, reminds me of Hillary Clinton. The general view is that she is "standing by her man." My view is a little different. I think she supports her husband for the same unromantic reason Stalin made his alliance with Hitler.

What Will History Say?

JANUARY 28, 1993

Suddenly Slick Willie has become Thick Willie. Supposedly a smart politician, he has begun his presidency by picking a fight he can't win over a red-hot cultural issue.

His stand on gays in the military has embarrassed his own allies in Congress. The Democrats know they can sneak almost anything through, as long as Rush Limbaugh doesn't find out about it. This was definitely an item that called for furtive midterm treatment. But the commander in chief decided to tell it to the Marines.

Liberals — those broad-minded people who define a bigot as anyone who disagrees with them — have decided that homosexuals are to be officially defined as a victimized group. It's now nearly taboo to suggest in public that there is anything wrong with homosexuality, when everyone knows otherwise, as the popular reaction shows. The media's hypocrisy about sex would amaze the Victorians.

Like impotence and many other disorders, homosexuality is a disability for marital life. No decent person would torment anyone for it, but no sane person would think it's normal. Despite all we hear of gay "pride," nobody wishes the condition on those they love. It's bizarre to imagine even the most liberal expectant parents hoping their child will be homosexual. People never say: "Susan and I don't care whether it's a boy or a girl, as long as it's gay or lesbian."

Yet the liberal chorus insists that Mr. Clinton's action is the equivalent of Harry Truman's decision to integrate the armed forces. This strained analogy is a clue to what's really going on. Today's liberals want to reenact the civil rights struggle, and they are using the gay rights movement as an opportunity to strike virtuous poses. See how tolerant we are! See how nobly we stand in contrast to our benighted opponents!

Liberals fear nothing more than being on the Wrong Side of History. They presume, of course, that History will ultimately be written by moralizing liberals like the people who write editorials in the *New York Times*. It never occurs to them that their moral fads may blow over in a few years, as nature inexorably reasserts herself, and that their views won't necessarily constitute the perspective by which future historians judge us. Let's not dismiss the possibility that future historians, surveying our age, will die laughing.

Gays and feminists, cognate political activists, hold pretty much the same ideology — one that belittles the centrality of the family. Those who don't share that ideology can see what the decline of the family has brought us: a social dissolution whose most volatile element is fatherless boys.

Yet liberals, of whom gays and feminists are merely two denominations, insist on asserting the same old precedents, which have lost their relevance and now can only mislead. And instead of offering evidence for their views — of which there is precious little — they condemn anyone who is reactionary enough to disagree with them.

The result is a severe reactionary shortage. Progressives have a terrible record of predicting the future; remember the Soviet experiment and the Great Society? But the reactionaries who saw only a dark future, though they had more sense, fell short. They had no idea how bad things were going to be.

Just as no monarchist or capitalist predicted that Communism would kill tens of millions of people, no Goldwater Republican or Bircher foresaw the rates of crime, disease, and abortion that now degrade and depopulate American society. And who, back in sunny 1964, prognosticated AIDS? Never mind what History will say. We can't even draw the right lessons from our own experience.

No, our gloomiest conservatives turned out to be utopian optimists. This is History speaking, folks. Absolutely nobody a generation ago had any inkling of what was to issue from social reform and experimentation and welfare and liberation — all those hot tickets of the Sixties.

Throughout this progressive century, only the pessimists have been prophetic. But not prophetic enough. If any segment of our society deserves to be nurtured and cherished and encouraged (I won't say subsidized), it's the doomsayers. The more hysterical they sound, the more respectfully we should listen to them. That's what recent history teaches.

Bad Language

JANUARY 21, 1993

"**W**ould you call it a great speech?" No sooner had Bill Clinton finished his inaugural address than the pundits started asking each other this rather anxious question. Americans believe in Great Presidents, and one augury of a Great President is a Great Speech at his inauguration.

No, it wasn't a great speech or even a good one. It was pure Bill Clinton in its evasive grandiloquence.

Anyone who doubts that the country is being run by a central conspiracy has to explain away the post inaugural banner headlines on the front pages of our two most important pro-government newspapers. The *New York Times*: "Clinton Takes Oath as 42nd President, Urging Sacrifice to 'Renew America.'" The *Washington Post*: "Clinton Takes Oath as 42nd President, Asking Sacrifice, Promising Renewal."

The word "sacrifice" is being bandied about Washington so freely that an ancient Greek or Hebrew wandering by might get the idea that we were about to make burnt offerings of fatted calves or poor little lambs. No, the animals are safe. It's the taxpayers who are headed for the sanguinary altar.

Mr. Clinton referred to "an economy ... weakened by business failures, stagnant wages, increasing inequality, and deep divisions among our own people." But these things are effects, not causes, of economic decline. He didn't speak of government that consumes more than a third of the nation's wealth as a cause of decline. On the contrary, he implied that the solution is for the government to take even more of our money.

He went on: "We must invest more in our own people — in their jobs and in their future — and at the same time cut our massive debt." Like "sacrifice," the word "invest" is one of the new Democratic euphemisms. Government is to "invest" (i.e., spend) more money while cutting "our" (i.e, the government's own) debt. How does Mr. Clinton propose to do both at the same time? By raising taxes.

In this way Mr. Clinton uses the rhetoric of thrift as a cover for the same tax-and-spend policies that created the mess he complains of. He poses as an economic reformer who will be both wiser and more humane than his two predecessors.

But if the Reagan and Bush administrations created the current deficit without helping "our own people," it would seem to follow that all the increased government spending of the past dozen years was wasted. And since federal spending has doubled in those years, the obvious solution to the debt would seem to be to cut the federal budget in half and return to the spending level of 1980.

For some reason Mr. Clinton doesn't offer to do this. Serious spending cuts aren't in the cards. Serious tax increases are. The taxpayers can begin baring their throats for the sacrificial knife.

The Elvis impersonator is also a Kennedy impersonator. He still thinks of the Sixties as a heyday of American eloquence, and John Kennedy as a model of leadership. Accordingly, his speech was full of words like "sacrifice," "vision," "bold," "resolve," "service," "responsibilities" and "energy," topped off with a verse of Scripture. He said we must "face hard truths and take strong steps," though he didn't specify any of either. It was all meant to sound inspiring rather than menacing.

The *New York Times* account called this "brutal frankness." Not hardly. Brutal frankness would have included the sentences Mr. Clinton went out of his way not to utter: "Forget what I said during the campaign. I'm going to raise your taxes."

Unless you read between the lines and saw the implicit threat to productive Americans, it was a singularly empty speech. Its real meaning lay in what it avoided saying outright, but tried to disguise in bogus uplift and liberal circumlocution.

It was a bad day for the English language. But in Washington, the English language never has a nice day. Mr. Clinton proved only that he can be long-winded even in a short speech. It was fitting that his address was accompanied by Maya Angelou's embarrassing poem, about which the kindest thing you can say is that in its peak moments it achieved doggerel.

America the Virtuous

JANUARY 26, 1993

I should have expected it, but the inaugural rituals evoked such excesses of silliness as to make a sober man blush. Anchormen burbled on and on about what a uniquely wonderful system we have, in which power is transferred peacefully. Hadn't any of these gentlemen ever heard of coronations?

Somehow I felt I was learning a lot more about our country a few nights later when I listened to a Peruvian tell me what he thought of American women. I won't repeat it here, because it might get back to Gloria Steinem. But right or wrong, it was amusing and refreshing, after a few days of fulsome patriotism, to hear how we actually look to foreigners.

Americans have a terrible need to feel superior, as if America is worthless unless it's the best. Well, I'm sorry, but it isn't the best. Italy is. Let's keep things in perspective. We can't claim superiority to the nation of Dante and Chianti.

One thing I'm pretty sure America leads the world in is self-absorption. After last week, I'm convinced. We not only feel lucky to be Americans, we feel it's a virtue. We are convinced that everyone in the world aspires to be an American. We assume that the greatest blessing that can befall any country is to be Americanized — politically, culturally, technologically. This is the new Manifest Destiny.

I was mildly stunned by an article on the Manhattan Project in *The New York Times Book Review* this week. The whole thing was written on the bland assumption that the creation of the atomic bomb was an unambiguously good thing, another American contribution to the betterment of mankind.

And that's what I was raised to believe. Most of us were, at one time. Everything around us seemed to attest that this was one of the great American achievements. In fact this may still be the prevalent view. We like to say that the bomb "shortened the war." We admire Harry Truman for making the "tough decision" to drop it.

Well, suppose we'd never made it. Suppose we'd won World

War II without it. And then suppose that when we occupied Germany, we'd discovered that the Nazis had been close to building it. What would we have said?

I know exactly what we'd have said. We'd have cited the Nazi version of the Manhattan Project as more evidence of their fiendish evil and utter inhumanity. Just think: They were secretly working on a weapon that would have been able to obliterate whole cities in a flash!

And we'd have had a point. But what does that say about us?

Never mind. The patriotic mind can transmute everything into proof of its own country's virtue. I know. I used to be very good at it.

Not that America is especially wicked. Most countries would have done just what we did with that bomb. I presume the Greeks would have used it on Troy. But that's the point. We aren't as different from the rest of the world as we insist on believing we are.

It's time we discarded most of our patriotic propaganda. But that's easier said than done. The French theologian Jacques Ellul observes that propaganda isn't just something that blares out of loudspeakers; it's inseparable from modern life, hard to detach from our rational beliefs. It's woven into our education and our everyday language. If you aren't careful, it can shape your mind unawares. (Ellul notes the paradox that educated people are more easily taken in by propaganda than the illiterate, who have a certain immunity to abstract thought and its abuses.)

The very people who denounce "isolationism" are likely to be mentally isolated from the rest of the world, unable to believe that America is only one country among many and that the rest of the world could survive without us if it really had to. Does any other country have these Messianic mood swings?

"And so, my fellow Americans, let us resolve ... " No, no, no, Mr. President! Let us not resolve! Let us open a bottle of good red wine and pretend we're Italians and sing! Let us — if it's not too un-American — enjoy life for a change!

Seduced and
Abandoned

JANUARY 19, 1993

T he Clinton administration seems to be unraveling ahead of
schedule. The new president didn't wait until he took his oath
of office to renege on his promise to cut taxes for the middle
class.

He now says he's been puzzled that the press had made such a big
deal of a few sweet nothings he'd murmured somewhere along the
campaign trail. The taxpayers may have thought it was true love, but
to him it was just a one-night stand.

What's surprising is the man's perverse consistency in the arts of
public seduction. You'd think a politician mocked as "Slick Willie"
and "Pander Bear" would go out of his way to improve on his reputation and build confidence in his word. Instead Mr. Clinton seems bent
on vindicating his detractors, from Paul Tsongas to Gennifer Flowers
to Dan Quayle. The charge that he can't be trusted was something
more than Republican sleaze.

The news media are now giving Mr. Clinton the business for his
double-talk on taxes and other matters. Only it's a little late for scrutiny. It would have been nice if he'd gotten some tough coverage during the campaign. The belated postelection candor falls into the category my journalist friend Tom Bethell calls the "Now They Tell Us"
story. The voters must be informed — but only after they've voted.

Mr. Clinton's semi-pledge on taxes was sucker bait. During the
campaign he told a *Time* magazine interviewer that he'd been careful
to avoid Mr. Bush's mistake in saying "read my lips." He hoped to cut
taxes, he said, but he didn't want to close his options, since future economic considerations were unpredictable. That should have tipped us
off that he never meant it.

A candidate who wins with two-fifths of the popular vote has no
public confidence to spare. But Mr. Clinton doesn't blame himself for
the mistrust he inspires. In fact, the *New York Times* reports that he is

still sore at Al Gore for failing to defend his character against Mr. Quayle's taunts during the vice-presidential debate in October.

It may well be that Mr. Gore was honestly troubled by his running mate's habitual duplicity and didn't want to invite a national, prime-time horse laugh by arguing the point. Any riposte would have risked amplifying the accusation; a rash assertion of Mr. Clinton's probity might have taken its place beside Richard Nixon's "I am not a crook" in the annals of political risibility.

Mr. Gore's refusal to tell a blatant lie suggested that there was at least one honest man on the Democratic ticket. He was wise enough to accept some damage by letting the charge stand rather than risk disaster by trying to refute it.

There is no great mystery about Mr. Clinton's fancy stepping. As a liberal Democrat, he is espoused to the governing elite and its millions of dependents. But these are still a small minority of the country, so in order to get elected he had to flirt with the taxpayers just enough to convince a critical number of them that he was on their side. That's why he disingenuously campaigned on tax cuts for middle-class Americans. The seduction accomplished, he has dropped the pretense and gone back to his wife, as it were.

In the pretty much eternal class struggle between the rulers and the ruled, the taxers and the taxed, Mr. Clinton wanted each side to feel it had his sympathies. This is his modus operandi. But it's clear which side he was on all along, even back during the primaries, when he emphatically promised tax cuts. He had no intention at all of keeping that promise.

Now, even before taking office, he has squandered whatever credibility he may have had. He has been caught in the same kind of betrayal that ruined George Bush. But unlike Mr. Bush, he didn't even mean what he said at the time, and he didn't have to be pressured into breaking his word. He was simply cynical.

"One may smile, and smile, and be a villain." Yes indeed.

Majority Rule

DECEMBER 1994

T he November elections showed that something is changing deeply in this country. I have to confess that the size of the Republican victory startled me. I knew Middle America was angry, but I didn't realize how intensely that anger was focused against the Democrats.

In 1992 Ross Perot won 19 per cent of the vote. In some midsummer polls he had had nearly twice that much (until he betrayed his supporters by suddenly pulling out); which meant that more than a third of the electorate, even then, was willing to leave the sacred two-party system. So much for pundit-chatter about the voters' "surly mood" this year.

White Christians are leaving the Democratic Party.

The Republican victory doesn't mean that the country has fallen in love with the Republicans. It means that Bill Clinton managed to chase the Perot vote away from the Democrats. And no wonder. He worked hard at it.

Clinton has broken all records for bad imagery. He began with a pointed mention of AIDS in his inaugural address, serving notice that he regards infected sodomites as martyrs. Then, in his first full day on the job, he made the stupidest move any new president has *ever* made. Given his military record and his sleazy reputation, what could have been more ill-advised than to announce at the outset that he means to homosexualize the armed forces? There went the loyalty of the men in uniform, the symbolism of the commander in chief, and the respect of Christian America — three assets a president should enjoy automatically.

He proceeded to name a cabinet that "looks like America" — well, maybe P. T. Barnum's America. It recalled the wisecrack that cost James Watt his job, the one about having (if memory serves) a black, two Jews, and a cripple. Add a couple of drawfs and lesbians, and you've got Clinton's formula. He capped it with Joycelyn Elders, who made Andrew Young look like Adlai Stevenson. Oh, and I nearly forgot Maya Angelou.

On top of all this, Clinton's past—and his wife's—caught up with him. He'd used state troopers to procure women for parking-lot trysts; both he and Hillary, the priggish scourge of greed, had long records of shady business dealings. They put their only child into an exclusive private school. He got a haircut on the runway of a busy airport. Bad imagery.

And yet everything he did was fashionable, according to those who dictate fashion. National health care seemed to be an idea whose time had come. A health-care crusade led by the nation's First Feminist seemed, at first, irresistibly powerful. The Clintons cultivated all the right rich people, all the right celebrities, and all the right minorities.

Why did the country come to loathe them so deeply? Probably because they embodied everything we hate about politics: its opportunism and its fanaticism, its glad-handing and its bullying, its officious compassion and its hypocrisy. They want our children to have condoms, but they don't want us to smoke.

Law making has become a lawless process, and these two are a pair of crooks. Multiplying laws is not the same thing as the rule of law. The rule of law begins with constitutional restraint — something nearly forgotten but keenly missed anyway. Today's politicians are in it for themselves, and even when they make the laws they can't be bothered to obey them. Rostenkowski, in a word. The Clintons only dramatized what was wrong with the party. But though they fully deserved him, and brought him on themselves, the Democrats didn't need a leader like Clinton. Now they are stuck with him.

The *New York Times* election poll showed a remarkable breakdown. The Democrats didn't lose lopsidedly in the aggregate vote, but they lost consistently, along a clear fault line.

One large pattern emerges from the poll stats: white Christians are leaving the Democratic Party.

The Democrats got only 42 per cent of the white vote. They got only 24 per cent of white born-again Christians. They were wiped out in the South, where a mere 35 per cent of whites voted for them — remarkable, considering that the last three Democrat presidents have been Southerners.

On the other hand, the Democrats got landslides among their pet alienated minorities: 88 per cent of blacks, 78 per cent of Jews, 70 per cent of Hispanics, and 60 per cent of homosexuals. And with the departure of white Christians, who have gotten the message, those minorities control the party. A fifth of the remaining Democrats in the House are black. More than a tenth are Jewish. The party stands for special treatment for these groups, who are now overrepresented, but not for whites or Christians.

Both Clinton and Newt Gingrich understood the Democrats' problem right away. Immediately after the election Gingrich urged a school prayer amendment and Clinton quickly tried to follow suit — only to have his Jewish supporters protest that he was betraying them, whereupon he just as quickly backed off. That illustrates the problem, except that for the party's ruling minorities it isn't a problem. It's the way they mean to do things, win or lose. It's only a problem for the party's remaining white Christians who want to regain majority support more than they want to appease the minorities.

The Democrats don't look like America. They look like America's dying cities, infested with mutually hostile minorities, many of whom are on the public payroll and the dole while bankruptcy looms and the most basic public services break down — as the whites, facing the combination of crime and ruinous taxes, scurry to the suburbs with their children. Just as the whites know the cities aren't theirs anymore, they know the Democratic Party isn't theirs anymore, either.

The 1994 elections exposed the idiocy of the 1992 Clinton campaign's slogan: "It's the economy, stupid!" No, it's race, and religion, and parasitical petty tyranny, and social decay. Consider the phrase "social issues." There didn't used to be social issues. Franklin Roosevelt never heard the phrase. America in his day was still, in its public moral code, a solidly Christian country. Illegitimacy was a disgrace, abortion and homosexuality were unmentionable, and criminals were *bad people*. In those days whites looked on New York City as rich, clean, glamorous, and, it went without saying, safe.

As things have gotten worse, far worse than our grandparents could have imagined, only liberalism has insisted it was all "progress." And now liberalism has finally outworn its function of rationalizing social regression. It can no longer fool us into thinking the disruptions are only the makings of a better world, like a torn-up highway temporarily under construction. We know better. Those who have torn down so much of Christian civilization aren't going to build a better one; they aren't going to build anything. And what's more, we are saying so to each other in public, with Rush Limbaugh leading the hoots at liberal folly.

It's finally sunk in: liberalism is at war with Christian culture. The most ardent believers have long realized this; so now do what might be called the pious unbelievers, whose faith may be weak but who still respect Christian morality. The "liberal" Christians are mostly those who have adapted their creed to accommodate liberalism, discarding as much of tradition and Scripture as that project requires, while pretending there is no conflict and aiming their poison shafts exclusively at orthodox Christians.

America is a big place, and more than a place. It's chaotic, unpredictable, hard to generalize about. But its white people and its growing Asian population, though not monolithic, are basically Christian, in creed and in culture, and they don't like the results of the twentieth-century welfare state, even though many whites have their own attachments to it.

In retrospect, the Cold War saved the welfare state. Conservatives — who are mostly ardent Christians — put up with mammoth, unconstitutional socialist spending programs because they were convinced the country faced an emergency that made huge military budgets a necessity of sheer survival. I thought so too, and I now think we were wrong. This country's geographical position does for us what armed borders may have to do for other countries. No enemy can possibly invade, conquer, and occupy it (though a nuclear attack could devastate it).

The *evil* of Communism is hard to overstate, but its specific threat to us was exaggerated. The real threat was really our own government.

Conservatives hated Communism more because it was anti-Christian — it was called "godless" and it really did persecute

Christians — than because it posed any direct danger to the United States; just as American Jews hated Hitler because he persecuted Jews, not because of any danger that Germany would conquer the United States. And we all tend to confuse threats to our most cherished values with physical threats to our survival. It's interesting to study the shifting alignments of Christians and Jews during the Hitler and "McCarthy" eras. Just as it was hard to mobilize the great mass of Christians against Hitler, it was hard to mobilize Jews against Communism.

Now that the Cold War is over, the federal government can no longer pretend to be our great protector. This fact has severely impaired its legitimacy. As long as the government could claim necessity against overriding foreign and domestic crises, it could get away with inflicting many lesser evils of its own. So we faced German, Japanese, and Soviet threats, as well as the Depression (which ended long ago, but haunted most voters until recently). In other words, huge numbers of Americans, including many in the country's white Christian core, were convinced that their lives literally depended on the federal government, and most of all on its military power.

And that is why Clinton's immediate estrangement of the military was the most foolish step he could possibly have taken. The very people who are now being accused of "isolationism" — which was, significantly, Franklin Roosevelt's pet word — are largely conservatives who reflexively favored military intervention when they saw it was related to genuine defense. Just as liberals automatically support "social" spending, conservatives automatically supported "defense" spending. The Cold War at least had a clear (if misguided) *defensive* rationale, which can't be said of deploying U.S. troops to Somalia or Haiti.

Most states, even tyrannies, don't make war on their subjects' culture and religion. (As I like to put it, how many lesbians does Saddam Hussein have in his cabinet? Would he appoint a Joycelyn Elders?) It's a remarkable fact that the "isolationists" who are most skeptical of the federal government, at home and abroad, are by and large people who used to be called "superpatriots." And their "superpatriotism," ironically, kept the welfare state from collapsing long ago.

Liberals were quite right to accuse conservatives of being "obsessed" with Communism. What they never realized was that everything they wanted the federal government to do *required* that obsession. Only such a national obsession can keep up the morale the superstate requires. Lyndon Johnson could never have passed the Great Society programs liberals loved without waging the Cold War liberals hated.

With the United States unchallenged at the pinnacle of global power, it will be hard to convince most Americans that they face a foreign threat — or that they have much need of the federal government that has been bullying them and despoiling their country. If ever there was a chance to restore limited, constitutional government, it is now.

We shall see whether the Republicans really want to restore it. They have no particular *political* motive to do so. Their "Contract with America" pledges popular but superficial reforms (mostly tax breaks) but leaves intact the liberals' warped constitutional system; in some ways it even reinforces that system, by drawing the federal government into areas where it has no business: crime, family law, and so forth. The Republicans promise to increase the already monstrous "defense" budget; the military is, after all, the Republicans' welfare state. (The phrase "common defense" has been as preposterously stretched as its twin, "general welfare.")

The Republicans are vultures, not eagles. They have acquired the skills of opposition, but not the vision of leadership. Taking the path of least resistance, they will most likely continue to prefer winning the game to revising the rule book. We'll soon find out whether they want to curb power, or just redistribute it.

The Well-Adjusted President

JUNE 1996

O ur young president recently explained why he supports Boris Yeltsin's brutal efforts to crush Chechnya's war for independence: "I would remind you that we once had a civil war in our country in which we lost, on a per capita basis, far more people than we lost in any of the wars in the twentieth century over the proposition that Abraham Lincoln gave his life for: that no state has a right to withdraw from our Union."

What an odd way to define the mission of our great national martyr! Yet it's not far off the mark. At times you can tell Bill Clinton was educated in the South. Any Yankee will tell you that Lincoln gave his life to abolishing slavery, but Clinton has kept his eye on the ball. The real lesson of Lincoln hasn't been lost on him.

The Civil War was about consolidation — that devil-word of the Founding Fathers, who dreaded the possibility that the sovereign states might be swallowed up in a monolithic central government. The Confederacy is not among the many themes over which Clinton gets moist-eyed; he isn't waiting for the South to rise again. Notice that he speaks of "our Union" — not the accent of one of the Civil War's sore losers. Clinton is triumphantly what the social scientists used to call "the well-adjusted personality"; there isn't an alienated bone in his body. He's game for any kind of change.

Shortly after the Civil War ended, the Confederacy's vice president, Alexander Stephens, wrote precisely that "consolidation" had been the real issue:

"The conflict in principle arose from different and opposing ideas as to the nature of what is known as the General Government. The contest was between those who held it to be strictly Federal in its character, and those who maintained that it was thoroughly

National. It was a strife between the principles of Federation, on the one side, and Centralism, or Consolidation, on the other.

"Slavery, so called, was but the question on which these antagonistic principles, which had been in conflict, from the beginning, on divers other questions, were finally brought into actual and active collision with each other on the field of battle."

The Republican Party, from its inception, was a party of consolidation; the last gasps of "states rights," a generation ago, were still heard from Southern Democrats, oddly out of step with everyone else in both parties. Clinton represents the "new" South, eager to consolidate further — married to a Yankee feminist-liberal, big on "civil rights" and national health care — which is why he is so unpopular in the South generally.

Clinton is one of those baffling people who actually feel right at home, like a gator in a swamp, in a land of alphabet agencies, numberless regulations, arcane welfare programs, crisscrossing subsidies, inflation, and every sort of needless complication. He appears to have neither nostalgia for a simpler life nor the instinct to simplify for the sake of principle or efficiency. He has no qualms about jettisoning traditions or cutting himself off from the past. Northerners who take him for a hick couldn't be more mistaken; he's the ultimate city slicker. He grew up in the gambling town of Hot Springs, not exactly a pastoral setting (it's more like a Mafia Shangri-La), where playing the angles is a way of life. If he knows any hog-calls, they're probably Sicilian.

Meanwhile, the Republican Party has long since lost its own enthusiasm for the Lincoln revolution. Though it has by no means reverted to all-out federalism, which it has never understood, its sullen resistance to the socialist frenzies has made it the lesser evil to most Southern whites.

One consequence of our enormous military establishment is that it's absolutely unthinkable that any state, or any combination of states, should attempt secession again. You can't fight a nuclear superpower with a state militia, let alone a private one. It's surprising that Chechnya has held out as long as it has; but of course even the ruthless Yeltsin has to be reluctant to nuke one of his own provinces. As for Montana's Freemen, they may be making some sort of point, but they can't even keep a few acres of wild country land out of federal control.

Try to imagine Clinton participating in a hopeless rebellion. (It's easier to imagine Bob Dole dancing in *Swan Lake*.) He may be many things, but a Quixote he's not. He may be the most nimble politician ever to sit in the White House. If conservatism is the wave of the future, why, he'll ride that too; by November he may have the country convinced that he, not Dole, is the conservative candidate.

Most wars, by their nature, occur between neighbors, who are most apt to annoy each other. But the United States keeps attacking countries far from its own borders: Panama, Somalia, Iraq, Yugoslavia. In order to prevent the Yugoslav war from spreading, Clinton's spreading the war.

◆   ◆   ◆

Clinton is a cynic defended by an army of fanatics.

Clinton's America

APRIL 1998

The polls tell us that a sizable number of "the American people," as we are collectively and reverently called, approve of Bill Clinton's presidency no matter what his "private life" is like. His "private life" includes any adultery he may commit in the Oval Office on company time.

Sometimes I wake up and wonder what country I'm in. The morning papers, the disc jockeys, the movies, and prime-time TV all keep reminding me that this isn't the country I remember, where the tone was set by Norman Rockwell, Bishop Sheen, Walt Disney, Dwight Eisenhower, Bing Crosby, Art Linkletter, and other grownups. (Teenagers, though widely deplored, were still a cloud no bigger than a man's hand.)

Bill Clinton is in the White House; the stag film is obsolete.

I don't yearn for the Fifties; I only wish there were more continuity with them. Certainly they could have been improved on; but the people who despise them most superciliously are themselves pretty sorry advertisements for progress. In those days most of our current media celebrities would have been confined to stag films. It's a sign of the times that the stag film has become an obsolete art form.

We did away with the old pieties and hypocrisies, and instead of honesty we got Clinton. The Fifties were a time when people wanted to be adults and thought it was safe to have children. There was not only prosperity, but, more important, a Baby Boom. The adults knew they could trust other adults — particularly politicians, movie stars, athletes, and others in public life — to try to set good examples for their kids. Scandal, as Ingrid Bergman learned, was still a bad career move. In those days men like Clinton went to prison long before they got near the White House. (Prison, or stag films.)

America was bound to change a lot, but it didn't have to change this way. Those who prefer the Nineties to the Fifties want to make the current situation seem not only better, but inevitable. But the sorry moral and cultural state of this country owes a lot to a few arbitrary and fraudulent rulings of the U.S. Supreme Court, which were by no means inevitable. No more inevitable was the silent acquiescence of a large part of the clergy, especially the Catholic bishops, who illustrate the truth of Charles Peguy's prophetic aphorism: "We will never know how many acts of cowardice have been inspired by the fear of seeming not sufficiently progressive."

Christian conservatives saw the Cold War as a final, apocalyptic struggle between Christian civilization and godless Communism. But when the Soviet Union finally collapsed at the beginning of this decade, they found that the society they'd thought they were defending no longer existed. It was just gone. In the first post–Cold War election, the new America chose Bill Clinton, a glib, irresponsible child of the Sixties, to lead it.

For a while I thought Clinton was a mistake that my beloved country would correct at its earliest opportunity. The first Clinton scandals made me doubt that the boy from Hope would finish his first term. Just as George Bush had seemed invincible after the Gulf War, Clinton seemed supremely vincible. The Republicans agreed, and thought the surest way to beat him was with a safely moderate candidate like, oh, Bob Dole.

Even after Clinton beat Dole (with less than half the vote), I blamed Republican stupidity for his reelection. It wasn't until those polls showed Clinton's popular approval soaring with his worst scandal that I began to realize how deeply the country has changed. It's finally sinking in. As an all-knowing pundit I blush to admit it, but I've recently come to feel that I've been awfully naive — not just about this country, but even about human nature. A large part of the human race is far more cynical, mutable, and manipulable than I imagined possible. But I can't say the evidence was concealed from me.

A lot of people support Clinton even though they don't doubt that he committed sexual offenses (not all of them "consensual"), perjured himself, solicited perjury from others, lied to the public, and generally broke laws to cover up his offenses. Our traditional morality, public and private, has seriously eroded. The "idealism" of the Sixties has rotted into the nihilism that was always latent in it.

Clinton himself embodies the process. He's a born cynic who feels no promptings of honor. This makes him an acceptable leader for a country whose sense of honor has been enfeebled by religious and moral skepticism. Clinton's America measures its health only in economic terms, sees nothing unseemly in soft porn, and isn't revolted by abortion. Worse, it doesn't really remember anything very different. It has neither the moral compass nor the historical memory to compare the present with anything earlier or better. After all, its official sages — the journalists — constantly defame the past and treat divine law itself as mere opinion. "Values" have replaced "virtue."

Clinton didn't bring all this on us; all this brought Clinton. It made him, a fast-talking con man who knows all the latest clichés, normal. He hails from a troubled home, headed by the alcoholic stepfather from whom he takes his surname; that's now a normal pedigree. He might be praised for rising above his background, if he'd improved on it; but he seems to have turned out worse than one might have predicted, with, moreover, the talent to get away with his crimes. Things being what they are, he has risen to the top, and pundits talk solemnly of his "policies." It's his country now. You and I are just passing through, puzzled, disgusted, and as thoroughly out of place as a pair of rusty Royal typewriters in Silicon Valley.

How did this come about? When I say I don't idealize the Fifties, I mean that the process leading to Clinton was already far along by those days, no matter how different the country looked then. The Constitution, which shouldn't be idealized either, had long since ceased being a serious obstacle to the centralization of political power — just as its original opponents had foreseen, proving once more that the most pessimistic reactionaries generally underestimate the trouble ahead. (As a rule they're only marginally more far-sighted than the optimists.)

From the Civil War to the New Deal, the Constitution had actually been converted, by sophistical jurisprudence supported by powerful interests, into an instrument of centralization. To earlier generations, this would have meant tyranny; in the twentieth century, it has meant "progress." Fascism and Nazism, now denounced everywhere, were just different versions of the same thing — vanquished sects of the progressive faith.

Not for nothing was Franklin Roosevelt's America (though partly modelled on Mussolini's Italy) allied with Joseph Stalin's Soviet Union: both men sought to make the state economically omnipotent, with the population dependent on it. It's a common error to suppose that tyranny always means an entire populace quaking in terror; no tyranny can exist for long without many beneficiaries. Plenty of people owed their prosperity to Roosevelt and Stalin alike, despite the net results for everyone else.

But the Soviet model was too successful for its own good: as the state destroyed all independent institutions, the parasites destroyed the sources of production and the system itself finally imploded. It lasted as long as it did thanks to the black market — i.e., the illicit free market — which it was increasingly forced to tolerate.

In America the productive sector has been allowed to exist and create enough surplus to support the parasites, albeit burdened with mounting taxes and restrictions. Through the income tax and other controls, this country has adopted the category of what the Soviets called "economic crime," giving the state the power to police and punish formerly free modes of exchange.

In the name of "democracy," the parasites are allowed to vote themselves benefits that must be paid for by taxing the producers. Roosevelt himself boasted that "no damned politician" would ever be able to dismantle "my Social Security system"; and how right he was. Later presidents, notably Lyndon Johnson, have added new entitlements, nearly as popular — and as untouchable. In fact a chief measure of a president's "greatness" is now his ability to pass ambitious new "programs," thereby creating new parasite constituencies.

Even the radical democrat John Stuart Mill warned that the franchise must be limited to the productive and withheld from those who receive income from the government; otherwise, he said, the vote would invite people to "plunge their hands into their neighbors' pockets." But this principled advice has been ignored; nobody in American public life today would dare to utter it.

Newt Gingrich, the chief spokesman for the Republican Party, now hails Roosevelt as "the greatest president of the twentieth century" and scolds conservatives who criticize FDR — that mortal enemy of the limited, constitutional government Gingrich professes to favor. The welfare state is now, and has long been, bipartisan, with Republicans pledging to "save" Social Security and Medicare from the Democrats. If the Clintons had succeeded in imposing their national health care plan, the Republicans of the next generation would no doubt bow their heads at the name of Clinton.

As a result of all this, we live under what Hilaire Belloc called "the Servile State." Before the Russian Revolution, and long before the Cold War, Belloc predicted the advent of a system that was neither capitalist nor fully socialist, in which the state would compel one part of the population to support the other. The beneficiaries would be dependent on the state; the victims would live in dread of it. Well, here we are! Without, I might add, a Cold War to distract us from the reality.

Meanwhile, Belloc's friend G. K. Chesterton, with equal prescience, foresaw the virtual abolition of the family. The legalization of divorce, he argued, meant the nonexistence of marriage itself; utter sexual license would soon follow by the logic of things, no matter what the "reformers" of marriage intended. Chesterton also understood that the Servile State would favor what we now call the "sexual revolution."

The sexual revolution is a real revolution, and the abortion clinics form its Gulag Archipelago. At first glance it may seem odd that the omnipotent state, while increasing other restrictions, should be permissive about sex; but Stalin himself favored sexual freedom and (until the Russian population began to diminish more than he deemed desirable) abortion on demand.

The truth, as Belloc and Chesterton saw, is that the family, like private property and religion, is a barrier to the total state. Just as private property creates material bases of independence, the family creates rival loyalties. And the state wants nothing between itself and the individual. For the state, citizenship — membership in the state itself — should be the only claim on the individual's loyalty, the only meaningful identity. Abolishing the sanctity of sexual relations within marriage achieves this end. Demoting religion to the status of mere opinion (in the name of the separation of church and state) likewise weakens rival sources of authority that may counter and inhibit the power of the state.

As the state releases us from our duties to our own flesh and blood, it reciprocally increases our duties to the state itself. You can leave your spouse, abort your children, and abandon your parents, but you can't divorce the state. Its claims are absolute, when nothing else is. So it gladly dissolves the bonds of real kinship, while it uses the cozy rhetoric of "family" and "village" to describe our relations to the remote fellow "citizens" we are taxed to support.

Sexual relations (including, for this purpose, abortion) are among the few areas still officially recognized as "private." You may wonder why, if sex is so private, you're watching it on TV; but let's not quibble. Just be grateful that something is still considered private, sort of. At least the concept of privacy still gets lip service.

Everything else is the state's business: our earnings, our food and drugs, our health, our treatment of our children, our children's education (including sex education). Nearly everything is now actually or potentially a "federal concern" — that is, a proper subject of the centralized state's power. The Constitution can always be adapted for the purpose at hand, thanks to such rubberized and decontextualized phrases as "interstate commerce" and "equal protection of the laws." New "rights" can be multiplied endlessly, because "rights" are no longer areas of privacy the state is bound to respect, but claims against others' privacy that the state is empowered to enforce. My freedom ends where your "civil rights" begin.

C. S. Lewis says somewhere that the modern world makes religion a purely private matter while shrinking the sphere of privacy itself. That sums it up. I'd add only that the state now decides what is, and what isn't, private, redrawing the boundaries as it pleases.

There is no specific mastermind or secret conspiracy behind all this; it's the natural result of godless man following his nature; governed by his sloth, perhaps, even more than his lust. The order he forms is like that of a hive of insects, who form an observable design without knowing it, just by obeying their instincts.

At some point in this degenerate process a chief insect like Bill Clinton emerges. He no more plans it all than the queen bee plans the hive. He's just supremely at home in it, among people who don't know any better than to vote for him.

Clinton's chief significance in our history is that he's the first president to make the sexual revolution part of the conscious program, promoting abortion, homosex, feminism, and the rest, and even weaving them into the system of entitlements. His Bible has told him that the kind of sex he likes best isn't adultery, and he carries that Bible, even flaunts it, as he comes out of the church with Hillary every Sunday morning. He's a good and photogenic family man, right down to his new dog. It must be symbolic that Buddy has been neutered.

If termites could talk, I always say, they'd call what they're doing to the house "progress." And from Clinton's own point of view, he's the acme of progress. He's not the only one who thinks so.

Impeaching Clinton — who's not about to resign in shame — would be a laudable act, but it may be too late to do much good. At this point, killing the termites may not save the house. The damage is probably irreversible. The day after he leaves the White House, suitably tarred and feathered, we'll still wake up to find ourselves in Clinton's America, with patriotic Republicans determined to save it.

The other night I watched the old movie *Invasion of the Body Snatchers,* in which, as you may recall, creatures from outer space take over the bodies of earthlings. The hero comes to realize that his old friends and neighbors are no longer themselves, but aliens, recognizable as such only by subtle personality changes. I'm starting to feel that way about a lot of my fellow Americans in the Age of Clinton. The Americans amongst whom I grew up would have gotten rid of this guy in a flash when it turned out he had monkeyed with a young intern in the Oval Office and lied to us about it.

The Age of Nonjudgmentalism

MAY 5, 1998

L et's not mince words: things just keep getting worse. The U.S. Government doesn't have to worry about making profits; it can take unlimited amounts of money from the American people. Yet it has managed to fall more than $5 trillion dollars in debt. And it still presumes to tell others how they should run their businesses.

For most of this nation's existence, its rulers didn't even have to use the word "billion," unless they were discussing astronomy. Now they are up to multiple trillions. At the present rate, they're going to have to come up with an equivalent of "light years" as a shorthand for units of federal spending. The word "astro-

From high-school Greek to remedial English

nomical" will assume connotations of parsimony, as in: "This heartless skinflint wants to cut Medicare back to astronomical levels!"

This has become a country in which Thomas Jefferson couldn't get elected mayor of a medium-sized city, let alone president, yet Bill Clinton goes right to the top — with high approval ratings. It used to be a country where high-school students learned Latin and Greek; today its college students take "remedial English" and can listen to Cliffs Notes on audiotape. And we're told our best days lie ahead of us!

Am I complaining? Yes, but not for myself. I was lucky. The worst thing I ever had to worry about in school was being beaten up by bigger kids. Nobody even thought about bringing a gun to school. We had fewer laws, but they were enforced. Today the people who don't want to enforce existing laws are always eager to make new ones.

We Baby Boomers may be the first generation in history that can tell our juniors how easy we had it. In our day it was still unusual to come from a "broken home"; nowadays many kids have never lived in any other kind, since their parents didn't bother getting married in the first place. *Sports Illustrated* has just done a cover story on multi-millionaire athletes who have kids out of wedlock, ignore them, and often try to avoid paying a few bucks in child support.

Meanwhile, "queer studies" have become fashionable at the university level, and a noted Shakespeare scholar has saluted "gay and lesbian theorists" as "men and women of the greatest independence of mind." Which just goes to show that you not only have to accept change; you also have to pretend, with a silly smile, that the new way of life is a big improvement over the old one.

In every generation, we're always reminded, there are old codgers yearning for the good old days and denouncing the degenerate youth around them. But the old days weren't this bad, and it's moral insanity to deny it. What's more, today's youth aren't to blame for the changes; they're the victims of trendy elders who have abdicated both authority and responsibility. When bishops go ape, don't expect children to behave like little angels.

Everything, in short, is getting worse. (Except maybe car stereos. There's always a bright side.) Not just worse, but exponentially worse. Worse cubed.

It's all summed up in the word "judgmental." This idiotic word says it all: the final censure of a relativist age. It's wrong to say anything is wrong. You must be punished for advocating punishment.

Egad. We live in the Age of Nonjudgmentalism, eloquently attested in Clinton's approval ratings. I expect to see an ominous bumper sticker any day now: "I'm nonjudgmental and I vote!"

Can it be an accident that back when people were more judgmental, they didn't shoot each other quite so often? It may seem paradoxical, but it's quite natural. Simple, even. When you have commonly accepted moral standards, you don't usually need to resort to force. But when moral rebuke no longer exerts its restraining influence, there is a human temptation to blow the offending party away, as it were.

I realize that to say that things keep getting worse is highly judgmental. So maybe I should say that they keep getting worse from a judgmental point of view. From a nonjudgmental perspective, of course, everything is fine.

True Colors

JULY 1998

One of the minor revelations of Bill Clinton's trip to China was a topic that didn't come up. In his brief and tactful reference to human rights, Clinton mentioned such items as "the right to be treated with dignity" — not exactly the sort of thing that would make Thomas Jefferson jump out of his chair. And I thought Roosevelt's "Four Freedoms" were woolly-minded!

The only "right" Clinton has ever been willing to fight for is the right to abortion. Like all abortion-pushers, he insists he's not pro-abortion, he's "pro-choice." Likewise Hillary and her feminist fans.

If "choice," rather than abortion as such, is the point, you'd think the Clintons and the feminists would be outraged by the Chinese policy of forcing women to have abortions after the first (or in some cases, the second) child. It's hard to imagine a more barbarous tyranny.

Opponents of abortion oppose forced abortion because it's abortion, not just because it's forced. But advocates of "reproductive freedom," as it's also called, ought to be indignant about it precisely because it's forced. The Chinese policy is an easy test of their sincerity. How did they score?

Clinton said nothing about it during his trip. Not a word.

In her syndicated column the week of the trip, Hillary ("It takes a village") Clinton wrote about the problems of Chinese women. She cited jobs, education, workplace discrimination — but not forced abortion. Apparently the government's power to control women's bodies with the most total and cruel rigor isn't an important concern among them.

Neither did feminists at home make any noise about forced abortion. Some of them have been known to say, when confronted with the question, that you have to understand China's population "problem." They show no sympathy for a woman strapped down against her will while her healthy baby is killed in her womb, even at the end of her term. (These are the sort of people who like to accuse conservatives of "lacking compassion.")

Is it just that American feminists are willing to make allowances for foreign countries with different cultures? Hardly. They profess to stand for the rights of women everywhere, and multiculturalism be damned. One of their current causes is the abolition of female circumcision, traditional in parts of Africa and the Middle East.

The feminists are incensed that foreign women should be deprived of orgasms, but not that they should be deprived of their children. This speaks volumes about their mentality. In essence, they want to export the sexual revolution — minus the right to have children, the one freedom that most normal people all over the world would probably consider more basic than any other.

One way to put it is that feminism and the sexual revolution are quite compatible with totalitarian government. But this really isn't news. The Soviet Union, even under Lenin and Stalin, permitted free love and abortion on demand.

These people are no more "pro-choice" about abortion than they are pro-choice about home schooling or the income tax. They are pro-abortion, and they are willing to countenance the denial of choice to a woman who wants her baby.

In his grand jury testimony, Clinton attacked several women, showing naked bitterness toward Gennifer Flowers, Paula Jones, Kathleen Willey, and Linda Tripp. And despite his fond words for Monica — "that woman" became a "good girl" with a "good heart" — he contradicted her testimony too. Why do so many people lie about the poor man? Why are so many of them women? And why are their lies so similar?

The Devil's Own

OCTOBER 8, 1998

"**I**'ve hesitated to say this," a friend told me the other day, "but I keep wondering if Clinton isn't literally Satanic." Coming from an intellectually rigorous man who measures his words carefully, this startled me. I asked him to explain. Did he mean Clinton is a conscious agent of the devil?

"Well," he said, "a saint doesn't think of himself as a saint. He just habitually obeys God's will until he is so close to God that God constantly acts through him. Maybe it's the same way with a man who gets too close to the devil. After a while he becomes the devil's instrument."

An interesting thought. Civility requires us to presume the good faith of those we disagree with, in politics and elsewhere. But of course this is no more than a polite fiction. Sometimes our opponents are cynical people who take advantage of this presumption in order to deceive us. In that case we don't owe them the benefit of doubt.

Clinton has always been notable and notorious for slippery language. Is it overwrought to suspect him of more than that?

Under pressure, Clinton lies, feigns innocence and moral indignation, evades, equivocates, quibbles, and dissembles in every imaginable way. His absurd semantics in his grand jury testimony — even the word "is" became problematic — have become a joke. But maybe it's no laughing matter.

Language is not just a means of conveying information and feelings; it's a moral bond. It depends on honor, sincerity, loyalty, and trust. Clinton habitually exploits our presumption of these qualities in order to "betray us in deepest consequence," as Banquo warns Macbeth about the witches' prophecies, though those prophecies may be literally true (or "legally accurate"). Clinton even betrays his own family. Nobody can trust him.

For eight months he used the entire executive branch, including his cabinet, to purvey a self-serving lie. He didn't merely make a pro forma denial and clam up; he organized and drove a furious campaign of deceit. That's enough to mark him as an evil man. But he has done much more, and his long trail of slime leads back to Arkansas. His sexual sins are only one of many signs of a deeply disordered soul. But they tell us less than his mendacity; he is a son of the father of lies.

Posing as a Christian, carrying and quoting the Bible (Shakespeare also reminds us that the devil can cite Scripture for his purpose), Clinton has shown conviction on only one issue: abortion. Here again we have something more than an honest difference of opinion. In Arkansas, until the early 1980s, Clinton publicly opposed abortion, though Gennifer Flowers says he gave her $200 to abort their child. He reversed his position as soon as he deemed it politically opportune.

Are we really supposed to believe that abortion advocates are driven by an abstract belief about when life begins? Our biology teachers, without deferring to theology, taught us, before abortion became a subject of political contention, that life begins at conception. It's a simple matter of fact that two parents combine, in the higher animals, to generate offspring, and conception means the precise point when this occurs.

The phony professions of doubt about this are exactly like the phony professions of Clinton's partisans that they believed his transparent lies (and their equally phony professions of belief that he is now really, really sorry he lied). Clinton and his ilk are willing to kill children on the very verge of birth, and the phrase "partial-birth abortion" concedes too much: it isn't "abortion" except in a "legally accurate" sense. It's the murder of an infant. The technique of extracting the brains and crushing the skull was developed precisely to stay within the law as the U.S. Supreme Court has warped it.

Too much is at stake for us to continue granting the benefit of doubt to people who deal with us in bad faith. They don't have different "beliefs" about embryos and fetuses; they simply don't care whether abortion is evil. And if they lie about that, they'll lie about anything.

Clinton's defenders are warning that his enemies are intent on staging what the lawyer Alan Dershowitz calls "a Christian coup." And they point to abortion as the crucial issue. If Clinton falls, abortion may become illegal again! The theme has been repeated so often that there can be no doubt that abortion is at the heart of their fanaticism.

How can there be so much moral passion on the side of evil? Again, it's hard to doubt the diabolical element: rejection of Christ and rebellion against God, which involves even the denial of nature.

It was sad to learn that Henry Hyde, who has been such an exemplary public man, had once had an adulterous affair. But Hyde, being a Catholic, accepts a moral standard given by God and inherent in nature. He didn't lie or justify himself when the fact was published. That's the disadvantage of the Christian side: we expect to be judged by norms we didn't create or edit to suit our desires.

The liberal side, by contrast, claims the right to choose a self-serving moral code. Barney Frank can't be blackmailed, because he's an open and self-righteous pervert. But liberals don't merely decide the standard they themselves wish to be judged by. They use that standard to sit in judgment over the past; they want to rule today's society by that same standard; and they want to use that standard to shape the future, starting with our children. At the same time, they accuse Christians of bigotry and arrogance for submitting to the traditional standard.

In a "pluralistic" society, the heretic has the upper hand. He decides what constitutes "consensus": it means whatever he chooses to accept from the traditional code. Whatever he rejects becomes, by his volition, "sectarian," and to insist on it is to "impose one's views." He refuses to recognize God's law, or natural law, as a coherent whole. He asserts his prerogative to take it apart as he pleases. He may agree to keep the old rules about rape, but not the rules about sodomy; he will continue to forbid some kinds of murder, but he finds others acceptable.

Old-fashioned Christians find the heretic confusing and baffling to deal with, because he maintains an illusory partial agreement with them. They don't realize that even the areas of seeming agreement are, for him, matters of not of obligation but of mere convenience. He pretends they are matters of obligation so that Christians will remain submissive to the "consensus."

The heretic may even be, in his arbitrary way, very militant on some points of his mutilated morality, so long as they serve his purposes; but for him morality is ultimately manipulable, because he is his own lawgiver, his own god.

Thanks to modern education, this sort of heretic is no longer a very exceptional type. The polls show he's quite common. And his idea of a good Christian is Bill Clinton. Maybe that's what this fight is all about.

I keep wondering: How can a man bear to make himself so contemptible in his own daughter's eyes? How can he bear to shame his own child before the whole world?

The *Salon* mag dirt on Henry Hyde's adultery, thirty years ago, when he was a private citizen, was a Clinton operation, in spirit if not in fact. (But probably in fact.) It followed the Clintonites' terrorist threats and modus operandi. At the very least it was What the Boss Would Have Wanted. And it backfired, just as antagonizing Paula Jones, Linda Tripp, and Kenneth Starr backfired. Hyde has always been an honest and genial legislator, and as chairman of the House Judiciary Committee he has bent over backward to be fair to Clinton ever since the Lewinsky story broke. Clinton's tactics have become mortifying even to the Democrats.

Hustler's Man of the Year

DECEMBER 24, 1998

I t would be interesting to see the White House coffee tables these days. The divergent aspirations of the First Couple seem to be defined by two magazines, *Vogue* and *Hustler.*

Hillary Clinton appears on the cover of the current issue of *Vogue,* while the defense of the president is in the capable hands of *Hustler*'s publisher, Larry Flynt. The president's amatory practices would be right at home in *Hustler,* which may be where he picked them up. Flynt is also a friend of James Carville, who appeared in the recent movie glorifying him. If *Hustler* honored a Man of the Year, it would have to be Bill Clinton.

Flynt is lending a hand to the besieged Clinton by publishing the sexual sins of Republican politicians, for which information he has paid lavishly. And some of this dirt may really have socially redeeming value — if, for example, it transpires that important congressmen have literally gotten into bed with lobbyists. But such revelations would be equally scandalous if they involved Democrats.

Flynt explains his desire to expose Republican adulterers on grounds that he is against "hypocrisy." Pornographers always pretend to oppose hypocrisy, even as they justify porn as honesty.

If Flynt really hated hypocrisy, he'd hate Clinton, who totes and quotes the Bible in public, then sneaks off to "private" trysts in the Oval Office. What a prize catch for the hypocrisy-hunter! And don't lies, perjuries, feigned remorse, and phony reformation count as hypocrisy? How about lamentations over "the politics of personal destruction" after a career of engaging in same?

No, pornography isn't at the opposite pole from hypocrisy. Its pretense to oppose hypocrisy is itself hypocritical. It merely wants to reduce decency to its own level.

Unlike some pornographers, Flynt doesn't even love the body. He merely hates the soul. He delights in degradation, as in his famous cover showing a woman being fed into a meat grinder, or his equally famous (and equally witty) cartoon showing a noted preacher committing incest in an outhouse.

In the latter case, the Supreme Court ruled that the Constitution protected him against a libel action; Flynt apparently construed the ruling as a vindication of his honesty. He has a Clintonian gift for self-serving construction, and he naturally sees Clinton as a kindred spirit.

The revelations about Clinton's "private" life are disgusting because they are so *Hustler*esque. Whether dropping his trousers in a hotel room or playing doctor with a cigar in the Oval Office, he makes you embarrassed to belong to the same species.

Anyone can understand certain sins; an unhappily married man — like all those French presidents we hear about — may seek love with another woman. But we expect the woman to be a grownup, and we expect a certain affection and respect between them, along with discretion and concern for their families. And no tobacco products.

Clinton has a certain point when he says that what he does isn't really sex; truly, much of it hardly "rises to the level of " sex. For most people the question isn't whether it's a sin, but why it's a temptation.

He finds it easy to trash women when he is through with them because, to him, women are trash in the first place. His preference for oral sex, the leitmotiv of his scandals, says volumes about his regard for the opposite sex. So does his inability to remember Monica Lewinsky's name after several sessions.

It isn't just women and sex; you have to wonder if any other human being is real to this guy. He even uses his daughter as a photo-op prop. Well, why not? If Larry Flynt can help, maybe Chelsea can too!

Jesse Jackson used to intone a bit of doggerel about advancing "from the outhouse to the White House." Clinton has brought the White House down to the outhouse.

When the original *Psycho* was released in 1960, one reviewer, not wishing to give away the plot, noted that "mother-love has been dealt a blow from which that sentiment may not recover." The dignity of the presidency has received a similar blow from Clinton.

COMMANDER IN CHIEF

Bill of the Balkans

DECEMBER 1995

Bill Clinton has certainly come a long way. After a youth devoted to opposing the Vietnam war and full of "loathing for the military," he is launching an unpopular military expedition to Bosnia—sending 20,000 soldiers as "peacekeepers," assigned to help keep a "peace" that exists only on paper.

There's a sense of psychodrama about the whole thing. Never mind the merits of the Bosnian intervention. What is Clinton trying to prove?

He seems miscast as commander in chief of the greatest aggregation of sheer force in world history. And not only because he avoided military service in his youth, but because, in some larger way, he has never made any of the traditional rites of passage to manhood. He's the eternal student-council president who happens to have nuclear weapons at his disposal.

This just isn't like Bill. He's a domestic guy. He goes in for health care and stuff. He's never had a job in the real world. And he's definitely a ladies' man, not a man's man. He's surrounded by women — his late mother, whose memory he frequently summons, Hillary, Chelsea, and whatever bimbos lurk in the background. No father, no son. In fact there have been very few men in his life, aside from political and Whitewater cronies. (The Arkansas state troopers make my point.)

In his televised speech explaining the Bosnian mission, Clinton failed to explain how any American will be better off even if the mission succeeds. His argument was that our global responsibilities, our ideals, our values, our hopes for a better world, our vital interests in the region, and dire necessity all, in perfect harmony, require our intervention. While he spoke, there was a vague plausibility about his lulling aphorisms, if you didn't listen carefully. Did he really think he was being eloquent, or did he think we'd think so? Afterward it was hard to remember a word he had said. Henry V's record is safe.

It's nauseating the way politicians always pretend that the right thing, the advantageous thing, and the immediately tempting thing are all the same thing. They never admit that there might be tension between "vital interests" and "ideals." Clinton is even more at home with phony talk than most. I kept thinking how refreshing it would be to have a president who'd say something nice and cynical: "Look. We have a chance to grab most of English-speaking Canada right now! They're no match for us, and we just can't pass it up. I know it runs against our democratic values and all that, but a hundred years from now, who's going to care?"

I'm grateful that Clinton isn't a Henry V. In fact he fails the most basic test of a leader: nobody wants to be known as his follower. He doesn't appeal to national pride; he shames it. Despised in the North, disowned in the South, hated in the West, he's not "one of us," except in the embarrassing way a disreputable relative is. No credentials can make him seem anything but an impostor.

But for the moment he's in charge of the empire, and he seems to want to act the part, even to glory in it. He has just made two successive trips to Europe, where he has found more respect and popularity than at home, with vast crowds welcoming him as a savior and cheering his most banal platitudes. I'm afraid it will only encourage him.

Clinton's Gut Issue

NOVMEBER 18, 1997

There is no popular demand for war with Iraq or anyone else, and President Clinton knows it. The pressure for war is coming from the usual quarters: those who, for various reasons, want the United States to dominate the Middle East.

The op-ed hawks are framing the issue as whether Clinton has the "character" (read: guts) to bomb Iraq. If there is one issue where he is vulnerable, it's character. He is easy to caricature as a draft-dodging hedonist who lacks principle and courage. And the caricature requires only slight exaggeration. Clinton is no saint, and the kind of saint he least resembles is a martyr.

As a young man, Clinton saw Lyndon Johnson and Richard Nixon devoured by a long, futile, unpopular war. That was Lesson One.

Lesson Two came later. As a presidential candidate in 1992, Clinton faced a president who had just waged war on Iraq. It was the opposite of Vietnam: a short, popular war that cost few American lives and ended in overwhelming victory. During the campaign Clinton himself was widely derided for his evasion of military service and for his subsequent lies about it. Yet he won, and George Bush, a decorated war hero, lost.

What Clinton learned from his own election was that even a successful war president can't count on reelection. At one point the polls had shown public support for the Gulf War at over 90 per cent. Yet that support didn't translate into electability for the commander in chief the following year.

So the lesson of Iraq was added to the lesson of Vietnam. What people will endorse passively is not the same thing as what they want passionately. Some of the op-ed warriors praised Bush for showing "leadership" in going ahead of the polls at an earlier phase, when those polls had shown most Americans reluctant to step up hostilities. Though the later polls swung in his favor, Bush's support was shallow. His political fate proved that 90 per cent verbal approval isn't the same thing as 90 per cent enthusiasm.

From Clinton's point of view, Nixon's fate is the worst-case scenario and Bush's is the best he could hope for. Furthermore, Bush was lucky. Nothing went wrong in his war, and he had enough sense to quit while he was ahead without toppling Saddam Hussein and trying to occupy Iraq, as some hawks had urged.

Right now the elites within the Beltway are eager for war. The cries for "action" against Iraq are deafening. Just this past weekend various talk-show panelists, liberal and conservative alike, called for everything from "carpet bombing" (Nina Totenberg of National Public Radio) to "ground troops" (William Kristol of *The Weekly Standard*). Leaders of both parties in Congress want Clinton to act — i.e., attack.

Yet there is no grassroots pressure for war. Most Americans don't see their own welfare threatened by Saddam Hussein, however they may despise him. The European allies of the United States — more precisely, the ruling elites of Europe — don't want war either; they dread the hostility of the Arab masses and the wider Muslim world. And they may be thinking that if Iraq is crippled, Iran will become the dominant power in the Middle East — in which case many of the same American voices who are demanding war with Iraq now will demand war with Iran later. Some of them have already named Iran as our chief enemy.

How many enemies do we want? We have the power to make an unlimited number, provoking terrorist retaliation in the short run and who knows what in years to come. And to what end? American military domination of the globe? Why is that desirable? What could it cost us?

As with Vietnam, the hawks are making it as awkward as possible for a president to behave with discretion and restraint. They threaten him with charges of cowardice if he retreats, while offering redemption if he attacks.

The real question is whether Clinton will have the guts to endure being called a coward by people whose courage is measured by their willingness to send others to die.

The Bombs of August

SEPTEMBER 1998

W hen, in mid August, Bill Clinton ordered missile strikes against sites in Sudan and Afghanistan, ostensibly in retaliation for the two terrorist bombings at U.S. embassies in Kenya and Tanzania, most people were immediately suspicious of his motives. Was this a "Wag the Dog" distraction from his personal troubles?

Yes, but maybe not quite in the way it's generally believed. It tells you a lot about the mentality of this country that a president can try to regain some of his lost moral stature by killing people. I heard one Republican (I forget who) tell an interviewer that he *Our anti-Muslim foreign policy*
found it reassuring that Clinton would bomb something, though he reserved judgment on whether he'd bombed the right targets! It was the principle of the thing, I guess. Reach out and touch someone.

No sooner had the missiles struck than the Sudanese government angrily denied that the pharmaceutical factory manufactured a nerve gas "component," as the U.S. Government had said in justification of the strike. A British engineer vouched for this, explaining that the factory lacked the safety features that would be necessary if it were making such dangerously toxic materials. Nor was there any clear evidence linking the factory to the guerrilla financier Osama bin Laden. Our leaders held their ground, but rejected the Sudanese demand for a UN investigation to settle these questions. Later reports made it clear that the plant had been targeted on little more than a hunch.

The Muslim world, meanwhile, was furious. It saw only outrageous violence, compounded by typical American hypocrisy about "terrorism." Most other Western governments were decidedly cool in their support for the U.S. action, while Russia's Boris Yeltsin fiercely condemned it.

Osama bin Laden must have been pleased. The episode elevated him from marginality to heroic status in the Muslim world.

Clinton too won heroic status in some quarters. In an open letter to him, published in the *New York Times,* the American Jewish Committee wrote: "We applaud your decisive actions against terrorist training bases in Afghanistan and a suspected chemical-weapons facility in Sudan.... We encourage you to press on in this battle against terrorism — wherever it leads and, within the bounds of law and U.S. policy objectives, whatever it requires." The letter barely mentioned Israel and called the missile strikes "bold acts of self-defense."

Thus a "suspected" culprit warrants acts of war — "self-defense" — against the country in which he, she, or it resides. This is the Zionist way.

Days after these bold acts, Clinton addressed a "civil rights" group on the 35th anniversary of Martin Luther King's "I have a dream" speech. He recalled that he'd wept "uncontrollably" when he heard the speech as a youth in 1963 — a lie as transparent as his earlier "vivid and painful memory" of black church burnings in Arkansas at about the same time. (It transpired that no black churches had been burned in his home state.) He also sang a chorus of "We Shall Overcome." The speech was warmly applauded.

What was Clinton doing? In both cases he was responding to his personal crisis by appealing to his minority bases: bombing for the Jews, emoting for the blacks. This was no time for subtlety. He'd have made a similar appeal to feminists, but he didn't need to: those whores have already shown their absolute loyalty to him by siding with him against all the women he's defiled and dropping sexual harassment from their agenda as of January.

Before his crisis, Clinton sought peace in the Middle East and, in general, avoided provocative military action abroad. But in his desperation, he was willing to gamble with this country's future by inflaming the whole Islamic world against the United States.

"Terrorism" isn't a specific enemy. Like "war crimes," it's a term used more often for polemical than descriptive purposes, which is why it's applied almost exclusively to the other side. Muslim bombings are "terrorism," American and Israeli bombings are "self-defense."

Secretary of State Madeleine Albright explained, in the manner of an irritable schoolmarm, that the Muslim terrorists act as they do because they hate "democracy and freedom." No mention of U.S. support for Israel, of murderous U.S. sanctions against Iraq, or of other U.S. policies in the Middle East that reek of greed, arrogance, cruelty, and exasperating hypocrisy. You wonder whether Albright is displaying the level of her own intelligence or deliberately insulting ours.

Even if the latest missile strikes were somehow warranted, the fact remains that their result has been to enrage three-quarters of a billion Muslims, not just a few "terrorists." This can only increase the number of Muslims who are willing to resort to horrible tactics against Americans in the near future. In the past few months there have been bombings, kidnappings, murders, from South Africa to Pakistan. We can expect more.

We should also brace ourselves for surprises in this country. In fact the U.S. Government is already preparing for them in downtown Washington, by beefing up security everywhere (with barricades around the Washington Monument, for example). Airports, of course, are likely targets. There are far too many soft targets for even the most stringent security measures to prevent.

The real nightmare scenario has already been sketched here and there. In the former Soviet Union, more than a hundred compact nuclear weapons, easy to smuggle, have turned up missing and are believed to be available on the black market. Shoppers no doubt include rich and fanatical Muslims like bin Laden — private operators who don't need state sponsorship to drive them on. Intelligence experts believe some of these bombs are already in this country.

If, one day soon, one of these bombs is detonated in Washington, New York, St. Louis, or Seattle, we'll pay dearly not only for Bill Clinton's sins, but for our politicians' fifty-year habit of pandering to the Jewish lobby by sacrificing America's interests to Israel. The shock will dwarf the memory of Pearl Harbor.

The danger is obvious to anyone who pays attention to U.S. foreign policy, but few Americans do. The great majority of us have only a faint conception of how bitterly we are hated abroad, and not only by

Muslims, for our government's swaggering, compounded by the ugliness of American cultural influence.

There is precedent for it. The Roosevelt administration conducted a secret and illegal campaign to provoke war with Germany and Japan, so that Pearl Harbor came as a total surprise to most Americans; to this day, "Pearl Harbor" remains a synonym for an unprovoked ambush, which shows how little we've learned about our ruling elites.

Back in March, Vice President Al Gore gave a speech to the American Israel Public Affairs Committee (AIPAC), in which he said in part:

"Our admiration for Israel has never been greater; our commitment to Israel has never been stronger; our friendship with Israel has never been deeper; America stands by Israel now and forever. Our special relationship with Israel is unshakable; it is ironclad, eternal, and absolute. It does not depend on the peace process; it transcends the peace process. Our differences are momentary, not permanent. They are about means and not ends. And let me say to my fellow citizens here in the United States, to our friends in Israel, and let me say especially to the citizens of any nation who may wish Israel ill, don't you even think for one minute any differences about this or that between the governments of the United States and Israel belie [sic] even the slightest weakening in our underlying unity of purpose or will shake our relationship in any way, shape, or form." He concluded with a prayer: "May God bless Medinat Yisrael [Greater Israel]!"

For some reason, this ringing declaration of "unconditional" support for Israel wasn't published. In a departure from custom, Gore's office hasn't even made it available to the public. It had to be leaked to *The Spotlight* and then posted on the Internet (of which — O irony! — Gore is such an enthusiast).

In other words, it was a more or less secret speech.

In late August, the American Jewish Committee, in an open letter published in the *New York Times,* praised Clinton for having bombed a "suspected" nerve gas factory. This probably reflected the sentiments of the major Jewish organizations and most big individual Jewish donors to both parties (with little effective opposition from the now-impotent Jewish Left).

Again, the Great Taboo prevails. The role of the Zionist lobby in pushing this country toward a terrible disaster is hardly reported or publicly mentioned. Anyone who aspires to a future in either politics or journalism knows better than to discuss it openly. Contrast the activism of the Christian Right, which is amply covered and freely denounced for its efforts to change public policy.

Suppose things were different. Suppose this country's foreign policy were pro-Arab and anti-Israel. Suppose the president's cabinet were full of men with names like Mohammed, Omar, and Abdul; suppose many of the major media were owned by rich Arab-Americans; suppose much of the working press, including many of the most famous pundits, were also of Arab ancestry.

A parallel situation? Not quite. You also have to suppose that if anyone were to point out that we were hearing only one side of the story in the Middle East, and that U.S. interests were being sacrificed to Arab interests, he'd immediately be branded an Arab-hater and his career might be severely damaged, with his colleagues afraid to defend him even if they secretly agreed with him. Just imagine.

Legacy

APRIL 8, 1999

A s he ordered the bombing of Kosovo, Bill Clinton assured the nation that he has been "reading up on the history of that area." That's a load off! The great wartime presidents have always realized that before you bomb a country, you should read up on it.

Clinton described the decision as "a moral imperative." He shouldn't use the word "moral" without blushing; but then, as we learned last year, he doesn't blush easily.

With Clinton, there is no such thing as a moral imperative. There is only what's good for Bill Clinton. And he has never seen any percentage in going to war, except when he has needed a momentary distraction, as he did several times last year.

Clinton's political style has always been selling and swapping favors — you give to me, and I give to you, as the song goes. That's normal politics, and though it's corrupt, it tends to keep a country out of war, which interrupts the peaceful exchange of graft.

On several counts, making war is out of character for Clinton. He saw what Vietnam did to Lyndon Johnson and Richard Nixon; he also saw, and profited directly from the fact, that George Bush's victorious conduct of the Gulf War didn't endow him with lasting popularity, though his approval rating had peaked at 92 per cent. Besides, Clinton's draft evasion and hostility to the military make him an incongruous commander in chief, and he has no feel for military affairs. As a rule he likes to be in complete control, but he has to rely on others' judgment when he contemplates committing bombers and troops.

So why is he waging war? Has he merely bluffed — and had his bluff called — too often? Have the hawks in his administration worn down his resistance? I doubt such explanations. If he could withstand the pressures of 1998, when more than a hundred newspapers called for his resignation, he can withstand the nagging of Madeleine Albright.

I can only speculate by trying to imagine the world as it appears to Clinton himself. Let's briefly review his presidency. He entered the White House in 1993 with high hopes. He had a Democratic Congress on his side. His "legacy" was going to be national health care.

But the health care plan flopped, scandals began to erupt, and even his wife lost her halo. In 1994, to everyone's shock, the Republicans took over both houses of Congress. It looked as if Clinton would be lucky to get reelected in 1996, let alone to bequeath a "legacy": the Republican Congress wasn't going to pass any big social program of his.

Clinton won in 1996; but he still couldn't get 50 per cent of the popular vote, his campaign produced more scandals, and the Republicans kept Congress. He'd proved only that he was a brilliant, devious survivor with no coattails.

This set the stage for the biggest scandal of all. As the Monica story consumed the media, everything Clinton did to save his skin had a cost. His lies, perjuries, subornation, and dirty tricks proved that he had no honor whatsoever. He was impeached, and his private life became the subject of scorn and ridicule such as no previous president had ever had to endure; he'd become a national dirty joke, his dignity annihilated. By the time he was acquitted he was held in almost universal contempt. There are strong rumors that his wife wants a divorce.

Though the Republicans failed to convict him and lost ground in the 1998 elections, they are going to control both houses of Congress for the rest of Clinton's presidency, and the impeachment brawl has left a residue of bad feelings toward him. So he can forget about big legislative achievements.

In the meantime his sex scandals refuse to go away. Monica is touring the world like Princess Di, basking in her sordid celebrity and reminding everyone of what Clinton would prefer to forget. And Juanita Broaddrick says, very believably, that Clinton raped her in 1978.

If he wants to be remembered for something other than his gross affair with a fat young intern, Clinton is going to have to take a new departure. He may see a war in the Balkans as his last chance to put his stamp on history and to upstage his own troubles. Congress won't declare war, but it will condone an undeclared war, at least until it goes bad.

This is impossible to prove. But notice that in his televised speech explaining his decision to bomb, Clinton listed Serbian atrocities, with the interesting exception of the mass rape that has been such a horrifying feature of the Yugoslav war for several years. Though everyone else has dwelt on it, Clinton seems not to want to bring up the subject of rape, which might connect his scandals with his war in the public's mind.

In other words, we may be at war for no better reason than that Clinton has a personal interest in distracting us, and future historians, from the sordid activities that will otherwise define him forever. This interest may even prompt him to escalate the war by sending ground troops if the bombing doesn't achieve its nominal goals, as seems to be the case.

The major news media assume that Clinton's scandals are "behind us," trivialities unrelated to the Balkan war. But those scandals may be intimately related to this war. Would Clinton really sacrifice many lives, at risk of a wider war, to his own hope of a "legacy"? Of course. He might even prefer being remembered for a Vietnam-scale disaster to being identified for all time as Monica's kinky beau.

Public men always have their private motives, but some of them manage to subordinate their personal interests to their country's good. This isn't the way most observers would describe Clinton. Nobody can predict how his life will end, but I think we can rule out hara-kiri.

When Clinton took the oath of office in 1993, an exciting world of possibilities lay open to him, including presiding over "the most ethical administration in our history." Six years later time and character have taken their toll, and war is one of the few options he has left. He wouldn't be doing it unless he thought it was good for him.

What will history say of him? Seymour Hersh has written a book about "the dark side" of the Kennedy administration. I doubt that anyone will ever refer to Clinton's "dark side." It would be a little like referring to the "dark side" of Stalin: there is no other side that matters.

The Sad Bomber

APRIL 15, 1999

P utting Monica, impeachment, and the Chinese espionage fuss far behind him, Bill Clinton continued to play his latest role: war president. In less than a fortnight he'd made it clear he didn't have the foggiest idea what he was doing.

Like Madeleine Albright, Clinton takes a schoolmarm approach to foreign policy. He thinks of bombing as a form of spanking, to be administered to bad boys who ignore his scolding. And a good little war gives him a welcome opportunity to pull up his trousers and act "presidential."

Yugoslavia's defiant president, Slobodan Milosevic, has been listening to Clinton's sermonic threats for years. Clinton seems not to think beyond the move he threatens to make, but Milosevic has already taken that move into account and is prepared to endure it. Clinton didn't foresee what Milosevic would have foreseen.

So Clinton had to pretend he wasn't surprised — though he was completely unprepared — when the bombing resulted in an even fiercer Serbian campaign against minorities and an immense flood of refugees from Kosovo. Even the attack on Belgrade failed, merely uniting Serbs behind Milosevic without impeding his troops.

Professional military men had tried to warn Clinton that bombing without ground troops was worse than useless, but he disregarded this advice and so far is trying to achieve his goal with air power alone. He assumed he could win with overwhelming force and an underwhelming plan. So everything that was wrong in the region two weeks ago is already much worse now. Asked what he would do if the bombing doesn't work, he was at a loss; he had to refer the question to his advisor, Sandy Berger, who said that in that case the bombing would be intensified. If at first you don't succeed, compound your original blunder.

Clinton is a con man caught in a street fight. He doesn't know what to do next; Milosevic does. Furthermore, Clinton appears not to know how to extricate himself when his efforts fail: the hawks insist that "credibility" — NATO's and "ours" — is at stake. Even some who opposed military action in the first place, such as Henry Kissinger, now say the United States can't afford to back out.

Clinton, meanwhile, has given a speech calling for cultivating good relations with China. But if China has any inclination to beat its swords into ploughshares, it's not likely to be encouraged as long as the United States is actively claiming global hegemony, arrogating to itself the right to intervene anywhere — even in the internal affairs of a single country.

One of the most serious long-term dangers of this war is the dangerous precedent it sets for violating national borders, which used to be the very definition of aggression. Borders are always somewhat arbitrary, but they at least stabilize things. The United States went to war with Iraq because it had violated the highly artificial borders of Kuwait, imposed by the British in 1922. Now the United States and NATO take the position that they may transgress Yugoslavia's borders for "humanitarian" reasons.

Since Clinton believes abortion is a woman's right, why shouldn't we bomb countries that deny that right? By the same token, why shouldn't countries that abhor abortion bomb the United States, if they could get the upper hand? It's easy to imagine infinite pretexts for war on such grounds. There is no logical limit on the enforcement of rights, especially when rights can be arbitrarily defined and redefined by the powerful.

As a practical matter, Clinton has now established that the United States won't be deterred from military attack by mere national borders (though it also reserves the right to attack others for violating those borders). Borders are like property rights: they are sometimes hard to justify in the abstract, but they are nevertheless a convention we dispense with at our own risk. The United States may never be directly attacked, but from now on it will have to deal with a New World Disorder, in which other countries may follow the Clinton precedent against their neighbors.

By Clinton's Balkan logic, we should also bomb China as long as it occupies Tibet and violates the rights of its own people. This thought may have crossed the minds of the Chinese rulers. Clinton doesn't realize that the rest of the world sees the United States not as the champion of justice, but simply as the most dangerous force on earth. After all, "our" sanctions against Iraq — also imposed for lofty-sounding reasons — have killed more people than Milosevic has.

This war wouldn't be justified even if it could achieve its stated goals. It isn't defensive and it hasn't been properly declared; one of the chief purposes of the Framers of the Constitution was to create a limited presidency, in contradistinction to a permanent monarch, so that no single man would have the power to plunge the nation into war.

The war hasn't consumed all of Clinton's attention, however. With boundless effrontery, he said in an interview with Dan Rather that his impeachment was not "warranted," but that it gave him the opportunity to "defend the Constitution." (And here we thought he was just lying to the country and smearing his critics to save his own skin.) Clinton is also calling for federal "hate crime" legislation, likening random murders of homosexuals to Serb-style "ethnic cleansing."

Not that the war is meeting much Republican opposition. Most (not all) of the Zionist neoconservatives ardently support it, criticizing Clinton for doing too little and demanding that he send in the ground troops; Arizona's Senator John McCain, the media's favorite "conservative" (the torch has been passed to him from Bob Dole), has been appearing on every network with the same message. Nobody seems to question the premise that the United States should be a world empire. The only question is whether Clinton is up to the job of emperor.

To their credit, Senate Republicans voted overwhelmingly (38 to 16) against the bombing. But no good deed goes unpunished, and this only earned them a stern rebuke from the neocon *Weekly Standard:* "Is this the party of Reagan or the party of Buchanan?"

The editorial went on making nostalgic references to Reagan — "the Reagan mantle," "the strong moral and strategic foundations of the Reagan era" — and approvingly quoted McCain's description of the United States as "the greatest force for good in history" (so much for Christ and the Church). But there's no danger of the Republicans becoming the party of Buchanan, alas.

Balkan Bill

APRIL 22, 1999

I 'm not alone in the cynical assumption that Bill Clinton sees war in the Balkans as an opportunity to put you-know-what "behind us." Unless he can upstage his own scandals, he'll be chiefly remembered in history for his total void of character. And knowing that we tend to rank presidents as "great" in proportion to the number of people they get killed, he's gambling on redemption through warfare, adopting a moralistic — and almost messianic — posture as he rains bombs on Yugoslavia.

Nobody has explained what's in this war for those Americans who don't happen to be perjurious presidents. But Clinton has now resorted to military force more often than any recent president — and mostly since he got into girl trouble last year. Maureen Dowd of the *New York Times* wrote the other day that war used to mean "old men sending young men to fight"; whereas with Clinton it seems the other way around — the "boy-man in the White House" sending abroad soldiers who seem more grownup than he does.

The Balkan war is a new departure, being an intervention into the internal affairs of a sovereign country on purely moral pretexts. The first condition of a just war is that it be defensive. Wars are normally fought between neighbors for that reason: one attacks, the other defends. But Clinton has established a precedent for any country, anywhere, that chooses to make war far from its own borders, provided it can come up with a suitably moral excuse. By this standard, any country could declare war on any other. In practice, of course, powerful countries would make war against weak ones. Thanks to Clinton, borders have now lost their inviolability in international relations. And to think this decade began with a war against Iraq for defying the borders of Kuwait! Those borders were of course set by the British in 1922.

Incidentally, Slobodan Milosevic has probably killed far fewer people than UN sanctions against Iraq, which have deprived the

CHAPTER 3 : COMMANDER IN CHIEF

people of Iraq of clean water, electricity, food, and medicine, hugely increasing infant mortality. The Muslim world accepts the number of Iraqi deaths as 500,000 or so. Most of the world doesn't share Clinton's assumption that the United States is the globe's moral exemplar. To the contrary, the United States is widely seen as the globe's greatest danger, a hugely powerful and hypocritical bully.

Communist China and Russia reject Clinton's justifications for the Balkan war. To their hard-headed rulers, all this war signifies is the American claim of a unique right, denied to other countries, to intervene militarily anywhere on earth. To their ears, what Clinton calls "resolve" means "aggressive intentions." The whole globe is our "sphere" of interest.

Meanwhile, as Monica Lewinsky arrived in Helsinki on her book-promotion tour, Judge Susan Webber Wright, back in Little Rock, found Clinton in contempt of court for lying under oath in denying his sexual relations with that woman. Apparently rejecting his claim that he was "defending the Constitution" by lying, she has ordered him to reimburse the court and Paula Jones's lawyers for the expenses incurred as a result of his perjury. Clinton is going to have to escalate his unconstitutional war considerably if he hopes to make us forget the defining events of his sorry presidency.

Fareed Zakaria, managing editor of *Foreign Affairs* (published by the Council on Foreign Relations), writes in the *Wall Street Journal* that conservatives are divided over the Balkan war. "The rise of liberal interventionism," he observes, "has confused conservatives," who are "generally in favor of vigorous assertions of American power." He notes that conservatives favor such actions when they seem to defend or advance American interests, whereas liberals favor military action only when it's free of any taint of national self-interest.

I don't always agree with Zakaria, but he's right in his observation that "many conservatives who believe that the state can do nothing right at home think that it can do nothing wrong abroad. (If things go badly, why, more money, bigger bombs, and ground troops will straighten it out.) Many who are scornful of social engineering at home seem sure it will work beyond our borders. They seem convinced that good intentions and a burst of state power can transform the world. How conservative is that?"

Most conservative criticism of Clinton's war is based on the same few objections: that he "isn't doing enough," lacks the will to win, isn't prepared to pay the necessarily bloody price of victory (which would require ground troops), and has gutted the armed forces with budget cuts; it also rarely fails to mention his own Vietnam-era avoidance of military service. But relatively few conservatives have raised the most basic objection: that this is a war we should stay clear of. If it's not necessary to fight, it's necessary not to fight.

A controversial new book, *The Pity of War,* by the Scottish historian Niall Ferguson, argues that Britain should have avoided war with Germany in 1914. The British turned a European war into a world war, which led to the Communist and Nazi revolutions and eventually to a second world war. If the Kaiser had won the war, he argues, Germany would have dominated Europe, but its rule would have been civilized and tolerable, especially compared with what actually happened.

I'm not sure why Ferguson's thesis is even controversial. At the very least, it's highly plausible. War rarely comes out the way those who wage it hope it will, and even the victorious countries would usually have been better off if they'd kept out altogether. Nobody knows where the Balkan war will lead, but the Russians are warning that it could culminate in a third world war.

Besides, what are American boys fighting for in the Balkans? A Christian society? That has been taken from us by our real enemies, who are here at home. The real goal is a godless, U.S.-led New World Order, as witness the sort of people who support it.

The real question is what's good for America — not as an empire, but as a potentially Christian republic. But none of our policymakers think in such terms. The ruling circles need a moral consensus right now, but they've already destroyed the consensus we once had. It's fitting that a man like Clinton, Bible in hand, should lead them.

Chinese Shadows

JUNE 3, 1999

T he Cox Committee's explosive report on Chinese espionage has finally been released, and it's a damning account
of lax security about what is supposed to be secret military information. Though the problem began in the Seventies, it
has worsened during Bill Clinton's presidency, and Clinton himself has lied to the public about it, falsely claiming never to have
been briefed about the Chinese quest for American secrets.

Did surreptitious Chinese contributions to his 1996 reelection
campaign have anything to do with it? It's hard to believe that
even Clinton would sell the country out directly; on the other
hand, the Chinese may well have calculated that as long as he
remained in the White House, American secrets would continue
to be easy pickings. If so, they were right.

"I can assure the American people that their nuclear secrets
are now safe at the labs," said Energy Secretary Bill Richardson.
He forgot to add that those "labs" are in Beijing.

One columnist, Sandy Grady of the *Philadelphia Daily News,*
has already expressed his fear that the new revelations could lead
to a new McCarthy era, with "the paranoia, suspicion, and hysteria of the red scare era ... witch-hunt ... fear, xenophobia, and
anti-Commie pathology of the McCarthyite nuttiness."

Grady admits that the Cox report is "scary," and that Clinton
has lied. But he still doesn't grasp, in spite of all the recent dis-
closures from the Cold War archives, American and Russian, that
McCarthy actually underestimated the full extent of Communist
penetration of the U.S. Government.

Anyway, this is a different era. Soviet infiltration succeeded
because many liberals did have Communist sympathies. Franklin
Roosevelt set the tone with his moral and material assistance to
the Soviet Union and "Uncle Joe" Stalin. In those days the Soviet Union was looked on as a light unto the nations, the fulfill-

ment of the progressive dream. "I have been over into the future, and it works," said the journalist Lincoln Steffens. Walter Duranty of the *New York Times* lied to curry favor with Stalin, reporting that there was no famine in Ukraine. Joseph Davies, Roosevelt's gullible ambassador to the Kremlin, wrote a book defending Communism as compatible with Christian principles, and even approving of the notorious show trials of the late Thirties, in which Stalin framed many of his old Party comrades on absurd charges of sabotage in collusion with "fascists."

To call Roosevelt "soft on Communism" is a little like calling Hugh Hefner soft on fornication. Soft on it? He loved it! No wonder his administration was full of Soviet agents like Alger Hiss and Harry Dexter White; no wonder Stalin was able to obtain the know-how to build the atomic bomb by 1949. Even many of the scientists in the Manhattan Project were Soviet sympathizers.

By contrast, there is no such ideological sympathy today for the ambiguously Communist People's Republic of China. China simply doesn't inspire the perverted idealism that Stalin's regime did. Though still tyrannical, it's more nationalist than Communist; it doesn't offer itself to the world as the model for other countries; and it doesn't seek to propagate its creed, if it even has one. All of which makes it hard to imagine that China has more than a handful of fellow travelers in this country, and most of those that do exist seem to be ethnic Chinese rather than true believers in any cause.

Clinton is hardly a true believer type: in order to accuse him of harboring a secret loyalty to China, you have to posit that he can harbor loyalty to anyone but himself, which is manifestly unrealistic. (Hillary is the Bolshevik in the family.) But he is strangely eager to curry favor with the Chinese. He still insists that his policy of "engagement" is bearing fruit — "I strongly believe that our continuing engagement with China has produced benefits for our national security" — and he continued to make abject apologies for accidentally bombing the Chinese embassy in Belgrade even when the Chinese regime had retaliated by spewing insults and sponsoring mob attacks on the U.S. embassy in Beijing. Such fawning behavior suggests that he believes the Chinese have something on him.

How much of a threat does China pose to the United States? Hard to say. It's doubtful that the Chinese rulers plan a military attack on this country, but that may change. Ambitions tend to grow as power expands, and in a generation they may decide it's feasible, and desirable, to attack the United States directly. What they certainly want in the near future is sufficient power to dominate Asia, driving the American Empire out of the region. Even at that, they haven't been especially aggressive toward their neighbors lately. Walter Pincus of the *Washington Post* notes that the Chinese military budget is only a small fraction of ours.

As his conduct of the Balkan war shows, Clinton doesn't understand military matters very well, and it stands to reason that he might be somewhat nonchalant about military secrets. Worrying about that stuff is for old fogies like George Bush the Elder. So what if the Chinese have grabbed a few documents?

But Clinton's indifference has now blown up in his face, in a scandal that alarms even people who thought he shouldn't have been impeached for perjury and obstruction. Clinton has interpreted his acquittal as exoneration. He doesn't seem to comprehend that he is universally recognized as a shameless liar who has run out of credit.

In a way, Clinton may be lucky that he has already been impeached, because his enemies' failure to convict him the first time may immunize him against impeachment for allowing treason on his watch. The idea of having an impeachable president, according to Alexander Hamilton, was to have an officer who could be held responsible for all misconduct in the executive branch, if only by negligence.

Harry Truman's famous motto was "The buck stops here." Clinton's motto is "How was I supposed to know?" He passes the buck more adroitly than anyone in American history, as the Republicans have learned time and again. Maybe he'll try to bury the Chinese scandal by getting the resignations of Janet Reno and Sandy Berger, tacitly blaming them for letting Chinese agents get away with so much. But it will be hard even for him to evade responsibility for permitting espionage that could conceivably result in millions of American deaths.

Here is a new dimension of the Clinton Legacy: corruption that "rises to the level of " virtual treason.

CHAPTER 4

THE POLITICAL HOUDINI

The Selfless President

JANUARY 25, 1996

B
ill Clinton is a New Democrat again. Having tarred the Republicans as extremists, he is filching their themes, thereby displaying one of his defining qualities: an utter incapacity for embarrassment.

Maybe he doesn't know the meaning of self-contradiction. Or maybe it's his guiding principle. You have to catch your breath at his audacity. For sheer quick-change conviction and philosophical acrobatics, we shall not look upon his like again.

Mr. Clinton assures us that the era of big government is over, and proceeds to unroll an agenda of dozens of programs that didn't occur to Lyndon Johnson. You'd think nobody would be gullible enough to believe him, but he shares H. L. Mencken's opinion of the American public, except that he doesn't complain about it. No, he turns it to his advantage.

Even the skeptical sages of the media fall for him. They describe his myriad state-of-the-Union proposals as "conservative" because he talks about crime, morality, and the family, all of which he treats as proper concerns of the federal government. Few point out that a new batch of programs is hard to square with his professed concern for cutting the federal deficit.

Operating on the practical assumption that the American public is stupid, Mr. Clinton has risen to the highest office in the land. If he thinks 51 per cent of the public will believe that cows are reptiles, you may count on him to say that cows are reptiles.

The key to Mr. Clinton is that it wouldn't bother him a bit that he was insulting the intelligence of the other 49 per cent. He is amazingly, brazenly sucker-oriented. Had he delivered the Checkers speech, he wouldn't have done it in the stiff Nixonian manner; he would have done it with moist eyes and an operatic throb in his voice, while holding up a picture of the dog, preferably in a body cast.

The wonder is that he stands a good chance of reelection, even though he has betrayed nearly everyone at some time or other. Perhaps his supreme feat occurred during the recent budget negotiations, when bitter Republican enemies, who didn't trust him going in, came out feeling double-crossed by him.

Richard Nixon got a bad reputation because in his day lying was still lying, since it was still believed that there was such a thing as objective truth. We are now in a post-Nixon phase of history, and what used to be called demagoguery is now called marketing. If enough people believe or "accept" an assertion, it is thereby "validated."

Virtues have become subjective "values." Nobody can say when life begins. Nobody can even say what Shakespeare means: literary texts, the bright new critics tell us, are "radically unstable" and have no inherent meaning, let alone truth. The Constitution is a "living document" whose historical meaning is irrelevant to today's jurisprudence. Government can be "reinvented."

Needless to say, such fluidity creates its own opportunities. This is the golden age of the con man. He is no longer a marginal figure staying on the move to keep one step ahead of the law. In the absence of stable principles — the Decalogue, Ciceronian natural law, the code of the gentleman — the con man himself makes the law.

Does he tell the truth? Never mind that. How do the control groups react? What do the polls say? Truth may be unknowable, but power is still measurable. Power, in one form or another, is all that's left.

Mr. Clinton grasps the rules of power in today's Washington like nobody else, and he has thrown himself into the game with headlong enthusiasm. He appears to have understood and used the rules in Arkansas with equally quick apprehension.

Shakespeare's Richard III, the hunchbacked murderer, delights in his own evil; he is wittily fascinated by the contrast between his ruthless inner self and his pious outward appearances. Yet that inner self still exists, and he finally suffers nightmares of guilt.

But Mr. Clinton hardly exists apart from his kaleidoscopic appearances. He feels no guilt because he has no inner self that can feel compromised. A chameleon has no true colors.

Ever the moral ham, Clinton continues to feign contrition, laying it on a little thicker with each attempt. Every time he sheds his skin, he wants us to believe he's no longer a snake.

The President's Honor

JULY 2, 1996

My all-time favorite political quotation is the outraged bellow of the Irish politician Sir Boyle Roche: "Half the lies our enemies tell about us aren't true!" (It rivals Yogi Berra's reputed comment on a certain nightclub: "Nobody goes there anymore. It's too crowded.")

Sir Boyle's classic roar of indignation came to mind again last week when the Clinton administration reacted to a new book with nuanced hysteria. In his memoir, *Unlimited Access,* the former FBI agent Gary Aldrich, who used to work in the Clinton White House, repeats a salacious rumor about the president sneaking off late at night to a Marriott hotel for trysts with an unnamed celebrity.

What even his defenders won't claim

There are two problems with this rumor. The first is that Mr. Aldrich can't back it up. The second is that the White House can't deny it.

The president himself, caught off guard by a reporter's question about the rumor during his trip to France, said he hardly knew how to respond. (That probably means he didn't yet know how much he could deny without being contradicted by witnesses.) His spokesman George Stephanopolos called the book as a whole a "fabrication," then passed the ball to a Secret Service spokesman, who said it was physically and metaphysically impossible for a president — even this president — to get away from his Secret Service guardians. (What did you expect the Secret Service to say? "Well, you can't expect us to know where he is every minute of the day"?) The president's partisans in the press have called Mr. Aldrich lots of unflattering names.

But notice what nobody said. Nobody actually insisted that the president is faithful to Mrs. Clinton. Nobody said that his honor was being unfairly impugned. That's where the indignation carefully and tactfully hit the brakes.

Is the president's sex life our business? No. But his honor is. Any man who commits adultery casually has to be a habitual deceiver into the bargain. In some unhappy marriages spouses tolerate a sort of monogamous adultery with a single lover or mistress, as Franklin and Eleanor Roosevelt seem to have done. But that's a different matter from constantly prowling for new flesh, as Mr. Clinton notoriously does. A married man can't be a lecher without also being a liar.

According to his biographer Roger Morris, Mr. Clinton began cheating on his wife during their engagement. One witness recalls that he even had another young woman — a local politician's daughter — believing she was his fiancée at the same time Hillary Rodham was under the same impression. Such audacious deception has rarely been equaled outside the early movies of Alec Guinness. It may stand as unduplicated duplicity.

Some of Mr. Clinton's defenders apparently can't distinguish between a character flaw and a total absence of honor. They dismiss questions about the president's "morality" as if these were the exclusive concern of prying prudes. But in myriad ways Mr. Clinton has already succeeded in defining presidential deviancy down.

His defenders are mostly liberals who used to insist that Richard Nixon was the father of lies. He "lied to the American people," as they used to put it with doleful gravity.

But Nixon lied out of what he felt was necessity; in a tight spot, he lied to stave people off. Mr. Clinton lies to take people in. He lies when there is no need to lie, as if it were a sort of game. His first instinct is always to invent, as when he said that the recent wave of church burnings in the South recalled his vivid memories of racist church burnings in Arkansas during his youth; it quickly turned out that there hadn't been any, so he revised the lie. He had meant to say "community centers," not churches. And once again the record refuted him.

It's amusing to see Mr. Clinton defended today by the same journalists who used to talk as if Richard Nixon had debauched this country so badly that they'd never be able to look an honest Third World guerrilla in the eye again. This president may lie to them, but they'll be true to him.

Interpreting Clintonics

FEBRUARY 11, 1997

T he pundits are having fun analyzing the president's oratory,
which does present tempting targets: the short list includes, in
alphabetical order, banality, bombast, demagogy, evasion,
hypocrisy, illogic, sanctimony, tedium, and vacuity.

All these vices have marked Mr. Clinton's inaugural address, his
state of the Union message, and his recent prayer breakfast speech lamenting the cynicism of the press (which, by
the way, is a little like a burglar complaining
that watchdogs lack faith in human nature).

Then there is Mr. Clinton's delivery. All the
rest would be bearable if only he didn't seem
so pleased with himself. He speaks with an
evident conviction that his vacuous exhortations are memorable additions to our national heritage.

The president laments our cynicism.

Such exhortations are now called "applause lines," meaning
that the audience is more or less embarrassed into clapping, because not to clap would be to let an obvious bid for approval fall
flat, thereby souring what is supposed to be an occasion of national uplift. You know an applause line is in the making, for
example, when Mr. Clinton begins a sentence: "I challenge every American to ..."

Or when he mentions children. You have to clap when a president
wants to help children. There is nothing more presidential than helping children. When a presidential sentence begins, "We must guarantee that every child ...", we must applaud, no matter how that sentence
ends. This is no time for cost-accounting or squinting over the fine
print of the Constitution.

"We face no imminent threat," the president said in his state of the
Union speech, "but we do have an enemy. The enemy of our time is —"
(dramatic pause) "— inaction." Say what?

At such moments I begin to think that the chief educational reform
of our time should be to teach Clintonics as a separate language. Only

Mr. Clinton himself can speak it, but the rest of us should at least learn to comprehend it, if only in self-defense. What may sound like boring nonsense may turn out to mean something very specific.

How can "inaction" be our "enemy"? Since that's nonsense when taken literally, we look for a figurative, or Clintonic, meaning, with inspirational overtones. If inaction is our enemy, "action" must be our "friend." But what kind of action? Just action in general?

Ah! I have it! Legislation! The president is saying that we must pass more laws, or we'll be destroyed, or ruined, or left behind by the Japanese, or something.

It turned out, as we all know, that the president was calling for lots of laws — federal programs, really — to make sure every child can read, operate a computer, go to college. Such programs will appeal to lots of parents, and they will mean billions of dollars for the teachers and "educationists" who are Mr. Clinton's chief supporters. So there is concrete meaning, real cash value, lurking in the vague Clintonic up- lift.

In the real world, there are grounds for treating this agenda with re- serve. But in Clintonics, proposals to expand the federal government beyond its current dimensions sound like platitudes nobody could possibly deny — the very stuff of "bipartisanship." We're all in favor of action, children, education, and keeping America Number One, right?

Mr. Clinton seems loath to admit that the cynicism he complains about is a natural reaction to such duplicitous rhetoric. Cynicism is the emotional form of what the intellect experiences as skepticism. Mr. Clinton is really objecting to honest skepticism of his pretensions. He affects to find it a morally troubling symptom of our time that people don't trust him.

One need not be a Clinton-hater to recognize this president as a deeply dishonest man. Even for his supporters this is not a judgment to be denied, but a fact that has to be worked around. His personal scan- dals are of a piece with his politics: both reflect the complete disjunc- tion between his facile words and moral reality.

No president since Lyndon Johnson has grasped the pure logic of politics as well as Bill Clinton. He has maneuvered us into reelecting him, even as he has made us ashamed to be Americans. No wonder we are cynical.

Clinton admits he lied to us once, but he reminds us that he has told us the truth "hundreds upon hundreds upon hundreds of times." He seems to think that if you lie less than half the time, you are, on balance, an honest man. And even though he has had a few flings, he's been a faithful husband hundreds upon hundreds upon hundreds of times.

Two Liars

MAY 1997

W eathermen, someone has observed, now talk like book-
ies. They no longer say it's going to rain; they say there's
a "60 per cent likelihood" of rain. That's one step from
saying there's a 50 per cent chance a coin will turn up heads.

In the same spirit, I'll predict that there's a 60 per cent chance that
Bill Clinton will be impeached. A preliminary impeachment inquiry
may begin soon in the House of Representatives, but don't hold your
breath.

Not that it wouldn't be an unmitigated delight to see Clinton and
the missus tarred and feathered; the trouble is that that's pretty much
all there is to a conservative agenda in Washington. Conservative pundits and intellectuals keep talking about it, but the Republicans in Congress don't even have the gumption to execute that much.

Bill Clinton is not the essence of the problem with the U.S. (alias
federal) Government, and getting rid of him is not the solution. It's
only an amusement.

But what an amusement! At a recent conservative gathering I
picked up a T-shirt with the legend "VISUALIZE IMPEACH-
MENT." I love it, and I prick up my ears like an old dog spotting a
squirrel whenever I see a new sign that our young chief executive may
be headed for the chute. Actually, I'd be content with a lot less than his
removal from office. I'd just like to have him get up every day of his
life after he leaves the White House and hear people using the word
"Clintonian" the way they use such eponymous tags as "Stalin,"
"McCarthy," and "Rodney Dangerfield" — names that stand for
qualities requiring no further explanation. I'd like dictionaries to have
entries like this:

Clintonian, adj. [fr. Bill Clinton, 42nd president of the United
States.] Egregiously dishonest and evasive; cheerfully unscrupulous;
ingratiating but untrustworthy. Syn.: **Nixonian.**

More or less the O. J. treatment, in other words. Clinton and
Simpson should be the two people the 1990s are remembered for. It

was fitting that Clinton's state of the Union speech should be upstaged by the second Simpson verdict; both men are excellent liars, but they represent opposing styles in mendacity. Simpson can say unflinchingly that he's never owned the Bruno Magli shoes he's shown wearing in thirty photographs right in front of his nose, with a jury watching. That's Simpsonian, not Clintonian. The Clintonian approach would be to say he'd had to borrow those Bruno Magli shoes from a friend for that single occasion, but never wore them again. (Another difference is that Clinton might be more easily forgiven by the American public for dispatching his wife, but I'm getting off the subject.)

By now you can divide Americans into those who still pretend to believe Clinton, and those who don't. Eleanor Clift is still playing Olive Oyl to Clinton's Popeye, and Garry Wills and E. J. Dionne Jr. are still giving him what Rabbi Korff (remember Rabbi Korff?) gave Richard Nixon: loyal denial. A competent epistemologist might make the case that we still don't *know* that Clinton has ever lied, just as we may not *know,* at a given moment, whether we are awake or dreaming.

It's puzzling. Are those who profess to believe an obvious liar lying too?

What about Juanita Broaddrick's charge that Clinton raped her in 1978, when he was Arkansas's young attorney general and she was volunteering to help his campaign for governor? It seems almost silly to doubt she's telling the truth. We've heard this story too many times, from too many women; the details are convincing, right down to Clinton's later "apology." She says he approached her in 1991 to assure her that "I'm not the same man I used to be." He's never the same man he used to be. That's one thing that never changes.

Billy Con

JANUARY 1998

B ill Clinton is an amazing politician. I recently compared him to Joe Louis: just as Joe was the perfect fighting machine, Clinton is an almost perfect political machine.

But a better analogy would have been Billy Conn. First, the name is an apt pun. Second, Conn was a great light-heavyweight who decisively outboxed Louis for twelve rounds, landing hundreds of stinging jabs and eluding Louis's bombs. But here the analogy breaks down. In the thirteenth round, far ahead on points, Conn decided to outpunch Louis too; a moment later, he was one more notch on Louis's belt.

Clinton wouldn't have made that mistake. He knows his limitations, and he sticks to fast jabs and footwork, avoiding slugging contests. He survives as long as nobody can lay a glove on him. And nobody does.

When his attorney general decided there were no grounds for asking for a special prosecutor to check out his 1996 compliance with campaign fundraising laws, we knew we were seeing the incredible luck of a man who makes his own luck. How did he arrange his latest escape? Did he take Janet Reno out to dinner? Did he make a discreet threat? I think we can rule out such crude methods. He must have thought of something the rest of us can't imagine, some indirect cajolery or admonition, perhaps delivered through a third party, that left no trace or record. He's not the man to leave a horse's head between your sheets, but he always gets his man. Or woman.

Take the recent report that Clinton had auctioned off plots in Arlington National Cemetery to people whose only eligibility for burial there was campaign donations to the 1996 Clinton-Gore campaign. It turned out to be untrue, or at least not true enough to draw Clintonian blood. But it *should* have been true, like all the quick ripostes ascribed to Winston Churchill. Only a genius in his field could inspire such apocrypha. If Clinton didn't think of raising money that way, it was a rare lapse on his part, for which he should be pardoned.

I still marvel that after five unbroken years of scandals, frauds, evasions, lawsuits, and whoppers, along with several indictments and convictions of dear ones, the press has yet to apply to Clinton the phrase it habitually used about the Reagan administration: "the sleaze factor." Reagan, an easy-going guy, didn't run the rightest ethical ship. He wasn't crooked himself, but the same couldn't be said for some of his hangers-on.

But there is a difference. Reagan attracted sleaze. Clinton *is* sleaze. Watching the liberties he takes with his office, a patriotic American begins to understand how patriotic Romans must have felt when the emperor Caligula appointed his horse consul. It's not that he is the worst of men; it's that this has become the kind of country where a man of his make can rise to the top. His qualifications, such as they are, are purely political; he has no significant existence or substance outside politics. We are used to thinking we are ruled by heroes, giants, or at least men of accomplishment and character. But we are now being ruled by a political specialist, who exemplifies the logic of our time.

To quote Edmund Burke: "Criminal means, once tolerated, are soon preferred."

The Ethos of Lying

FEBRUARY 26, 1998

Conservatives are bemoaning the cynicism of the American people, who keep giving Bill Clinton high marks for doing his job, even though most of them think he's lying about "that woman."

Those approval ratings are a puzzle. Clinton got less than half the votes cast in two straight elections, but he gets landslides in opinion polls.

Of course people are cynical. They sense their rulers lie to them, and for good reason. The ruling elites believe that lying to the public is justifiable. This isn't some furtive whisper, but an open and ingenuous conviction.

In the March 2 issue of *The New Republic*, a useful barometer of elite opinion, the philosopher Michael Sandel contrasts two famous presidential lies. During the 1940 campaign, Franklin Roosevelt pledged: "I have said this before, but I shall say it again and again and again: your boys are not going to be sent into any foreign wars." At the time, he was secretly scheming to get the United States into war. And during the 1964 campaign, Lyndon Johnson falsely denied that he was planning to escalate the war in Vietnam.

When should rulers deceive the people?

Sandel comments: "Both presidents deceived the public — Roosevelt for the sake of a just cause, Johnson for the sake of an unjust one.... Johnson's lie was less justified than Roosevelt's, not because it was any less truthful, but because it served an unworthy end."

This profoundly elitist view has become a platitude among the political intelligentsia. Liberals, conservatives, and those in between repeat it constantly: Roosevelt was justified in lying to the people for the purpose of taking them to war.

Nobody seems to notice the obvious implication about democracy. When does a ruler owe the people the truth, if not when their sons' lives are at stake? Is it up to the ruler to decide whether his ends are so "worthy" that he may use lies to inveigle the public into supporting them?

The intellectuals have already answered these questions to their own satisfaction. If they think Roosevelt was justified in lying for a "worthy end," they will naturally believe that any other ruler is justified in lying for ends they consider worthy.

And this flexible ethos is bound to be stretched further, to minimize the gravity of lying for unworthy ends — provided the liar favors generally "worthy" causes. Ask any feminist.

Nobody will say flatly that the end justifies the means, but President Clinton's supporters evidently feel that his ends are worthy enough to warrant winking at his criminal means. This is the logic of politics in general. Ordinary, nonintellectual people understand this well enough. Cynicism about politicians is merely realism. Only part of the truth ever reaches the public, and even that fraction is adulterated with falsehoods.

So when, say, the Iowa housewife hears about the latest Clinton scandals, her response is likely to be something like this:

"I know Clinton isn't perfect by every standard; he's probably committed perjury along with adultery. But just how many criteria for a president are there? My family and I are alive, prosperous, and safe. My son isn't going to be sent to fight on the other side of the world. That's all I know, it's good enough for me, and I see no reason to risk our well-being by getting indignant about whatever Clinton may have done in some little room in Washington. I have no way of knowing what's happening there; I can only judge by what's happening here."

That's a rational reaction. It may not be noble, but it shows a sane resistance to being stampeded. Since modern government is a potentially destabilizing force, the wisest course may be to leave well enough alone — not because rulers can be trusted, but precisely because you never really know what they may do next.

If our rulers don't think they owe us the truth, we have to deal with them on our own terms. That may sometimes mean supporting a president we neither like, trust, approve, nor respect, and wouldn't let within a mile of our children. If Bill Clinton has degraded our political life, who is doing anything to elevate it?

The Clinton defense cites such precedents as John Kennedy's lechery in the White House, as if Kennedy's conduct exonerates all successors who do likewise. The real moral is the opposite: the posthumous revelations about Kennedy have damaged our standards by allowing Clinton to hide behind Kennedy's example.

Moreover, Kennedy hid his adulteries because he knew perfectly well that they would expose him to impeachment. The fact that he resorted to blackmail to conceal them shows how dangerous he knew his situation was.

The Great Prevaricator

APRIL 9, 1998

W hen Monica Lewinsky made headlines in January, President Clinton said he would provide as many of "the facts" ("sooner rather than later") as he could, consistent with his "obligation to cooperate with the investigation."

This promise was followed by a complete stonewall, supplemented by his aides' trashing of the investigator and the witnesses, all in keeping with his wife's charge of a "vast right-wing conspiracy" headed by special prosecutor Kenneth Starr. Meanwhile, Clinton pretended, à la O. J. Simpson, that he was legally prevented from telling his side. It was dizzying, and it was meant to be.

At last— Clinton tells his side!

Now that the Paula Jones suit has been dismissed, *Time* has published an exclusive interview with Clinton. At last! He can tell us his side!

But guess what? After fighting for years to keep the case from going to court, Clinton now complains that the summary judgment in his favor has deprived him of the "chance to disprove these allegations in court. After going through what I've been through, I would have wanted to put all my evidence before twelve of my fellow citizens." He still denies Mrs. Jones's charges, but, alas, "it's in the nature of summary judgment that it doesn't give me the chance to convince twelve people that the factual allegations are not true."

But, the interviewer asks, what about Kathleen Willey's story? Again Clinton denies everything, adding: "But I'm not going to talk about it."

The interviewer points out that there have been other stories too, and asks whether Clinton has any regrets about putting himself in apparently compromising situations. "I have no further comment on these things."

Asked about Starr's investigation, the president says: "I won't depart from my policy of not commenting on Mr. Starr." Asked about his claim of executive privilege for himself and his wife, he says he's in the dark: "The first time I learn about a lot of these legal arguments is when I see them in the papers."

At this point the interviewer is incredulous. Here is the president of the United States, a lawyer who has taught constitutional law, saying he doesn't know why his legal team is invoking executive privilege! How can that be? "I'm just not going to talk about that."

Amazing. Clinton grants an exclusive interview, then stonewalls the interviewer — while complaining that he has been denied a chance to tell his side of the story. If he escapes impeachment, he'll no doubt complain that he's been robbed of the chance to clear his name.

If he's telling the truth, Clinton is in something like the predicament of Cary Grant in *North by Northwest*, who is photographed holding a knife over the corpse, except that Clinton is holding a lot more knives. In a situation like that, it's awkward to explain your innocence. What's more, many of Clinton's underlings are implicated in the things he insists he didn't do.

The simplest explanation is that Clinton is the Great Prevaricator. He doesn't merely fib a little. Lies ripple outward from him in great waves, through his aides, his allies, friendly members of the press. Getting others to spread his lies and smear his enemies is part of his modus operandi. This delegated mendacity makes it plausible that he has suborned perjury, tampered with witnesses, pressed his own secretary to change her story. He may have used Vernon Jordan, Nathan Landow, and others to dissuade women from testifying about him. Directly or through an underling, he may have tried to induce Linda Tripp to alter her testimony.

There's another possible explanation: Clinton is as innocent as he insists. If so, William of Ockham can put his razor away, because the simplest explanation is wrong and the truth is as complicated as a vast conspiracy fortuitously assisted by a hundred incredible coincidences that have joined to form a wholly misleading apparent pattern.

But the pattern chimes with reports from Arkansas that Clinton used state troopers to procure women and charges that he used his office to get an illegal loan. Either he has been abusing power for a long time, or he has a bad habit of creating the wrong impression.

Every Promise Is a Threat

FEBRUARY 2, 1999

I 've been nerdishly reading a government document: President Clinton's state of the Union address. It's longer than the letters I used to write to Santa Claus. A sampling:

"Fifth, to assure that our classrooms are truly places of learning, and to respond to what teachers have been asking us to do for years, we should say that all states and school districts must both adopt and implement sensible discipline policies....

"Also, I ask your support for a dramatic increase in federal support for adult literacy, to mount a national campaign aimed at helping the millions and millions of working people who still read at less than a fifth-grade reading level....

"We must do more to bring the spark of private enterprise to every corner of America — to build a bridge from Wall Street to Appalachia to the Mississippi Delta, to our Native American communities — with more support for community development banks, for empowerment zones, for 100,000 more vouchers for affordable housing. And I ask Congress to support our bold new plan," etc., etc.

Query: Just how many laws do we need?

It isn't just that Clinton's myriad proposals have no authorization in the Constitution. Who cares about that? Most of them won't be adopted anyway; they were meant as applause lines.

The trouble is that Congress did applaud. This kind of talk — a numbing litany of ambitious programs — has become routine political rhetoric.

The green-eyeshade analysts have already observed that Clinton's program package presupposes constant budget surpluses for the foreseeable future. True enough, but that's not the point.

It isn't just that the federal government shouldn't be doing all these things; neither should the states or counties or cities or townships. Has everyone forgotten that every increase in the scope of government is necessarily a further limitation on freedom, a further growth in power over the citizen, a further rise in taxes?

Government, as our first president reminded us, is not persuasion or reason; it is force. Government doesn't produce anything. It can only compel. Every benefit for you ultimately has to be taken from me, and vice versa.

It's not just a zero-sum game. The growth of government — of systematic social compulsion — lessens the value of everyone's efforts. It may not appear that way during prosperous times, when production outstrips taxation, but it's true. Everything has its cost, in liberty as well as in cash.

How many laws should a society have? Is there such a thing as too many? When these questions aren't even raised, it's a cinch that the laws have already far exceeded the requirements of justice. Which can only mean that most of them are unjust.

What used to go without saying is now considered "right-wing." Our ancestors agreed that legislation should be kept to a minimum; that what is naturally unjust can't be made just by positive law; that it is wrong, as well as bad policy, to make some people pay for benefits for others; that people who don't pay taxes, or who get government money, shouldn't vote; that excessive taxation is extortion and imposes servitude.

It was understood that if you had no right to take something from your neighbor, you had no right to have the government take it from him for you. But the legacy of the twentieth century — of Bill Clinton and Lyndon Johnson no less than Lenin, Hitler, and Mao — is that what would be wrong for private persons is somehow legitimate for the state.

"Constituencies" are no longer territorial units of representation, but groups that seek privilege for themselves at others' expense. We now take it for granted that politicians will work more for powerful lobbies than for the people who elected them.

Proposals like Clinton's are treated as generous gestures, as if the man advancing them were going to pay for them himself. But

they are actually implicit threats against everyone but the beneficiaries, since they can only be implemented by force — an obvious fact that can't be escaped, but is generally ignored.

Does government have the right to do such things? Never mind.
It has the power, and that's what counts.

Idle Thoughts

SEPTEMBER 10, 1998

T his week I'm taking a vacation from logic and giving way to a flow of impressions arising from Bill Clinton's predicament. So please don't look for much coherence or continuity in what follows.

Even during Clinton's visit, Russia's Duma was convulsed with mirth at one member's suggestion that he divorce Hillary and marry Monica. The pro-Clinton columnist Garry Wills confesses: "I was shocked when my son returned from a 22-month bike trip around the world and told me that the ordinary people he met all over the globe reacted to his saying he was an American with snide jokes or questions about his President's sex life."

And yet, back home, a CNN poll found that if an election were held today, Bill Clinton — the laughingstock of Western Civilization at the close of the second millennium — would still beat Bob ("I'm elect-able!") Dole, 46 to 36 per cent. This ought to be the last word on the Republican Party.

It reminds me of my early days in New York City in 1972. One night I asked a cab driver what he thought of Richard Nixon. I will file an affidavit, if necessary, to affirm that this is a true story: most columns involving cab drivers or bartenders are sheer inventions, but this really happened. You have to believe me! Anyway, the driver let fly with a stream of invective, profane and obscene even by New York standards, about what a blankety-blank liar Nixon was.

When he finally paused for breath, I asked him if he was vot-ing for George McGovern. "Are you crazy?" he asked. I forget the exact words, but he was voting for that blankety-blank liar Nixon. And today a large part of the public prefers that blankety-blank liar Clinton to Bob Dole. I think I understand, even as an unabashed Clinton-hater.

By the way, what's wrong with "hate"? Liberal rhetoric as-sumes that "hate" is not only bad but is the defining trait of conservatives. The truth is that hate, like love, is entirely natural. That's not all. God is love, but Our Lord himself tells us that we may have to hate our own loved ones for his sake! There is no virtue in feigning love for the hateful. Our Lord doesn't enjoin us to be idiots, hypocrites, or Episcopalians.

It all depends what you hate, and why, and how. Excessive, vengeful hatred is wrong, and so is revenge. But we naturally fear, and therefore hate, anyone who threatens us with harm. Even animals hate this way. Hatred is dangerous because it may easily lead to malice and revenge, and we may self-righteously confuse our irritation with God's judgment; but it's absurd to say that hatred is intrinsically wrong.

When a devious malefactor like Clinton has power over us, we do — and should — hate him and take measures to protect ourselves and our society from him. It would be wonderful if he converted, but praying for his conversion isn't quite the same thing as expecting it momentarily. And the absence (or denial) of hatred isn't the same thing as charity.

Clinton has done terrible evil by using the presidency to promote sexual license and its inevitable consequence, abortion. The policies he favors are distinct from his personal life, and they would be evil even if he were a faithful husband. And yet it's fitting that he should be punished by having his own sexual sins, including his onanism in the Oval Office, exposed to the world.

Clinton's rise to the top of American society ought to be a rebuke to our excessive patriotism. Americans are a self-righteous people, far too apt to equate their political system with virtue. In this respect I think conservatives are far worse than liberals.

It's become a cliché to say that "everyone lies about sex." This is a cynical insult to chaste people and an unconscious confession by those who say it. As Edmund Burke said: "He that accuses all mankind is sure to convict only one." Lust and lies go together — a truth Clinton exemplifies. And chastity and honesty go together. What do virgins and faithful spouses have to lie about?

As for the vagaries of the stock market, I have no idea what they mean. But Clinton's basic claim to presidential competence rests on "the economy, stupid," and the last fortnight has destroyed the illusion that "peace and prosperity" are a solid foundation for deeming him a success even in secular terms. He wants to be judged by the Dow Jones Industrial Average — though he carries his Bible to church for good measure.

And speaking of the Bible, the Mobile Clinton Defense Forces have now added King David to the distinguished line of adulterers in high office who furnish Clinton with precedents. You'd think licentiousness were the infallible mark of a great statesman.

The Clinton defense is rooted in the philosophy that private virtue — at the level of the family and the individual — doesn't matter; only government management shapes the character of society. "It's the economy, stupid" really means "it's the government, stupid." In principle Clinton and his partisans agree with Stalin. I'm not imputing principles to them; that would be an anthropomorphic error. They merely adopt a view that denies personal responsibility and justifies themselves in claiming power.

MR. AND MRS.

The Flying Clintons

JULY 1996

I keep catching myself hoping that Bill Clinton will be reelected. It isn't just that Bob Dole richly deserves to lose; it's that mere electoral defeat would be an inadequate comeuppance for the Clintons. They are headed for their own Watergate, and it would be a pity to see the drama aborted. I'm only moderately vindictive: I want them hounded out of office, not hounded after they've already left.

This is getting good. As I write, Bill's old pal Bruce Lindsey has been named an unindicted co-conspirator in the latest federal trial of the Arkansas mob. The Republicans want the special prosecutor to investigate three Clinton associates who may have perjured themselves before the Senate Whitewater Committee. Both Clintons are under fire for the abuse of FBI files, a new scandal that has turned over several interesting rocks and revealed unsuspected dimensions of skullduggery: the thuggish Craig Livingstone, who was in charge of the file operation against the Clintons' enemies, is a character right out of the 1972 Nixon reelection campaign. He also turns out to be close to Hillary, and even helped clean out Vince Foster's office after his death. The Clintons' original story of "an innocent bureaucratic mistake" with the files has been exposed as a lie covering up something far more sinister. Every week brings a damaging revelation.

Foster, according to a new book about the Clintons, was Hillary's closest friend — and her lover. This throws an interesting light on everything else, beginning with Hillary's amazing operation to take control of his office. The news of his death must have been the shock of her life. She was in Arkansas when it happened, and an innocent observer would think that her first reaction would have been to call her husband; after all, the three of them were old friends. If Foster's office contained damning material about their Whitewater and Travel Office misdeeds, it would have been in the interest of both spouses to remove it.

But it appears that she didn't call Bill in her hour of crisis. She immediately resolved to make sure her people got the records out of that office before anyone else entered it. She spent the night on the phone with her old pal Susan Thomases and her chief of staff, Maggie Williams, both of whom suffered from failing memories when the Whitewater Committee asked about the substance of the calls. Their explanation was that they were exchanging "condolences" with Hillary — in more than a dozen calls, some as brief as a minute or two.

We may never know the full story of that night. All that is clear is that she was up to no good, and it appears that she chose not to involve Bill or to seek his help. Was she hiding things from him too?

One early result of all these scandals is that Hillary's image as Bill's better half — the "ethical" member of the family — is shot. Moreover, there is no love lost between these two. They are like members of a trapeze act who hate each other's guts, but can't let go: if one falls, the act is finished.

The Clintons remind us of Tolstoy's famous aphorism: "Happy families are all alike; every unhappy family is unhappy in its own way."

The Secret Settlement

AUGUST 1996

W hen Bill Clinton gets into trouble, more often than not his wife seems to be at or near the bottom of it. Our first impression of this couple was that he was the wayward one, the slippery pol, the philandering husband, while she was the honest if strident feminist virago. When a columnist called her a "congenital liar," Bill himself said this would be a better country if everyone were as "ethical" as his wife. (She hasn't returned the compliment.)

The picture is changing. Hillary may well be more deeply implicated in the Whitewater crimes than Bill. She has been linked to Craig Livingstone, the curious keeper of the FBI files, though she has denied the rumor that she ordered his hiring. She orchestrated the possibly criminal coverup after Vince Foster's death.

Until recently I didn't realize how widely it was known that Hillary and Foster had been an item. A friend told me of asking a Bush employee whether he knew who was moving into a certain White House office at the January 1993 transition. He was told: "Hillary Clinton's lover." To wit, Foster. Even the Bush people knew.

In his headline-making book, *Unlimited Access,* Gary Aldrich says Livingstone once told him that Foster had killed himself because he feared that the press was going to reveal his affair with the first lady. Yet the story didn't break even when Foster's death itself created a sensation. The next time you hear "conspiracy theories" derided, remember how well Washington kept this little secret.

Aldrich also says the Clintons fought violently at the time of Bill's inauguration over whether Hillary would get what had traditionally been the vice president's office. Apparently she had expected this, which suggests that Bill had promised it, or (in his fashion) led her to think he was promising it.

All this casts a new light over Bill's use of Hillary during the 1992 campaign. She not only stood by her man during the Gennifer Flowers uproar; he offered her to the voters as a bonus. "Buy one, get one free." She even hinted to *Vanity Fair* that she would be a sort of "co-president," which does imply that she expected to outrank Al Gore.

During the first year of the Clinton presidency, Hillary played a grandiose role. She had a large say in appointments even at the cabinet level; she led her own campaign for national health care; she had her personal team of courtiers; she spoke of an ambitious "politics of meaning." In short, she became the most powerful and unpopular first lady in history. And it wasn't long before she also generated her own scandals.

It appears that the Clintons' marriage has been good and dead for a long time, and that the price of Hillary's cooperation in Bill's quest for the presidency was a share of the spoils. In other words, the White House became the object of a de facto property settlement in a bitter but unannounced divorce between two extremely ambitious people.

The Clinton Scandals

FEBRUARY 1996

W hether or not she winds up indicted, convicted, and/or imprisoned, it's delightful to see Hillary Clinton become a tarnished icon. The central scandal is not whether she has done anything technically criminal, but that she has already turned out to be the sort of devious and self-serving operator she used to denounce.

She was wont to pose as the champion of the Compassionate Sixties, in opposition to the spawn of the Republican Eighties — the Decade of Greed. Her comeuppance is a delicious deflation.

Why Mother Teresa doesn't rule the world

People who love power always denounce greed. And by greed they always mean the desire to earn and keep wealth through free exchange. Their antidote for this abhorred vice is to replace an economy of exchange with an economy of coercion, alias compassion. They don't regard the use of state power to get other people's money as a form of avarice. So it's not surprising that, as the royal family of Arkansas, the Clintons used their power as the means of enriching themselves.

Politics is a sort of market of coercion. Politicians offer to use state power to save their supporters from the onerous necessity of *earning* — of persuading others to give them money by offering something in return. This old racket used to be called patronage, back when it was relatively harmless and corruption was confined by low taxes and small budgets. But the modern limitless state has vastly expanded it, using every moral pretext available in order to commandeer the wealth of nations. The spoils system has been extended from a few officeholders to tens of millions of parasites.

Capitalism creates prosperity, which by its nature is always unequally distributed. Socialism is the promise of equal prosperity, which is radically impossible. Socialism follows prosperity as cockroaches follow food. In one form or another, it appears wherever there is surplus. It's wealth, not poverty, that brings on socialism; it's surplus, not scarcity, that brings out the parasites.

The parasite embodies true greed — consuming without producing. He disguises this elementary fact by ascribing greed to those who want to consume what they produce. His vocabulary is a lexicon of misdirection, in which words like *greed, compassion, fairness, sharing,* and *selfishness* take on perverse meanings and the element of raw power is concealed. Production becomes aggression, the refusal or inability to produce becomes victimhood, and plunder becomes protection.

This is the way of life the Clintons represent. It's been clear all along that Bill Clinton is a pure huckster, but Hillary seemed to be a true believer. Now it comes as a kind of relief to find she's made of the same stuff as her husband. Her fanaticism has never gotten in the way of her profit.

James Burnham described liberalism as "the ideology of Western suicide." The great old geopolitical analyst meant that liberalism rationalized every setback for Western *interests* as a triumph of Western "ideals." You could also say that liberalism is the ideology of simple opportunism. It disguises the shoddiest and most morbid appeals to selfishness as compassion.

There are many strings on the lyre of compassion — children, women, minorities, health, education, the environment — and the Clintons know how to pluck them all. They've become the Jim and Tammy Bakker of liberalism, milking specious sympathies to the last drop, until their fraudulence is completely exposed. Their compassion is reserved for the suffering of large and well-organized constituencies; they aren't averse to inflicting acute suffering on isolated people who get in their way.

If real compassion propelled people to the top, Mother Teresa would rule the world. It doesn't quite work that way. Power goes to people who know how to use power and use it for their own purposes. Politicians who lose elections merely seek other avenues to wealth and power. They don't become monks; they become lawyers and lobbyists.

The Clintons campaigned on the promise of "change," but real change was the last thing they expected. They assumed that the parasite politics of the New Deal tradition could go on forever, when it was already dangerously close to its practical limit and its slogans had lost most of their power to deceive.

To my mind any laws the Clintons break are no more than a minor scandal; the real scandal is what people like them can do *within* the law. But that's the generic scandal of socialism, that it converts law itself into the instrument of plunder. It avows the highest ideals and attracts the lowest types.

It always amazes me that political greed is so insatiable. You'd think that even criminal types could manage to be law-abiding when they themselves control and enforce the law. And yet so often they turn out to be like bullying children who make up games, then break their own rules in order to win.

The scandal has exposed Hillary too as a liar. When, in his August 17 speech, Clinton carefully said he'd "misled" his wife, he was misleading us. She knows him, she's not stupid, and she was also misleading us in January when she tried to divert blame to the "vast right-wing conspiracy." But she didn't want him to concede an inch, and it's likely that she only agreed to his pseudo-confession on condition that he exculpate her.

The Dysfunctional Clintons

AUGUST 12, 1999

T ina Brown's long cultivation of the Clintons, dating back
to 1992, when she was editor of *Vanity Fair* and continu-
ing through her years at *The New Yorker,* has paid off —
for Tina, not for the Clintons. Hillary has given Tina's new magazine, *Talk,* an exclusive interview in which she makes a total fool
of herself. But the publicity has given *Talk* a sensational launch.

As you've heard by now, Hillary discussed Bill in psychoana-
lytic lingo, excusing his philandering because he was "scarred
by abuse" by the age of four and was later unaware of the early
trauma that was "causing his behavior." What was the "abuse"?
His mother and grandmother used to fight! "A psychologist once
told me," Hillary said soberly, "that for a boy, being in the middle
of a conflict between two women is the worst possible situation."
It was a case of "dysfunction."

For ten years, up to 1998, Hillary thought Bill had "resolved"
and "conquered" his "weakness." But alas, as it turned out, "he
didn't go deep enough or work hard enough." But he's still "a
very, very good man," a superb president, and a husband worth
keeping, in spite of everything. And he's trying to do better: "He
has been working on himself very hard in the past year. He has
become more aware of his past and what was causing his behavior."

Is this how she really thinks? Or is it just how she thinks the
rest of us think? The glib psychobabble of Hillary's generation
has become so passé that it's a joke even to the comedians. Jay
Leno quipped that saying Bill has a "weakness" is like saying
Jeffrey Dahmer had an "eating disorder."

The interview was a disaster for the Clintons. Not even their
warmest supporters could take it seriously, and everyone else ridi-

CHAPTER 5 : MR. AND MRS.

culed it. Clinton himself felt constrained to say he made no excuses for his infidelity, and that Hillary hadn't made any excuses for him either. But that was exactly what she did. Once again she has made herself ludicrous while seeking that New York seat in the Senate.

Still, by talking publicly about Bill as a victim of emotional disorder, Hillary was subtly belittling him as a helpless creature of impulses he doesn't fully understand, casting herself as his superior in maturity and insight. Another historic first for the Clintons. A class couple. Al Gore must be writhing.

As for herself, Hillary felt "great anger," until she recalled that "Peter betrayed Jesus three times and Jesus knew it but loved him anyway." Actually, St. Peter *denied* Our Lord three times, as Our Lord predicted; when he said, "One of you will *betray* me," he meant Judas. In any case, Bill has betrayed Hillary more than three times; seventy times seven might be a better approximation. But that only underlines how forgiving Hillary is.

By saying all this publicly, for self-serving reasons, Hillary indirectly admits that she was lying when she played along with her husband's denials and assisted his smears of the "bimbos" and "vast right-wing conspiracy" who told the truth about him over the years.

But Bill wasn't the only straying Clinton. A new book — *Bill and Hillary: The Marriage,* by Christopher Andersen — says Hillary had her own affair with Vincent Foster, starting in 1977. No wonder she panicked when Foster suddenly died, frantically phoning her White House aides from Arkansas and ordering them to ransack his office. Who knows what investigators might have found there?

The affair was well known in both Arkansas and Washington. But the press didn't mention it in the enormous publicity attending Foster's supposed suicide. Now it's another Leno joke.

Andersen also says Hillary slapped Bill so hard she left a red mark on his face during the Monica scandal, screaming: "You stupid, stupid, stupid bastard! My God, Bill, how could you risk everything for *that*?" If this is accurate, it's interesting that she didn't ask, "How could you do this to Chelsea and me?" After all, Chelsea had been hospitalized several times for stress. But no, he was endangering their hold on power.

In 1982, according to Andersen, Hillary hired a private eye to see if Bill was cheating on her. The snoop reported back eight names of women Bill was seeing. In 1988 she demanded that Bill be checked for HIV; the test proved negative, but Andersen cites an informant who says he does have a venereal disease, which is why he has never released his medical records.

Back in Arkansas, Judge Susan Webber Wright fined Clinton $90,686 for lying under oath. In Maryland, Linda Tripp was indicted for wiretapping Monica. In California, Monica rolled her car over, suffering minor injuries. And they talk about the Kennedy Curse!

CLINTON AND PAULA JONES

Near-Victims

MARCH 1997

O f all the comments on the Paula Jones suit, the most interesting was made by Richard Cohen of the *Washington Post.*
Observing that the feminists haven't rallied to Mrs. Jones
as they did to Anita Hill, he reflected that she is precisely the
type of woman who is most vulnerable to what the Sisterhood
calls "sexual harassment": dowdy, working-class, without money
or education or social connections or ideology. Who these days
would dare to hit on a smartly dressed professional woman who
spoke fluent feminese?

Another way to put it is that a lecherous governor could have
sized up Mrs. Jones in a flash as a woman he could safely make a
crude pass at. Who would believe her if she complained? And
who among those who suspected she was telling the truth could
give her story resonance? Not even Bill Clinton, who thinks of
'most everything, could have foreseen that if he ever became
president of the whole U.S. of A., her story might find its own
avenue to the front page.

But Paula Jones may also stand as a symbol of something larger
than the admittedly large class of women who have received Bill
Clinton's attentions. She belongs to the class of people who fall
into a peculiar twilight zone — just above the victimhood line,
so to speak.

Some people earn just enough money to disqualify them for
welfare. They get little attention and less pity. In the same way,
some whites are ineligible for the aid and solicitude that go to
minority-group members at the same income and education level,
and some women — women of modest means, heavy makeup,

and big hair — don't qualify for feminist sympathy.

All these folk might be called near-victims. They are typically self-sufficient, job-holding whites without much ambition, which is not to say they lack purpose, industry, or self-respect. They may even have political passions. But they are more likely to spend their weekends building a garage than organizing a movement. They know they are better off without the victim status which they despise and which, in any case, isn't intended for the likes of them.

The establishment of any sort of victim status creates not only a class of victims, but a counterclass of invisible but resentful near-victims. They are audible on what's called "right-wing talk radio," as they phone Rush or Gordon or Ollie with their well-grounded gripes and homespun witticisms.

Progressive-minded people scorn them, and vice versa. There is no room for compassion for the near-victim in the liberal's bleeding heart; in fact, the near-victim's self-respect and self-sufficiency make him (or her) a rebuke and a bête noire to the liberal, as witness the liberals' acid dismissal of Paula Jones and the talk-radio audience.

The real controversy over Mrs. Jones isn't over whether she's telling the truth; it's implicitly understood on all sides that she is. The struggle is over whether a jury of ordinary people, including, in all likelihood, several near-victims, is to be allowed to decide between her word and that of the nation's victim-coddler-in-chief.

Our Debt to Paula Jones

JANUARY 22, 1998

Suddenly nobody is questioning Paula Jones's veracity any-more. Mrs. Jones told a simple story and has stuck with it, while the president has shifted ground, equivocated with his patented "carefully worded denials," and let his thuggish, blundering, and very expensive lawyer handle public relations.

The Clinton team's line, echoed by the major media until recently, has been that Mrs. Jones is "trailer-park trash" whose allegations are credible only to dirty-minded right-wing Clinton-haters. Never mind that her allegations are consistent with a great many other allegations from a great many sources.

The "respectable" press catches up.

The Clinton strategy was to scare her off, and then, when that didn't work, to make her character the issue, leaking their own allegations to the press.

But her tenacity created enormous pressure, forcing the president to make a humiliating appearance in her presence a few days ago to give his deposition — and possibly to try to tamper with other wit-nesses. Only he knows how many other potential witnesses there are.

The new charges of creepy lechery and criminality have finally cost Clinton his protective press. Though *Newsweek* spiked its own scoop, the story exploded anyway. All those journalists who have cov-ered for Clinton now feel he's yanked the rug out from under them once too often.

And it happened because a story they didn't want to dignify with coverage refused to go away. The story *Newsweek* spiked was written by Michael Isikoff, who had left the *Washington Post* in fury two years ago when the paper spiked a similar story he'd written on the Jones suit. But now the "respectable" press has finally caught up with the "crazy" press, leaving Hillary Clinton to repeat her usual gripe — Bill's just the victim of someone's political agenda — to an empty gal-lery.

Clinton is standing on a precipice, staring down at the abyss of impeachment and prison. One nudge — another story, witness, allegation, or tape recording — could push him over. And the market value of any damaging evidence has skyrocketed, with the media fighting fiercely for the kind of information they used to spurn. He's at the mercy of any bimbo who wants to step forward.

After being driven from office, Richard Nixon was able to make a comeback by claiming, however speciously, that his motive had always been to defend the dignity of the presidency. That's a claim Clinton won't be able to make. If he seduced a twenty-one-year-old White House intern and urged her to perjure herself for his sake, the dignity of the presidency was the last thing on his mind. Nor will he have the diehard it-didn't-start-with-Watergate defenders Nixon had. In Clinton's case, it started long ago in Arkansas.

He arrived in Washington with a trail of sleazy rumors, some of them substantiated. The "respectable" press ignored all that, including the fact that Gennifer Flowers had enjoyed rapid promotion as a state employee (and had tapes of Clinton urging her to lie about their liaison). It ignored "right-wing" reports that he'd used state troopers to procure women. Such stories illustrated his readiness to abuse power for sleazy purposes, but they were treated as cheap sex gossip. When Paula Jones told her story, it fit the pattern — but was rejected as unworthy of serious attention.

Now that the pattern is undeniable, Clinton is still Clintonizing — issuing new carefully-worded-denials, as if he might yet exculpate himself with verbal cleverness. It hasn't sunk in that he no longer has many supporters who will seize on any excuse for believing his version. His guilt isn't an epistemological puzzle.

Supporting Clinton has become extremely costly. He has destroyed the Democrats' congressional majorities in both houses, and though he managed to win reelection (by methods that will now get redoubled scrutiny), he has destroyed his own presidency. And his disgrace will be contagious.

The major media should not be allowed to ask: "How were we supposed to know?" It's their business to know — and to inform the public. But their job had to be done by Paula Jones and the "right-wing" press.

The Defection of David Brock

MARCH 10, 1998

D avid Brock has become the first journalist to confess his participation in the vast right-wing conspiracy to get President Clinton. Actually, he confessed it last year, but nobody was listening.

In an open letter to the president in the April issue of *Esquire,* Brock apologizes for his epoch-making 1993 article in *The American Spectator,* the one that gave "Arkansas state troopers" a special meaning, like "grassy knoll" as of 1963. Or, more to the point, like "bimbo eruptions" as of 1992 and "White House intern" as of 1998. The article also led, inadvertently, to Paula Jones's lawsuit.

The president has accepted Brock's mea culpa, but he may feel it's a little late for apologies. Confessing you started a forest fire doesn't make the trees grow back. This forest just happened to be unusually combustible. (Georgia state troopers probably don't have many colorful memories of former governor Jimmy Carter.)

Since 1993, Brock's career has taken some setbacks. His book on Hillary Clinton, for which he received a huge advance, died on the shelves, and he lost his high-salary job at *The American Spectator.* Vilified as a "right-wing hit man," he hasn't had a right-wing hit lately.

So now he's making a second career of defecting from the right wing. He's even trying to discredit the sources who made him famous: those blasted troopers "took me for a ride" and have since "greatly damaged their credibility."

Say what? As a reporter, Brock was supposed to be able to size up the "credibility" of his sources at the time, precisely so that he and his readers wouldn't be "taken for a ride."

So it was all a pack of lies? Here he hedges. "I'm not saying they made the whole thing up," he says now. "I do think there was probably room there for them to exaggerate." He admits that his own "ideological desire to damage Clinton" made him unduly credulous. He admits the same of his own book attacking Anita Hill, in which he says he was guilty of "hypocrisy."

But don't worry: "I've abandoned that form of journalism."

Great! But why not just abandon journalism? After all, he has virtually repudiated his whole career, which is not the smartest of career moves. Confessing your crimes is fine, but don't expect it to win you a job as a cop. And complaining that you were the victim of your sources doesn't burnish your credentials as a reporter.

Brock is now telling liberals that he has seen the error of his ways. Like many ex-conservative defectors before him, he is bidding for a niche among his former enemies by denouncing his former friends, including the good ole boys who gave him the scoop of his life.

Those troopers don't seem to have exaggerated much, judging from subsequent developments. Only Brock seems skeptical of them, just when history has vindicated them with a whoop.

Brock probably hopes to peddle one more book, titled something like *Nasty Right-Wingers with Whom I Should Never Have Allowed Myself to Have Become Entangled and Whose Money I Should Never Have Accepted but Have Already Spent, Alas.*

But the book to read will be the memoirs of Mike McCurry. Right now the president's press secretary has the safest job in America, including the president's.

Why? Well, *Spin Cycle,* a new book by Howard Kurtz of the *Washington Post,* tells a few inside stories about the Clinton White House and the press. One of them concerns a coarse crack McCurry once made to reporters about the Clintons' sex life, comparing Mrs. Clinton unfavorably to a mummy. Rush Limbaugh has already repeated it about fifty times, and McCurry still has his job.

Under normal circumstances, the president would have himself a new press secretary by now, with the hearty concurrence of the first lady. But he apparently understands that the moment McCurry leaves, the biggest publishers in New York will be bidding zillions of dollars for a book titled something like *Things Linda Tripp Never Dreamed of That I Couldn't Talk About until Now.* To paraphrase *The Godfather,* keep your friends close, but your press secretary closer.

CHAPTER 7

CLINTON AND MONICA

The X-Rated Presidency

FEBRUARY 1998

J ust as we'd — we thought — completed this issue, a big news story made the piece titled "Clinton without Sex" seem peculiarly untimely. So let me add a few words on the topic.

Yes, our president has been implicated in yet another scandal with the opposite sex: as I write, it appears that he had a liaison with Monica Lewinsky, a twenty-one-year-old White House intern, then urged her to perjure herself by denying the affair when she was to be deposed in the Paula Jones case. As usual, he insists he's innocent. But this time nobody believes him. He has pulled the rug out from under his allies once too often.

The President is exhausting his defenders.

It looks like curtains. Clinton finally seems to have used up all his luck, which he has so relentlessly pressed. His denials meant nothing; apart from being a habitual liar, he'd already sworn, in his own deposition, that he'd never done anything improper with Miss Lewinsky. The slightest admission would have been a confession of his own perjury.

Clinton has been trying to define his "legacy"; well, here it is. He's the Sex President. That's his essence, and that will be his reputation for all time. It goes deeper than mere "womanizing." He's both advocate and exemplar of the sexual revolution. He has used the presidency to promote everything from gay rights to late-term abortion. The notion that he's been a "nonideological" president is nonsense; his ideology is a fusion of Hugh Hefner and Gloria Steinem. His kind of statism is actually more subversive of family life and personal responsibility than old-fashioned socialism. But while the failure of economic socialism is generally acknowledged, the destructiveness of the sexual revolution is still denied.

In politics, the sexual revolution is chiefly focussed on abortion. This issue, more than any other, has won Clinton the support of the major media and turned their eyes away from his "private" life. They've obligingly (and anachronistically) treated his personal conduct as "irrelevant" to his conduct in office, despite the intimate connection between his philosophy and his lewd behavior. Sexual freedom, women's "liberation," and the materialist pursuit of happiness all depend on the legitimation of abortion, as media liberals understand very well.

The advocates of the sexual revolution avoid facing its results as resolutely as tobacco companies evade the connection between smoking and cancer. And Hollywood now glamorizes free love in the same way it used to glamorize cigarettes: no illegitimacy, disease, disgust, heartbreak, shame, dishonor, or damnation attends it. The same debased and carnal image of human nature that creates our entertainment also shapes our politics.

This explains Clinton's rise to the presidency better than any specific data of his life in Arkansas; his party almost unanimously favors the half-covert revolt against the Creator. The Sunday before the new scandal broke, he and Hillary were photographed coming out of church together, both beaming, he cheerfully carrying the Bible — presumably an expurgated edition.

Who was it who predicted Clinton would be forever remembered as the Sex President? But even that prophet failed to foresee the piquant details the Starr inquiry would unearth. He thought Clinton wanted to discourage young people from using tobacco products.

What's in the Trunk?

APRIL 23, 1998

Whenever the police pull me over, which I'm afraid is a common occurrence, I figure it's in my interest to be nice and cooperate. The offense is invariably minor — an expired sticker in my windshield — and there's no point in being ornery with the man who holds the discretionary power either to stick me with a $50 fine or to let me go with a warning.

It might be different if I knew that if a cop stopped me, he was bound to find that I was carrying a bullet-riddled body in the trunk. In that case, the logic of the situation might dictate a shootout. Being cooperative wouldn't get me far if the offense was serious.

Not that I can really picture myself shooting a cop; being nice is more my style, which is why I usually get in trouble for expired stickers rather than murder in the first place. But you see what I mean.

That's why it's interesting that Bill Clinton should be conducting a hate campaign against special prosecutor Kenneth Starr. And the key fact is that it began long before the Monica Lewinsky story broke.

Clinton's normal style is conciliatory and ingratiating. Like any good politician, he knows better than to make enemies he doesn't need, and you'd expect him to be the last man to antagonize someone who was conducting a criminal investigation.

And yet he and James Carville were accusing Starr of political motives nearly as soon as Starr took over the Whitewater investigation. Even a chief witness, Susan McDougal, suddenly refused to cooperate, blaming Starr for her abrupt change of mind. Writing in the *Wall Street Journal,* Chris Vlasto of *ABC News* recalls that this alteration occurred just as Diane Sawyer was about to interview her in New York: Mrs. McDougal's brother and fiancé arrived, and she clammed up. Eighteen months in jail for contempt of court have failed to break her silence.

Some interpret this as loyalty to Clinton, others as bitter hatred of Starr (her own explanation). But there is another obvious motive for both Clinton and Mrs. McDougal: fear.

If Clinton has, so to speak, a bullet-riddled body in the trunk, and Starr is the cop, Clinton realized that being nice wouldn't get him out of this jam. Knowing what Starr was bound to discover, he quickly went into the shootout mode, hoping to discredit Starr personally before Starr could announce what was found in the trunk.

Many people who knew things about the Clintons have been reluctant to testify. This fits an old familiar pattern: witnesses are often less afraid of crossing the government than of crossing the mob, whose sentencing guidelines tend to be unpredictable and uninhibited.

On this hypothesis, Clinton was never indignant about Starr's supposed partisanship or improper tactics. Clinton himself has a genial tolerance for loose ethics, as witness his use of private investigators against "bimbos" and his readiness to make illegal use of FBI files on Republicans. No, he was afraid — afraid of what Starr was likely to learn about the Clintons' illegal activities in Arkansas banking and real estate.

It was important to smear Starr early and often, though the public hardly noticed until the Lewinsky story brought Starr into the foreground. Since then the anti-Starr campaign has escalated with, from the Clintons' point of view, excellent results.

Even now, most of the public that gives Starr his dismal approval ratings doesn't remember that the Clintons were trashing him long before the most recent scandals. But the Clintons, knowing what was in the trunk, decided long ago that Starr was destined to be their mortal enemy no matter how they might try to "cooperate with the investigation."

For the guilty who hope to escape, cooperation with the prosecution is utterly irrational. The rational course is to frustrate and, if possible, destroy the prosecutor.

But just as Clinton's lawyers antagonized Paula Jones and Linda Tripp by trying to intimidate them, the attack on Starr and his team seems to have hardened Starr's resolve to see the case through. Everything will be explained when he tells us what he found in the trunk.

Clinton and His Enemies

MAY 21, 1998

F or some time now, Bill Clinton's supporters have taken what might be called the *faux français* position: "We are much too sophisticated to deny that he's a liar, but we distinguish between his private life — which may include frolicking with *demoiselles* in the Oval Office — and his performance of his presidential duties."

This was the theme of the movie *Primary Colors,* in which a Clintonesque character was depicted, warts and all, as the only available bearer of liberal hopes, the alternative being the Republican abyss. Voting for Clinton was made to seem like the sort of hard choice a world-weary Gaulois-puffing existentialist might have to make.

Alas, *mes amis,* Clinton belongs more to the milieu of Monsieur Larry Flynt and Monsieur Jerry Springer than to the Rive Gauche.

When the Monica scandal broke in January, the main debate was not between those who believed Clinton and those who didn't, but between those who didn't believe him and those who didn't care — as long as the Dow Jones was soaring and the president was "good on women's issues."

But Clinton never rests. Given the opportunity to define presidential deviancy even further downward, he'll always seize it.

Thus we now confront growing evidence that there was a nexus between his decision to waive export controls over sensitive military technology to China (against the urging of the Pentagon) and a generous albeit illegal donation to his 1996 reelection campaign from ... China.

Clinton says there was no connection. He didn't even know of any Chinese donation to his campaign, and it certainly didn't influence his policy decisions, which were made in what he believed were the best interests of the American people. He says.

In fact — he says — he "would support" an investigation into

133

HUSTLER: THE CLINTON LEGACY

any illegal Chinese contributions, evidently with all the ardor of O. J. Simpson pursuing the real killer or killers.

The Monica episode didn't finish Clinton off, but it put the finishing touch on his reputation. The question is no longer which of his predecessors he should be compared to, but which life forms.

Any earlier president would have enjoyed a strong benefit of doubt and presumption of innocence in a compromising situation like the Chinese business. The man who occupied the White House could be assumed to be sufficiently honorable that even his political opponents would hesitate to accuse him of selling national security to a potential enemy. He might be a crook, but at least you could count on him not to sell out his country or his mother.

With Clinton, all the old bets are off. Nobody knows what the limit is for him. If there is one, that is — and his allies don't know any more than his enemies do.

No matter what current scandal they're staving off, his defenders do know better than to mount what for most people would be the first line of defense character. "He's not the type of man who would ever do that." "How dare you impugn his integrity!" "Are you implying that Bill Clinton is the sort who would cut corners?"

On the Chinese question, it won't do to have Hillary come forth once more to do her stuff. Or to blame Kenneth Starr and the VRWC (the vast you-know-what). Or to let James Carville and Sidney Blumenthal attack the question. Or to have Clinton himself construct more of his patented labyrinthine equivocations.

Even those who excused his lies about the Lewinsky case had to acknowledge that he was lying. That meant he'd used up the credit he'd need for the next scandal — the inevitable next scandal — while exhausting his allies in the process. How many times can the most loyal Democrat pretend to believe him?

Manipulative people often fail to understand that it's dangerous to push loyalty to the breaking point. In the long run, nobody is going to hate Bill Clinton more than those who feel he has trapped them into supporting him, at great cost to themselves. If the China deal turns out to be what it appears, his enemies may one day forgive him; but his friends, never.

The Dark Side

JUNE 11, 1998

W ell?
Isn't anyone going to say something?
I'm way-ting ...!
That's right. Monica Lewinsky has posed for some mildly sugges-
tive pictures in *Vanity Fair,* and none of
the president's defenders are indignant.
Why the strange silence, Mr. Car-
ville? Mr. Begala? Mr. Blumenthal?
Aren't you gents worried that someone
may get the wrong impression from
Miss Lewinsky's naughty hints — the
heavy lipstick, the feather boas, the bare shoulders?

Why do lawless people want to govern?

The premise of the layout (and forgive any doubles-entendres
here; I'm sincerely trying to avoid them, no matter how much revising
it takes) seems to be that Miss Lewinsky has had some kind of liaison
with an important personage. It's difficult to understand why the
magazine would bother with this fancy spread unless the editors assumed she was some sort of scarlet woman. And this could lead the
magazine's readers to conclude that the president and the intern were
both lying when they said, under oath, in interviews, and at press conferences, that there was no sexual relationship there.

The president's defenders have a new theme. Special prosecutor
Kenneth Starr's investigation has now lasted, by the count of former
White House counsel Jack Quinn, "1,450 days, longer than it took us
to win World War II." Clinton advisor Paul Begala has a similar perspective: Starr's investigation has reached "Day 1,400" and has
"lasted nearly as long as the Second World War."

William McDaniel, White House aide Sidney Blumenthal's lawyer, has a similar perspective too: Starr has been at it "longer than
World War II lasted."

Or, if you like these wartime analogies, you could put it this way:
Bill Clinton has now held out longer than Adolf Hitler. The president

might prefer a Cal Ripken parallel, but Cal is up around 2,500. This brings us to another disturbing development. The other night, while entertaining a South Korean delegation, the president shook hands with a man whose trousers, at that moment, dropped to his ankles. Nor was the man wearing underwear.

The president handled the incident with tact and aplomb, but it took several hours to convince the first lady that it wasn't the work of the vast right-wing conspiracy. She refused to believe it could just be destiny.

Possibly it was karma for Paula Jones. That, of course, is sheer metaphysical speculation, but the thought must have flashed across Clinton's mind. Whatever the cause, the incident seemed to bear a chilling personal message, as when the last voice you hear before everything goes black tells you: "Michael Corleone says hello."

Meanwhile, *Arkansas Mischief,* a book by the president's late crony, Jim McDougal, implicates said president in several felonies, including serial perjury. But the book isn't an attack on Bill Clinton; it's a matter-of-fact memoir of the way things were done in one-party Arkansas, where the Invisible Hand had a greasy palm, and legal technicalities were never allowed to stand in the way of friendship. Clinton just happened to be part of the flow for a few years.

Which raises a question. Even on the darkest Republican estimate, Clinton is neither the first, the only, nor the worst criminal to hold high office. As rulers go, he may even be above the 50th percentile. Think of — to confine ourselves to the recently deceased — Pol Pot, Sani Abacha, and Sam Yorty. Judging from the editorial pages, Yorty was the most brutal of these, but we needn't quibble about that.

The point is that governing — making and enforcing law — somehow seems not to attract, as you might naively suppose, the most ardently law-abiding, moral, and ethical part of the population. On the contrary, those who have ruled throughout history seem to have been disproportionately recruited from the lower percentiles.

"Public service" is an inapt expression for politics. The only term limits most politicians might support would be limits on the length of prison sentences. How does it happen that we are so often "represented" by men who seem to embody not our aspirations, but our dark side? And why have we come to expect this?

CHAPTER 8

THE *OTHER* OTHER WOMEN

The Trash Team

APRIL 1998

I t didn't take long. No sooner had Kathleen Willey described the way Bill Clinton groped her in her hour of need, right in the Oval Office, than his Trash Team produced a stack of warm letters she'd written him after the Oval Office interview, in one of which she called herself his "number one fan." The next day a publisher said he'd rejected a book proposal from Mrs. Willey in which she'd described the incident in a somewhat different tone. Then a former friend contradicted her in an affidavit. You had to admire the celerity with which the Trash Team manages to create a blur around every new bit of evidence and testimony.

Mrs. Willey wasn't the "Clinton-hater" of liberal stereotype; she inspired respect and trust, and she had been a loyal Clinton supporter who had testified against him, reluctantly, only under subpoena. (Even then she might have denied everything or toned down the details; apparently she was too scrupulous to lie or fudge.)

Her story rang true. Clinton had spotted her on the campaign trail in 1992, gotten her name and phone number, called her at home, and tried to arrange a tryst, saying he could shake off his Secret Service guardians. She turned him down. In 1993 her lawyer husband was charged with embezzling hundreds of thousands of dollars, and she hoped Clinton could help her get a job. She went to the White House, not realizing that her husband was about to commit suicide that very day; to her shock and astonishment, Clinton — her friend, her husband's friend — took crude liberties with her, telling her he'd always wanted to "do that."

Mrs. Willey told this to Ed Bradley of *60 Minutes* on a Thursday (for Sunday broadcast). On Friday Paula Jones's lawyers released 700 pages of depositions from other witnesses, all of whom described Clinton's conduct in similar terms. Clinton's lawyer Bob Bennett, who had earlier promised to make Mrs. Jones's sexual history part of Clinton's defense, gamely but lamely dismissed the depositions as "a pack of lies."

But all these adverse descriptions of Clinton, made for the record, were totally congruent with Monica Lewinsky's description of him in what she had thought were private conversations with Linda Tripp. In addition to trying to disparage Miss Lewinsky's remarks, the Trash Team dug up, and released to a friendly reporter, embarrassing information about Mrs. Tripp (a minor arrest in 1969, when she was nineteen).

And who can forget the assault on Kenneth Starr and his assistants? Before March 13, it had been convenient (if mendacious) to blame the damaging testimony on leaks from Starr's office. But that was only one of the Trash Team's ad hoc tactics, quickly abandoned as soon as it ceased to help.

All this was in keeping with the Clintons' modus operandi in containing "bimbo eruptions": get dirt on witnesses and, if it doesn't scare them out of talking, use it to smear them. The Trash Team has even rehired some of the same hardball private investigators it used in Arkansas. Even if some witnesses testify, others will be contained by a firewall of fear.

The ruthless crudity of Clinton's defense is of a piece with the very crudity his accusers attest. Clinton himself, of course, is the captain of the Trash Team, and his methods of self-preservation illustrate his criminality.

Query: How would you like to have been a female slave on Bill Clinton's plantation?

Entrippment

OCTOBER 1998

Throughout the endless brawl over the Lewinsky affair, Bill Clinton's partisans have reserved a special indignation for Linda Tripp. As a key witness against Clinton, she has turned out to be one more of those women on whom organized feminism refuses to confer sisterhood.

She is attacked for betraying poor Monica by secretly taping their intimate conversations, and in Mrs. Tripp's case there is no extenuation, no talk of "waiting until all the facts are in." A Maryland prosecutor (a Democrat) has charged her with a felony, though nobody thinks it will stick; it's pure vendetta. Even her looks are fair game for ridicule.

After giving her testimony to the special prosecutor's grand jury, Mrs. Tripp finally made a short public statement this summer. She said that she'd told the truth and that these last six months had been an ordeal because of the cruel treatment she has received in and through the media. There was no reason to doubt her on either point.

Meanwhile, two interesting details about her have leaked out. It transpires that hers was one of the hundreds of raw FBI files the White House improperly got hold of; and she and her family have apparently been threatened. It's been reported that Clinton's pal Bruce Lindsey told her she would be "destroyed" if she told what she knew about the Kathleen Willey incident, and Monica relayed an ominous warning from Clinton himself.

These stories were briefly mentioned in the news, then forgotten. Yet they put everything in a different light. They certainly explain why Mrs. Tripp might feel she needed to protect herself by taping Monica. If true, they fully justify her in doing so. But they have had no effect on the trashing of Linda Tripp.

Mrs. Willey has also been in the news again, equally briefly. She told a reporter she'd been approached by a stranger in a car recently while jogging near her home. The man referred to the disappearance of her cat and the flattening of her tires a few weeks earlier; he mentioned her two children by name; then, warning her to watch her step, he drove off.

So this whole thing is "only about sex"? It sounds rather as if it's about some very nasty people who are willing to go to some lengths not only to commit and suborn perjury, but to silence adverse witnesses.

Yet this angle has failed to penetrate the public discussion of Clinton's conduct as the nation's chief law-enforcement officer. Nobody seems curious about whether threats against witnesses can be traced to his circle, even though it fits the Clinton team's modus operandi from the days of yore when they were heading off "bimbo eruptions" with the aid of some unsavory private investigators.

It's only about sex. Everyone lies about sex. Perjury about sex is never prosecuted and wouldn't fall under the heading of "high crimes and misdemeanors." So maybe intimidating witnesses wouldn't be serious either, as long as it's about sex?

Clinton insists he has never told anyone to lie. But he may have pointed out, to Monica and others, the hazards of telling the truth. Linda Tripp understood those hazards well enough to use a tape recorder; Paula Jones, Kathleen Willey, and other witnesses may wish they had done likewise.

Don't Change the Subject

FEBRUARY 23, 1999

W ill Hillary Clinton run for New York's open Senate seat next year? Probably not. She'd have to face too many questions about her own past. And what would her campaign slogan be? "Buy one, get one free"?

Her noncandidacy is just part of the Clintons' post-impeachment snow flurry to Change the Subject. Bill Clinton only thinks about bombing foreign countries when he's in trouble at home. He's not only still in trouble; he will remain so as long as there are other shoes yet to drop.

A big shoe dropped the other day — a Bruno Magli shoe, so to speak — when the *Wall Street Journal* ran an interview with a woman named Juanita Broaddrick, who says Clinton raped her in 1978 when he was attorney general in Arkansas. NBC has been sitting on her story for several weeks. But it's out anyway, and Congressman Christopher Shays, a Connecticut Republican who voted against impeachment, says Clinton should resign if Mrs. Broaddrick's account is true.

Why didn't she report the crime at the time it happened? Well, it's obviously awkward to bring a charge of rape against the state official who is supposed to be punishing rapists. ("You are now entering Arkansas. Beware of attorney general.") Besides, Mrs. Broaddrick admits she was herself engaged in an adulterous affair at the time, making her situation all the more awkward.

Clinton's lawyer, David Kendall, calls the rape charge "absolutely false." As further details emerge, look for a three-pronged defense: (1) if it happened at all, it was consensual; (2) rape, though reprehensible, doesn't rise to the level of an impeachable offense; and (3) many presidents have been rapists.

Besides, even Mrs. Broaddrick admits Clinton has apologized. In fact that's the most Clintonian detail in her story. The *Washington Post* quotes her as saying he approached her in 1991: "It was unreal.... He kept trying to hold my hand. I can still remember his words: 'Can you ever forgive me? I'm not the same man I used to be.' ... I told him, 'You just go to hell.' And I walked away. I was shaking."

Those nine words she ascribes to him are as good as a DNA sample: "I'm not the same man I used to be." That's our boy: the same contrite man he used to be.

We saw his contrition about having "caused pain in my marriage" in 1992, when he assured the voters he was no longer the same man he used to be. And last year he turned over yet another new leaf, when he regretted that "what began as a friendship [with Monica Lewinsky] came to include this conduct." By "this conduct" he alluded delicately to the oral sex which, by Miss Lewinsky's estimate, occurred only ten minutes after the friendship began. (He couldn't remember her name until the friendship had continued for a while.)

Does it really matter anymore that Clinton is a liar and a criminal? It matters every minute. U.S. planes may soon be killing people and U.S. troops may be stationed in Kosovo because of Clinton's endless need to Change the Subject.

Others are giving lofty reasons for U.S. military intervention in a remote corner of Europe. The columnist George Will likens this country to the Roman Empire and says it has "a complex fiduciary responsibility for the universal values it embodies." If that's not an impressive reason for sending your boy to Kosovo, I don't know what would be. But please don't send mine.

Ask yourself a simple question: When has any country, anywhere, ever suffered by avoiding war? If Bill Clinton can be said to have a virtue, it's that he is reluctant to kill people except when he thinks his own personal interests require it — for example, when impeachment looms.

After resisting the counsellors of war for five years, Clinton resorted to military distractions several times in 1998, the Year of That Woman. If he faces recurrent scandals until he leaves office in early 2001, we must assume his gravest decisions will be guided, as always, by his own self-interest, rather than complex fiduciary whatever.

CHAPTER 9

IMPEACHMENT:
FAITHLESS EXECUTION

Impeachment Politics

MARCH 1998

T he president of the United States is the focal point of power in the modern world. His unofficial titles include Leader of the Free World and Manager of the American Economy. His fall is therefore a fateful event, and the live pos-sibility of impeachment can send shudders through Wall Street and around the globe.

The president is also expected — infor-mally but strongly — to provide moral lead-ership for the nation. When he's morally soiled, his general powers are weakened, and he becomes vulnerable to defeat and even impeachment. I think the job of moral leadership is inappropriate; but it's the natu-ral result of the excessive power, attention,

At least one courageous figure has emerged in the Clinton years: Paula Jones.

and reverence the presidency now enjoys. The myth of Great Presi-dents has raised our expectations; in just five years, Bill Clinton has drastically lowered them and still fallen short of them. Even normal dignity is beyond him. To say nothing of honor.

It's worth reminding ourselves that the president used to be more an opponent than an advocate of legislation. Most presi-dents before Lincoln, in their inaugural addresses, pledged above all to use the veto against any attempt by Congress to usurp pow-ers not delegated by the Constitution. The president was in a sense the embodiment of the Tenth Amendment; nobody expected the Supreme Court to do the routine job of checking Congress, and even proponents of judicial review never thought of this as the exclusive province of the Court. The president himself is sworn to "preserve, protect, and defend" the Constitution.

After Lincoln, and especially in this century, the president gradually came to be thought of as a charismatic leader, ideally the driving force behind legislation, proposing ambitious "programs," "running the country," and managing "the economy." This has become so conventional that few Americans now realize that it's radically at odds with the older conception of the presidency. Both Roosevelts have been canonized as "great" presidents, along with Lincoln, while Grover Cleveland is forgotten and Millard Fillmore ridiculed. Liberal opinion bestows "greatness" on those who succeed in centralizing power, in spite of constitutional obstacles. (And the Constitution was designed to be an obstacle to any power it didn't clearly authorize.)

In his state of the Union address, given at the height of the new uproar, Clinton tried with some success to buy popular favor by proposing a multitude of new federal programs — all, of course, unconstitutional. Republicans joined Democrats in applauding them. Some said the speech might save Clinton from impeachment. In a better world, it would have ensured his impeachment.

The real question about any president now is not whether he's going to enjoy colossal power — that's a given — but how he's going to use it. The presidency has quite naturally become a center of perpetual contention the Framers never meant it to be.

Impeaching a president really shouldn't be a momentous event. If he were confined to the relatively modest role the Constitution assigns him, his removal would be a serious matter, but hardly cataclysmic. But the concentration of power, real and symbolic, in the office has raised the stakes and also increased the incentive to impeach.

Impeachment was conceived as a remedy for corruption or tyranny. Of course it may be used with ulterior political motives. The only president to be impeached, Andrew Johnson, was more honest than the Congress that arraigned him: he'd refused to enforce a law he deemed a usurpation of power by Congress itself, and he escaped conviction by a single vote. But just as Al Capone went to prison for tax evasion rather than for murder, extortion, or selling booze, a president may be nailed for some minor offense rather than for the actions that really provoke his enemies.

Republicans, conservatives, and neoconservatives have been dying to get Clinton for reasons that are only tangentially related to his "alleged" crimes (which are hardly in doubt). I myself would love to see him impeached on any grounds, but my chief reasons have little to do with those crimes: he has accelerated the federal government's usurpation of power, promoted the awful moral decay that afflicts America, and supported even the most savage forms of abortion. He's been the Franklin Roosevelt of the sexual revolution.

One of the oddities of Clinton's hitherto charmed life is that he has rarely been accused of hypocrisy. Ronald Reagan was so accused because, while he was friendly to Christianity and "family values," he'd been divorced and rarely went to church. But Clinton ought to be doubly vulnerable to the charge. He's a flagrant adulterer who has always used the power of office to exploit women, while both espousing "women's rights" and ostentatiously simulating Christian piety. He quotes the Bible at every opportunity, but his chief interest in it seems to be whether it explicitly forbids his favorite sexual activity; his insistence that it doesn't is a telling leitmotif of all the rumors he denies. (He has taken the Protestant principle of Sola Scriptura to new lengths.)

But Christians are slow to accuse a professing Christian of insincerity, while feminists don't mind how he treats women personally as long as he's "good on women's issues." Their strictures against "sexual harassment" were clearly never meant to apply to politicians like Clinton or to protect women like Paula Jones; they're now lamenting that sexual harassment laws have "backfired" because they've been used against their chief ally!

That speaks volumes about their concept of law. If a law against murder is used to punish a real murderer, most people would say that the law has worked, not that it has "backfired," no matter who the murderer happens to be. This curious word betrays the fact that harassment law was meant to be used only against enemies of the feminists. They actually think it's been misused when it operates impartially against their friends.

As Tom Bethell observes, sexual harassment law is really a weapon of political blackmail, which the feminists expect will be enforced for their benefit. Such "law" is just one more instrument of the soft tyranny we've become inured to — a device for invading and policing formerly private domains. And the cunning Clinton has keenly understood this. Feminist leaders expressed no outrage when his behavior was exposed. (As one lawyer noted in the *Wall Street Journal,* the Justice Department and the Equal Employment Opportunity Commission would have swooped down on any corporation whose CEO had been accused of behaving as Clinton had.)

If Clinton could be impeached for jaywalking, that would be fine by me. But that he should be threatened not only with removal from office but with the special ignominy that now hangs over him gives the prospect of his ruin exquisite poetic justice.

The threat of impeachment, long dormant, was revived by Richard Nixon's political enemies; but it's generally forgotten that there had been talk among liberals, a few years earlier, of impeaching Lyndon Johnson for waging war in Vietnam. Even though Johnson was never in danger of impeachment, the talk itself lifted the taboo on a power of Congress that had been unused and almost unmentioned for a century. A new phase in American politics had begun.

Once liberals had used the power against Nixon (and tried, without success, to use it against Reagan in the Iran-Contra affair), it was inevitable that conservatives would try to use it against a Democratic president. Jimmy Carter was too scrupulous to afford an opportunity; Bill Clinton is another matter.

Clinton's behavior in the White House has ranged from dubious to disgraceful. Is it also criminal? The precise character of his conduct has been hotly debated from the first, with the argument swirling around a welter of topics, from his business dealings in Arkansas to his putative abuses of power in the White House, all of which have been complicated by sexual rumors, his wife's role, and strong suggestions of perjury. His defenders try to bracket as much of this as possible in the category of "private life," denying its relevance to public life and therefore to the congressional option of impeachment.

His opponents, naturally, try to argue that his misbehavior is pertinent to his leadership, and even that it crosses the line into criminality, which everyone (well, nearly everyone) agrees is intolerable. There is no "vast right-wing conspiracy," as Hillary Clinton alleges; her attempt to define opposition as conspiratorial shows the classic Bolshevik mindset.

But there's certainly a large body of conservatives who would love to see Clinton run out of office, as, by their principles, he should be. And many of these people do foster the darkest suspicions about him, demanding congressional inquiries, special prosecutors, and of course impeachment.

This "vast conspiracy" had difficulty keeping the embers glowing, until the major media (which have been far more ambivalent about Clinton than most conservatives realize) found a corruption story with the reliably sensational angle of sex. Sex may not be the central issue, but it did get everyone's attention in a way that real estate deals, billing records, cattle futures, and FBI files never quite did.

We are hearing a great deal about the French model of sophisticated toleration of sexual "peccadilloes." That is, Americans who find Clinton disgusting are acting like a lot of puritanical hicks. But Clinton didn't just keep a mistress in a discreet and private niche, according to the French mode; he brought a remarkably puerile and reckless libido into the White House.

This may not be an impeachable offense, if for no other reason than that it falls so far below and beyond what the Framers of the Constitution could imagine that they made no provision for it. Nevertheless, his vice seems to have led him to crime: perjury, witness tampering, obstruction of justice, and conspiracy. Any of these is certainly grounds for removal from office.

The president's chief constitutional duty has been almost lost among the powers modern presidents have usurped: "he shall take care that the laws be faithfully executed." At best, Clinton has constantly wriggled around the law, seeking every loophole for his own advantage and construing every ambiguity to his own convenience.

Now it's clear that he has broken the law. By the beginning of February the evidence had mounted so high that he made no attempt to talk his way out of it; this most loquacious of politicians clammed up. It was typical of him that he explained his silence by appealing to his "obligation to cooperate with the investigation," while he dispatched his wife and cronies to smear the investigators.

If no more evidence were to emerge — which is highly unlikely — it's virtually impossible to imagine an innocent explanation of what has already come to light: Monica Lewinsky's recorded words, her refusal to speak to the public or prosecutors, her boasts to friends of a presidential liaison, her reputation, her three dozen visits to the White House after she had moved to the Pentagon, her secret meeting with Clinton at the White House days before her fateful testimony in the Paula Jones suit, her ready access to Clinton's secretary, her awareness of arcane legal matters pertaining to perjury (why should she have been discussing perjury at all?), her denial to Jordan (according to Jordan) that she'd had sex with Clinton (and why did that subject come up in an innocent discussion of her "vocational aspirations"?), Jordan's role in finding her a job, Jordan's stonewalling, Jordan's earlier role in helping the convicted Webb Hubbell, and so on.

Clinton's own inability to fashion an explanation of these facts is itself a powerful fact. What imaginable story, other than the one that's taking shape, could possibly tie all these details together? We don't have all the pieces yet, but when you get a third of the way through a jigsaw puzzle you can have a pretty good idea of whether you're assembling a picture of an elephant. At least you know it's not a goose.

It's significant that the only other scandal Clinton has been unable to talk his way out of is the Paula Jones case. Mrs. Jones's charges describe the same man who has been disclosed by the Monica tapes: a man using his high office to procure sexual favors of a peculiar kind.

The smearing of the accuser is also of a piece with the Clinton team's traditional handling of "bimbo eruptions." The phrase it-self comes from Clinton's former aide, Betsey Wright, who had to deal with the problem all the time; private investigators were used to threaten and blackmail potential witnesses into silence. The phrase and the tactics bespeak not only a chronic Clintonian difficulty, but a habitual Clintonian method of dealing with it. The argument that Clinton is an honorable man and a faithful husband would never fly and is never even attempted. (His friends would no more say he's honest than his enemies would say he's stupid.) What is done, and what has usually worked, is to attack the accuser and to drag him — or her — down to Clinton's level.

Monica is now coming in for this treatment, in puzzling con-tradiction to the high recommendations she received from Jor-dan; the White House is discreetly putting out the word that she isn't the most reliable of witnesses. (True, but only when she's under oath. She tells plenty when she thinks it won't leave the room.) Even today, such tactics are still no doubt discouraging other women (there are "hundreds" of them, Clinton told Monica) from coming forward.

Whatever the polls may say about Clinton's popular approval, it's sinking in that he's a cornered rat and is fighting as such. He lets others do the dirty work, but they obviously do it with his blessing — and at his instigation. His "private life" includes not just lechery but thorough nastiness. The irresistible levity about his appetites shouldn't distract us from the darkest aspect of his abuse of power: his readiness to defame and destroy anyone who testifies against him. The women in his life know all about it.

This isn't something Clinton used to do in Arkansas. It's something his minions have continued doing — and are doing right now, before our eyes, to give other witnesses pause. And so far it's working.

Try to imagine defending Clinton by other means. Picture James Carville saying: "It's deeply saddening that the president's opponents find it necessary to impugn his character without evidence. But his character speaks for itself, and needs no defense from me. I'm confident that the American people will simply disregard these im-plausible charges." No, the kind of man Clinton is requires the kind of eye-gouging counterattack Carville specializes in. It's a crude warning to any potential truth-teller, at a time when a single new witness could finish Clinton forever.

The "Clinton haters" have been widely denounced for making wild charges, including charges that Clinton has had inconvenient people murdered. I myself used to regard those charges as far-fetched. Not now. As Hillary Clinton says, we shouldn't judge "until the facts come out."

Every fact that has already come out is damning. And the Clintons themselves are desperately trying to suppress any further facts. They've moved to prevent the Secret Service from talking to Kenneth Starr's investigation team. It's typical of Clinton that he gives his desire to "cooperate" with Starr as a reason for not telling his own side of the story (even as his underlings smear Starr along with the "vast right-wing conspiracy"). The implication, of course, is that if only he were allowed to, he could explain everything satisfactorily — when he obviously knows that any version of the facts he offers is bound to be inadequate and likely to be exploded by new revelations.

Newsweek reports that Clinton got an unpleasant surprise when he gave his deposition in the Jones suit. He'd thought he'd covered up his relations with Monica Lewinsky, only to be bombarded with questions about her that told him how much Mrs. Jones's lawyers (and probably Starr) already knew. He had to improvise answers, and he did so awkwardly. Among other things, he testified that he'd never been alone with Miss Lewinsky. That deposition may eventually send him to jail.

Let it be said that Paula Jones deserves credit for real courage. She has endured the scorn of journalists who accepted the Clintonites' smears against her and has refused to back down when Clinton's lawyer, Bob Bennett, promised even dirtier assaults on her character. Her story has held up, and nobody now calls her a liar, though a large number of people are withholding the apologies they owe her.

It's become a cliché of the current scandal that unlike Watergate it features no heroes. Not true. Mrs. Jones has stood up to a man who is as unscrupulous as he is powerful. She has also had to get along without the support of her feminist "sisters" in a case that put their avowed principles to the test. Meanwhile, she has been blamed for accepting the support of "right-wing" groups who oppose Clinton; apparently her case would be untainted only if she took on the president of the United States without assistance. And yet she has essentially won her case: Clinton is now exposed for all time.

If that isn't heroism, would someone please tell me what would qualify? We now know why she didn't bring charges against him in 1991, for which she has been so widely censured and ridiculed: she was a scared kid, with good reason to be scared. What chance would she have had, standing alone against the all-powerful governor of Arkansas? Her "interview" with him ended on a note of menace: he reminded her that he knew her boss and told her he knew she was "smart." Naive as she was, she got the point.

Ironically, she had better odds against the president of the United States — the same man as the governor, but with far more enemies. (He was also under much closer public scrutiny.) And those enemies, for their own reasons, were willing to listen to her and give her the help she'd never have gotten in Arkansas. It's now clear why Clinton reacted so strongly to her lawsuit from the start, hiring a very tough and expensive Washington lawyer to frighten her out of her lawsuit. He too remembered that day in the hotel room very well.

It would be an unfortunate irony if Clinton were saved by his image as a charming rogue, whose worst sin is lust. The fact is that the president of the United States is a pretty ruthless criminal.

"This isn't Watergate," the wise heads remind us. No, it isn't. Some of Nixon's crimes were more serious than some of Clinton's. On the other hand, Nixon tried to bribe people into silence. He didn't threaten them. And he didn't defile his office and his country as Clinton has.

We needn't exaggerate the virtues of the older America in order to realize how deeply sickened it would be at the spectacle of a president like this one. But Clinton is staking his hope of escaping impeachment and ruin on the practical theory that today's America has sunk to his level.

The Framers
versus Clinton

SEPTEMBER 1998

N o matter what happens to Bill Clinton, it's essential to understand what impeachment means in the American constitutional system. My friend Ann Coulter has written an indispensable book on the subject: *High Crimes and Misdemeanors: The Case Against Bill Clinton* (published by Regnery).

Americans have become muddled about impeachment. They confuse it with a criminal procedure; and they have also come to accept a grossly inflated role for the presidency in which the chief duty of the chief executive is not to see that the laws are "faithfully executed," but to take charge of "the economy" and so forth. The office has become huge and amorphous, and Clinton has taken full advantage of the erosion of the Framers' criteria for the job.

The Framers were preoccupied with monarchy, of which they had recently had unhappy experience. They didn't so much want to eliminate it as to reduce it to republican proportions. As Alexander Hamilton explained in Federalist No. 69, the person of the king of Great Britain was "sacred and inviolable." The only way to punish him for abusing power was the dangerous step of deposing him, a revolutionary act that had led to civil war in 1642.

The American presidency, by contrast, was to be a temporary office, and the president was to be responsible to the legislative branch, which could remove him by a peaceful trial. Far from signifying a "constitutional crisis," impeachment was to be a normal constitutional procedure, averting any need for violence.

"High crimes and misdemeanors," as Miss Coulter explains, meant any serious misconduct or abuse of power. In English law the phrase had never meant only crimes meriting imprisonment; it referred to acts that might warrant removal from office.

That's why the Constitution specifies that the president is also liable to separate criminal prosecution. Impeachment goes no further than removing the malefactor upon conviction (with disqualification from any other office). A criminal trial exposes him to loss of his personal rights of "life, liberty, and property."

Clinton may have to endure both kinds of trial, but they are distinct. In an impeachment trial, the president is not entitled to the protections due to a criminal defendant. His guilt needn't be proved beyond a reasonable doubt. It's enough, as Miss Coulter shows, to present a preponderance of evidence against him.

Moreover, he is responsible for any misdeeds committed on his watch. He may be impeached for acts of his subordinates that he failed to prevent, correct, or punish. In scandal after scandal, Clinton has pleaded that he didn't know what his own subordinates were doing. But as the Framers explained, this is precisely why we have an impeachable chief executive: he is ultimately to blame for any misdeeds in the executive branch. With Clinton, however, the buck always stops elsewhere.

"The very least President Clinton can be accused of is neglect of duty — an impeachable offense," writes Miss Coulter. "And this is the very claim the president invariably raises as his *excuse*." (Her emphasis.)

Clinton deserves impeachment several times over. Debauching the office with an adulterous affair with an intern is among the least of his offenses, but it would suffice by itself. So would perjury. So would using the presidency to wage a campaign of lies and smears.

But even if Clinton were a model husband and the Lewinsky scandal had never occurred, Miss Coulter shows incisively that there were at least nine prior separate grounds for impeaching him, and his conviction on any one of them would warrant ending his disgraceful presidency.

The Chain of Faith

AUGUST 25, 1998

C onsider: Bill Clinton played kinky games with a girl in a room next to the Oval Office, where dignitaries were waiting for him; independent counsel Kenneth Starr is trying to find out whether Clinton took criminal measures to conceal this weird behavior.

So which of these two gents is "sex-obsessed"? Why, Starr, of course! Clinton is merely trying to shield his "family life."

Under intense pressure, Clinton has vaguely admitted lying about Monica Lewinsky and Gennifer Flowers. But his other lies — about Paula Jones and Kathleen Willey, for example — still stand.

The lies he didn't retract

If he were truly "remorseful," as his sycophants say he is, he'd be apologizing and making reparations to those to whom his advances weren't "consensual." (Aren't you getting weary of these "legally accurate" defenses?)

Unfortunately, removing Clinton from office would leave most of his support group in place. Most people think he ordered air strikes in Sudan and Afghanistan to distract attention from his scandals. But it's also possible that his scandals weakened him to the point where he couldn't resist the pressure to bomb.

Either way, Clinton's scandals have given us a good look at the people who make fateful decisions on our behalf. Beyond the Clinton problem is the larger problem of the U.S. ruling establishment.

Secretary of State Madeleine Albright, who addresses the American public in the tone of an irritable schoolmarm, says the terrorists who bombed two U.S. embassies in Africa did so because they hate "democracy and freedom." Is this fatuously grandiose statement the measure of her intelligence, or is she deliberately insulting ours?

When the Lewinsky scandal broke, Mrs. Albright led the cabinet in declaring their belief in Clinton's denials. Now we're supposed to trust their judgment and honesty when they tell us that the retaliatory air strikes were based on solid intelligence that a Sudanese pharmaceutical factory was producing a component of nerve gas.

This isn't just a chain of command; it's a chain of faith. We are expected to put our faith in people who put their faith in Clinton. None of them are resigning in protest against his deceits.

The U.S. intelligence services, furthermore, are unreliable. They failed to predict, among other things, the collapse of the Soviet Union and India's nuclear weapons tests. Bureaucracies by their nature are ill-suited to digesting information and making judgment calls. But we're asked to believe that the intelligence services linked the terrorist bombings to the Sudanese factory faster than the FBI lab has analyzed the stain on Monica Lewinsky's dress.

The Sudanese bombing, which killed several civilians but no terrorists, has enraged the Muslim world, which already regarded America with hatred and disgust. Most Muslims regard the U.S. bombing itself as terrorism. (Like "war crimes," "terrorism" is always committed by the other side.)

A British engineer named Tom Carnaffin says the factory didn't have "the necessary safety factors" to manufacture lethal nerve gas. There is no evidence, apart from the word of our own ruling inner circle, that the factory had any connection with the guerrilla financier Osama bin Laden.

But don't worry. Clinton and his team can hide the vital information we need to judge their decision. An aura of secrecy helps maintain faith in the secret-keepers, and suppressing facts means never having to say "Oops!"

Where will it all lead? "We are involved in a long-term struggle," says Mrs. Albright. "This is, unfortunately, the war of the future." Before the terror bombs and even more horrible weapons come to our shores, do we get to debate the wisdom of provoking the Islamic world? Will there be a congressional declaration of war, as the Constitution requires?

The fewer facts we have, the more important "character" becomes. If we have to place blind trust in our rulers, they should deserve our trust. But Mrs. Albright and her colleagues no more deserve it than Clinton does.

Nobody deserves such trust. The real lesson of the Clinton scandals is that we have allowed power to be dangerously concentrated in the hands of a few people of limited intelligence, dubious character, and considerable arrogance. The solution is not to replace them all, but to limit their power.

The American idea of republican government is opposed to the arbitrary rule of one man. Conceived in contrast to European monarchy, it sought to distribute power as widely as possible. The president of a federal republic was to be the most important single official in the system, but he was never to be the quasi emperor he has become in modern times. The Founders would have abhorred the idea that the fate of the nation, the management of its economic affairs, or the decision to make war should depend on a single individual.

Liar, Liar

AUGUST 27, 1998

This morning's *Washington Post* reports that President Clinton's advisors are urging him to make one more public statement about his "relationship" with Monica Lewinsky. The reporter asks whether it's still possible for Clinton to "repair his credibility."

I never heard that phrase when I was growing up. When you lied and lied and lied, we took it for granted that there was no way to prove, when caught in your lies, that you were honest. You were not

Repairing your credibility

to be trusted. Your word was no good. You were a liar. Period. Nobody spoke of "repairing your credibility," as if it were a technique, separate from your character.

Oh, you might confess, apologize, change your ways, and slowly begin to earn the trust you had forfeited. And much later, after your new-found virtue had been tested, others might cautiously begin to accept your word. It wouldn't happen overnight, or even in a year. The idea that you could restore your reputation with one speech, however eloquent, was out of the question.

But in Washington people seem to think it can be done. If the public doesn't believe your first confession, sit down with your aides and lawyers and speechwriters and craft a better one, and presto! You've repaired your credibility. You're an honest man again. At least the polls will show that most respondents think you are, and that's what counts.

A few days ago Clinton gave a speech in which he sort of admitted he'd been lying for seven months, and it only compounded the belief that he's a liar. That short speech defined him as surely as the Gettysburg Address defined Abraham Lincoln, only not quite in the same way. The way Clinton "came clean" illustrated why he was already distrusted; the stingy way he told a little bit of the truth — the part he no longer dared to deny — was of a piece with all his lies.

When he said his earlier testimony was "legally accurate," you knew he was quibbling with the truth even if he was telling it. Maybe this speech too was "legally accurate"? His own phrase warned us not to trust the speech even as he was delivering it. Yet he seemed unaware, at that moment, of his own damning self-revelation. He just thought he was outsmarting us again.

A lie is not just a statement that isn't "accurate." It's a personal betrayal. It means you are a traitor to whomever you are talking to. You make him a fool for trusting you in the way we all have to be able to trust each other for life to go along. You're willing to turn his good faith against him for your own selfish advantage. You treat him not as your friend or fellow citizen, but as your prey.

Clinton preys on people. Not just women; people. He looks into their faces and lies. He lied to his wife, his daughter, his staffers, his cabinet, his supporters, and the general public. He counted on others, many of whom were more honest than he was, to relay his lies. He may even have deceived the people who were willing to lie for him. He has used all the resources of his office to support his lies. Through his henchmen, he has called witnesses against him liars, taking full advantage of the benefit of doubt Americans give their president.

How much of a liar is he? Well, we don't know that there was a single person on earth to whom he told the truth.

Has his conscience been tormenting him these seven months? There is no sign that it has. He was evidently lying in his denials of charges made by various women before Miss Lewinsky, but he hasn't even "sort of " admitted those lies. Back in Arkansas he was known as "Slick Willie." In Washington a Democratic senator has called him "an unusually good liar." I was watching him on TV last January, and he waved a censuring finger at me and lied to me. Possibly he lied to you too.

But maybe, just maybe, he and his cronies can cobble one statement that will repair his credibility.

President Falstaff

SEPTEMBER 17, 1998

W ashington is debating whether to impeach or censure Bill Clinton. The polls say a lot of Americans would just like to drop the subject, but that's no longer an option. Say — could we settle for a roast? Naw. It's too late for that. We've been roasting this president for nine months now. Longer, actually.

Remember shock-jock Don Imus at the National Press Club last year? Hillary Clinton glared as he delivered gross jokes about her husband that turn out to have been gross understatements.

Clinton: Tragic or comic?

Why is Clinton so funny? This is the question that needs to be addressed. We've gone through solemn questions of law, character, public trust, and stuff like that. They somehow fail to capture the man.

A few of our deep thinkers have compared the Clinton scandals to a Shakespearean tragedy. Personally, I don't see it. Our leader lacks the noble but flawed character of such tragic heroes as Hamlet, Lear, Romeo, Othello, Macbeth, Brutus, Antony, and Coriolanus. They bring disaster on themselves, but not in a way Leno and Letterman could get hoots out of.

For a Clinton analogue, we have to turn to Shakespeare's greatest comic character, Sir John Falstaff. Falstaff is a fat old knight whose many vices include lechery, but his capacity for sexual sin is pretty much a thing of the past — others marvel that "desire should so many years outlive performance."

What makes Falstaff hilarious is that he can talk his way out of any scrape — running away from a fight, misleading youth, cheating a woman out of her money with a promise to marry her, feigning death in battle. He can assume a tone of lofty sanctimony to excuse the basest action. His hypocrisy is even a kind of game: he impersonates respectability so wittily that even some of his victims are more amused than offended.

Falstaff is also Shakespeare's most theological character: he can always cite Scripture for his purpose. Like our Bible-toting president, he keeps a useful verse of Holy Writ handy at all times. Scolded for his behavior by Prince Hal, he replies: "Dost thou hear, Hal? Thou knowest in the state of innocency Adam fell, and what should poor Jack Falstaff do in the days of villainy? Thou seest I have more flesh than another man, and therefore more frailty." He's never at a loss in a tight spot.

Furthermore, he's always promising to repent, then succumbing immediately to the next temptation. His pious intentions are a running joke. The depth of his sincerity is open to question.

Falstaff is perennially funny because he's an abnormal man who can never quite be pinned down. His own inventiveness rescues him from the consequences of his enormous and reckless appetites, and nobody knows what he'll say next to save his hide. As one critic has put it, he's always in character, yet always surprising. Remind you of anyone?

Clinton is the first comic grotesque in the White House. The Starr report is being denounced as "salacious" (the word of the week), but it's actually a clinical recitation. Reading it, you wonder whether the special prosecutor realizes that he's supplying several months' worth of gags to the late-night comedians.

The president has not only lost our trust; he's lost all his dignity. He can no more recover the one than the other. His sexual follies might earn him a certain admiration if he seemed like a virile conqueror; but playing doctor with an intern in the office, while trying to outwit his own staffers, who are struggling to save him from his own famous inclinations? That's farce. And when he quibbles about the definitions of "sex," "alone," and "is" in order to get himself off the hook, we are in the realm of infinite jest.

We can now begin to see what the Clinton legacy will be. When all the serious issues are past when the impeachment question is settled, when he has left office, when perhaps he has completed a spell in confinement — we'll still be laughing. He is, beyond any comparison, the funniest president of all time.

Impeachment: A Crisis?

SEPTEMBER 15, 1998

T he current debate over whether Bill Clinton should be impeached is warped by a misconception. Most people think of impeachment as both a finding of guilt and a punishment for crime. It's neither. It's actually a trial of fitness for office.

If impeached, Clinton won't enjoy the advantages of a criminal defendant, such as the presumption of innocence; and by the same token, the prosecution won't bear the burden of proof beyond a reasonable doubt. The reason is that Clinton can't be deprived of things that are his by right: life, liberty, and property. He can only be dismissed from the office he temporarily occupies.

President or monarch?

The purpose of impeaching Clinton would not be to punish him, but to protect us. He may later be tried separately for acts that are criminal in nature, but that's a wholly distinct procedure. He could be convicted in an impeachment trial and acquitted in a criminal trial, or vice versa, or convicted or acquitted in both.

Some pundits speak of impeachment as a "constitutional crisis," showing that they aren't very familiar with the Constitution. Recourse to a procedure prescribed in the Constitution itself hardly amounts to a crisis; it's there in order to spare us crises, and it's probably used much less frequently than it should be.

In Federalist No. 69, Alexander Hamilton explained why the impeachment of a president is a necessary part of a republican system of government, by contrast with monarchy:

"The President of the United States would be liable to be impeached, tried, and upon conviction of treason, bribery, or other high crimes and misdemeanors, removed from office; and would afterwards be liable to prosecution and punishment in the ordinary course of law. The person of the King of Great Britain is sacred and inviolable: there is no constitutional tribunal to which he is amenable, no punishment to which he can be subjected without involving the crisis of a national revolution."

Just as the criminal trial is a way of avoiding the violence of private revenge, impeachment is a way of avoiding political upheaval and even civil war. In "confederated America," as Hamilton called it, a president would not be above the law; he would merely be first among equals. His removal from office for misconduct wouldn't be an earth-shaking event, because the whole system wouldn't revolve around him. The president is ultimately subordinate to Congress.

What about another popular idea — that impeachment would "overturn the results of an election"? Of course it would! Why shouldn't it, if the president abuses his office?

The Constitution provides for impeachment, but doesn't require the popular election of the president. It simply says that the legislature of each state shall decide how the state's electors are to be chosen, and that they, in turn, shall elect the president. It says nothing about the president as the embodiment of "the will of the people."

The people are represented in Congress. The president is an executive; he doesn't represent anyone. He isn't supposed to be a quasi monarch or "leader of the free world," and global markets aren't supposed to shudder when he's in trouble.

The anxiety impeachment excites nowadays shows that we have concentrated far too much power in the presidency. The principle of republican government is that no individual should control the fate of everyone else. Power is supposed to be widely distributed.

By every standard that prevailed before Clinton himself lowered our standards, he has disgraced the presidency and the nation. His vile sexual conduct in the Oval Office is bad enough; he has also committed perjury and probably other crimes.

It's reasonable to suspect that he refuses to resign chiefly because he fears criminal prosecution when he leaves office. While the rest of us debate whether his known offenses are impeachable, he behaves like a man who knows he has done things that merit not only the loss of office, but the deprivation of liberty itself — as in prison.

We may be getting what we deserve: having inflated the presidency far beyond its proper dimensions, we find it occupied by a man with no character or dignity.

IMPEACHMENT: A DISHONORABLE DEFENSE

The President They Deserve

MARCH 24, 1998

I was raised to believe it was wrong to take certain liberties with girls before marriage. It was even worse if you did it forcibly. (If they let you do it, you were hanging out with the wrong kind of girls.)

The general idea was that men should treat women with respect. It was an easy inference from this code that if you worked in an office with women, especially if you had authority over them, you didn't take advantage of them. You treated them the way you hoped other men would treat your mother or sister.

The forgiving feminists

The term "sexual harassment" hadn't been coined yet. In those days, grabbing a woman was usually called "molesting" her, and the law and public opinion dealt with it pretty severely. If a man was plausibly accused of it, he could be shamed and ruined, if not jailed. If he exposed his genitals to her, he had put himself outside the pale.

Beyond that, it was a matter of honor for men to show women special consideration — holding doors and chairs, standing when they entered a room, "watching your language," and if necessary risking your life to protect them.

Where did I get this idea? All over the place. My parents, teachers, scoutmasters, the Baltimore Catechism, old books, even the movies. Everyone understood and believed it implicitly, from Shakespeare to the corner barbershop. Nobody contradicted it. It wasn't contradictable.

We didn't talk about "the culture" in those days, but that's what it was: a cultural assumption so embedded that if you tried to isolate it and remove it, the rest of the cultural tissue would bleed. You could no more change it than you could maintain a coherent math system while denying that five and five make ten.

Later I was taught by feminist consciousness-raisers that the old culture "really" didn't respect women at all. It was "sexist" and "male chauvinist," and all its apparent considerations for women were "really" just masks of "oppression," cunning devices to "keep them in their place," sort of the way the capitalist system kept the exploited workers from understanding their "real" plight by giving them the illusory happiness of consumer goods. (A lot of feminists, in fact, were graduates from Marxism.)

The feminists were determined not only to expose the hypocrisy of the old culture, but to offer a newer and higher morality based on "true" respect for women.

I was set thinking about all this the other day when I read a piece by one of the celebrity feminists, Gloria Steinem, in the *New York Times,* defending President Clinton against the charges made by Paula Jones and Kathleen Willey.

Positing the truth of the charges in both cases, Miss Steinem argues that "Mr. Clinton seems to have made a clumsy sexual pass, then accepted rejection." She insists that these acts should be considered "private sexual behavior," and he should be forgiven for it even if he "lied under oath" to conceal them: to punish him would be to "disqualify energy and talent the country needs."

Miss Steinem is of course only the latest of the feminists to find excuses for men who behave abominably toward women, provided they support the feminist agenda on "women's issues" (chiefly abortion). After all, she says, the key point is that the president took "no" for an "answer." So his conduct was just his way of asking a question?

Such feminists consider stopping short of rape in the Oval Office sufficiently presidential. Unwelcome contact with, and/or exposure of, breasts and presidential genitals is "clumsy," but not criminal, or even disrespectful. At least not if the president supports women's issues.

If I have this right, "sexual harassment" means unwanted sexual advances by a Republican.

So here is the higher morality of the feminist movement. Bill Clinton is "really" better for women than men who uphold the traditional code. If a few women have to be sacrificed to his appetites, a Benthamite calculation will still reckon that a far greater number of women have profited by his administration.

This new morality has no need of old words like "honor" and "decency." Its advocates have the president they deserve.

Feminists and other liberals "forgive" Clinton's personal fouls against women because he's "good on women's issues." His acts of what they ordinarily call "sexual harassment" belong to his "private life." Does anyone remember Griffin Bell? When Jimmy Carter chose him as his attorney general, he had to resign from a segregated country club. There was no question of arguing that his personal associations were just his "private life," provided he enforced civil rights laws impartially: his private life was viewed as a predictor of his performance in public office. And liberals regarded his private life as very much their business.

The Clinton Coalition

MARCH 26, 1998

A t the beginning of his African visit, President Clinton was asked by a reporter whether he was going to claim "executive privilege" to cover not only his aides' conversations with him, but their conversations with his wife (who isn't a government official).

"All I know is, I saw an article about it in the paper today," the president replied. "I haven't discussed that with the lawyers. I don't know. You should ask someone who knows."

That's lawyers for you. They don't

An alliance of ignorance and cynicism

even tell their client, the president of the United States, what constitutional arguments they are going to make on his behalf! Who knows what they are pulling behind his back while he is in Africa, doing the job the American people have hired him to do? While the cat's away, the mice will play.

After two months, the president and the first lady are still being kept in the dark about the scandals swirling around them. It's an outrage. They have waited and waited for the "facts" to come out, but the only facts to emanate from the White House so far have been a few unflattering details and countercharges about the president's accusers and special prosecutor Kenneth Starr.

A cynic, especially if he belonged to the vast right-wing conspiracy, might suspect that President Clinton himself was behind the White House defense. It's at least barely possible that those White House lawyers, along with James Carville and Bob Bennett (the president's personal lawyer), are taking orders from their boss and defending him the way he wants to be defended.

The cynic might also suspect that in claiming executive privilege, the president is attempting the presidential equivalent of invoking the Fifth Amendment. The same cynic, ignoring the wisdom of the U.S. Supreme Court, might assume that the guilty are more likely than the innocent to take the Fifth.

The cynic might even infer that an innocent man would have released all the facts he had by now, letting the chips fall where they may. The cynic might further infer, from the White House's stonewalling, that there are few hidden facts that would, if published, put the president in a more favorable light.

Such a beady-eyed cynic might also guess that when the president implied that he was legally unable to defend himself publicly, he was using the same ploy Johnnie Cochran used when he implied that O. J. Simpson was being denied the right to testify in his own defense (as if Simpson himself hadn't chosen to take the Fifth). These tactics seem designed only to confuse ignorant people; they won't impress anyone who follows the current scandals closely.

And maybe the purpose of the dirt we hear about the women who say Bill Clinton groped and flashed them is not just to discredit the accusers themselves, but also to intimidate other potential accusers. Cynical, I know, but possible.

The real motive for the sliming of Kenneth Starr may not be honest indignation about his tactics, but fear of what he is likely to find. If (let's be cynical again) the president has a lot to hide, he may figure that his best strategy is to discredit Starr early and often, in order to neutralize the damaging revelations that will eventually come forth.

An innocent man passionately wants to look innocent. He craves vindication. He is tortured by false accusations and their residue of unjust suspicions. He isn't content with a technical acquittal that leaves a permanent stain on his reputation, because dishonor itself is an agonizing punishment. Just being free to play golf the rest of his days isn't enough.

So why is President Clinton content, at every step, with a defense that makes him look guilty? He has removed all doubt in the minds of his enemies, and it has reached the point where few of his friends believe he is innocent. All sides are reaching a tacit consensus about his character.

His approval ratings are still high, but — speaking of cynicism — a large proportion of his supporters think he's guilty but simply don't mind. The Clinton coalition is now an alliance of the cynical and the ignorant. But this president seems content with it.

Right to the point: The columnist Paul Craig Roberts observes: "If the evidence were not enough to convict Mr. Clinton, then he would not be withholding it."

The Hidden Bottle

JUNE 16, 1998

K enneth Starr sounds just awful. If you listen to Bill Clinton's partisans — including Steven Brill, publisher of the new magazine *Brill's Content* — the special prosecutor, driven by partisan political motives and obsessed with sex, has illegally leaked grand jury testimony, forced a mother to testify against her daughter, tried to abolish attorney-client confidentiality, threatened the integrity of the presidency, and violated the First Amendment.

The president as victim

Well, Starr's defenders counter, Clinton has the power to get rid of him at any time. They are right. It's absurd that Clinton should tolerate grossly improper, illegal, and even criminal behavior in a prosecutor who ultimately answers to the president.

In fact, the case can be put much more strongly. If Starr is really as bad as the Clintonites make him out, Clinton should be impeached for failing to fire him!

Like O. J. Simpson's legal "dream team," Clinton's public relations trash team is depending heavily on keeping the jury confused. Take the idea that Starr has forced Monica Lewinsky's mother to testify against her daughter.

The key word is "against." Properly speaking, Starr forced her to testify "about" her daughter. The word "against" implies that she has knowledge of her daughter's guilt, which implies that her daughter is guilty (of perjury, among other things), which implies that Clinton is guilty too.

That's not quite what Clinton's partisans want us to infer. They want to give the impression that Starr has done something cruel to Monica's mom, but they don't want to acknowledge that if Monica were honest and innocent her mother's testimony would help exonerate her.

The Clintonites' task is to make Starr's pursuit of facts sound sinister at every turn, while making Clinton himself the innocent and helpless victim, even if all this involves grotesque contradictions.

At first Clinton stressed his eagerness to provide the public with "facts," and "sooner rather than later," in keeping with his "obligation to cooperate with the investigation." But soon he was implying, falsely, that this "obligation" prevented him from giving his side of the story, while Starr was taking mean advantage of the situation with illegal leaks. Several months later, Clinton has ceased pretending he is trying to cooperate. He is using every imaginable pretext to suppress information.

There is one fraying thread of consistency, though: Clinton still claims victimhood. But whereas he was formerly victimized by the nonexistent prohibition against telling us his side, he's now victimized by the demand that he provide information.

If Monica dropped into the White House for at least thirty-seven visits after she was transferred to the Pentagon, what does this suggest about Clinton? First, of course, he was flatly lying to us when he glared into the camera and told us he had had no sexual relationship with "that woman."

But much more important, in a way, is the nature of the relationship. It wasn't just sexual; it was habitual. Clinton didn't merely succumb, once or twice, to the passion of a moment; he kept Monica at hand the way an alcoholic keeps a hidden bottle in the desk drawer, with systematic planning and deception.

Others — apparently including Clinton's secretary Betty Currie and his pal Vernon Jordan — were made parties to his lies and intrigues. They probably felt they had to cover for him, at great risk and no profit to themselves.

Everyone seems to be forgetting Starr's ace in the hole: twenty hours of tape recordings of Monica's confessions and complaints about "the big creep." When their contents become known, they are likely to blast away all the distractions of the last five months, and even Larry Flynt is apt to feel that he knows more about his president than is strictly necessary.

Everything the Clinton camp has said about Starr has turned out to be a dodge, a bluff, or a stall. Starr, for his part, has acted as if he can afford to wait, enduring abuse with puzzling patience. He has something big, and Bill Clinton is one of the very few who knows what it is.

Starr illustrates why integrity in public office is so important. If he had had any dirty secrets in his past, Clinton's people, who surely looked for them, might have used them to blackmail him and kill the investigation. In other words, good character is the best armor against men like Clinton himself.

Everybody Knows

JULY 16, 1998

C an you identify the speaker of the following words? "I've known Bill Clinton since we went to school together, and I've never known him to lie. Just the opposite. I've known him to tell the truth, many times, even when it could cost him. As far as I know, he's always been a faithful husband. And it's unthinkable that he would sell out his country for partisan advantage. I can't imagine him doing any of the things he's being accused of."

The correct answer is "I give up." Nobody ever spoke those words, and nobody in his right mind would. Bill Clinton is being accused of deeds for which there is not only evidence, but antecedent probability. If he wouldn't commit them, one might ask, who would?

Unfamiliar quotations

Clinton has a thousand apologists. What he doesn't have is a single character witness. Not even his wife. Least of all his wife.

Hillary Clinton is the key to this whole story. If she hadn't sprung to his defense in the first days after the Lewinsky scandal broke, Al Gore would be president by now. As soon as she sent out the signal that she didn't care what her husband had done, the Democrats had their marching orders.

Mrs. Clinton is playing a curious role. She is the senior wife in what amounts to a walk-in harem. As long as she retains her primacy, she appears not to be jealous of the other women.

The president's defenders are likewise protecting the façade of the Clintons' marriage. They don't really think he never went beyond a handshake with Monica Lewinsky; they make pro forma professions of believing Clinton's shabby denials and help him avoid a showdown with the facts.

Another thing nobody has ever said is this: "Bill Clinton is innocent. Let's hear those tapes. Let's hear the testimony of Monica Lewinsky, Betty Currie, the Secret Service, the Chinese lobbyists, and let the chips fall where they may. The full truth will vindicate the president and confute his accusers."

Clinton's apologists argue that the Secret Service shouldn't be forced to testify against him. Note the preposition. Why "against"? Why not "for" or "about"? Because they assume the facts are damaging to Clinton — as do Clinton and Attorney General Janet Reno. The words "full disclosure" sound awfully quaint in today's Washington.

Clinton's chief hatchet man, James Carville, who prefers velocity to veracity, has been oddly quiet lately; the duty of defending the Democrats' alpha male seems to have devolved on Barney Frank, the man least likely to censure *l'amour clintonaise,* as I believe the urbane Parisians call it. (Barney recently split up with the gent who has been his main squeeze these last ten years, so now's your chance to grab him on the rebound.)

Barney is far too canny to suggest that Clinton is telling the truth, but he has perfected the rhetorical technique of violent nitpicking against Kenneth Starr. Starr, like Linda Tripp, has a way of outraging people who aren't outraged by adultery on the rug in the Oval Office.

But to the point: Has Clinton committed "high crimes and misdemeanors"? The phrase means approximately "abuses of power and disgraceful behavior." Andrew Johnson, though no criminal, was impeached for far less than Clinton has done.

In the private sector, any corporate executive who sexually exploited an intern would be quickly dismissed under the standard moral turpitude clause of his contract. The word "misdemeanors" in the Constitution may be understood as a virtual moral turpitude clause. So Clinton's fling with Monica in the Oval Office should suffice for impeachment and removal from office, even without graver abuses of power and setting aside Clinton's congenital venality.

But Clinton, with his usual cunning, has insinuated the dual notion, first, that a president can be impeached only for offenses that would land a private citizen in prison, and second, that a president faced with impeachment is therefore entitled to all the protections of a criminal defendant (on top of the privileges of the presidency).

This confuses removal from office with penal incarceration. Clinton may well deserve both, but they are totally distinct. Removing a malefactor from office should be easier, not harder, than sending him to jail.

Clinton's spokesmen continue to accuse Starr, groundlessly, of illegally leaking damaging information about Clinton. But Starr, apart from being honest, is clearly not a man who likes to tip his hand. Why should he have leaked? If he'd wanted to hurt Clinton by doing so, he could have put out details about Clinton's perversions as early as January 1998, when he got Linda Tripp's tapes. Instead, he managed to suppress the most embarrassing details for seven months.

The Tripp File

JULY 21, 1998

W ell, well. We haven't heard much lately about those raw FBI files the White House had illicitly obtained a couple of years ago. Until now. It transpires that one of those files was Linda Tripp's.

Will the people who have been denouncing Mrs. Tripp for violating the privacy of Monica Lewinsky now denounce the Clintons for violating the privacy of Mrs. Tripp? Will those who have complained that Kenneth Starr's investigation of the Clintons is "out of control" now

What a White House employee saw

add, with scrupulous fairness, that the Clintons themselves seem to have been a little out of control too?

I'm waiting. The suspense is terrific.

Maybe Mrs. Tripp taped her conversations with poor little Monica because she knew what sort of people she was dealing with, even if she didn't specifically know that they had her FBI files. Those files aren't the only example of the Clintons' keen interest in controlling sensitive information.

Long before she began taping Monica, Mrs. Tripp knew about the files and the Clintons' inability to explain how and why they had arrived in the White House. She was there when Vince Foster died mysteriously and Mrs. Clinton had his office cleaned out with frantic haste, forestalling a full investigation. She had seen the Clintons arrange the false prosecution of Billy Dale of the White House Travel Office. She knew about the measures taken by private investigators against "bimbos" of the president's acquaintance.

So by the time the president's lawyer attacked her veracity as a witness in the Kathleen Willey case, Mrs. Tripp may have begun to form an impression of the Clintons — the same impression millions of others have formed from afar, with the added vividness proximity lends. And after two Clinton cronies who possessed damaging inside knowledge of the First Couple — Foster and Commerce Secretary Ron Brown — suddenly bade this world good night, she may even have reached the paranoid conclusion that more than her job might be at stake if the Clintons discovered that she knew things they preferred to keep unknown.

Any such paranoia on her part has been vindicated by subsequent events. She can hardly have been surprised to find that the White House had her FBI file; it would have been surprising if it hadn't. The Pentagon illegally leaked private information about her to a reporter friendly to the White House and hostile to Mrs. Tripp; it was duly published. Now she is facing an unprecedented prosecution for illegal taping by a Democratic prosecutor in Maryland. And she has endured a campaign of smear and ridicule, not for lying, but for recording information the White House desperately wants to conceal.

Meanwhile, the White House has launched an even more vitriolic campaign against Starr — again, not for lying, but for trying to uncover the facts. And along the way, it has tried to discredit Paula Jones, Mrs. Willey, and other witnesses to Clinton's sexual cynicism, including the Arkansas state troopers who have told their stories. By now any Secret Service agent who testifies that he has witnessed Clinton's improper or illegal behavior knows what to expect.

Throughout its many scandals, the Clinton White House's tactics have included delaying, stonewalling, hiding evidence, scaring and smearing witnesses, attacking the investigation, claiming bogus privileges, creating distractions, distorting the issues, and outright lying. Not to mention equivocating ("There is no sexual relationship") and acting injured (by "the vast right-wing conspiracy").

The Democrats have disgraced themselves by abetting the White House, even to the extent of joining the assault on Linda Tripp before hearing her testimony or the crucial tapes. As for the party's feminists, they consider Clinton the alpha male of the sisterhood, and any woman who crosses him is on her own.

Just after the revelation of Monica Lewinsky's links to Clinton and his pal Vernon Jordan, a few Democrats called on Clinton to come clean. But when he refused this advice, even these voices fell silent.

The entire Democratic Party has become accomplice to the Clintons. It sees only a political problem, not a moral one, in — what's the phrase? — the most unethical administration in our nation's history.

Clinton's defense depends on cynicism. Nobody who defends him wants to raise our standards of public and private conduct. He has the kind of supporters Alger Hiss, Marion Barry, and O. J. Simpson had: his offenses don't really offend them. They want us to forget that anyone has ever behaved honorably.

Later Rather
Than Sooner

JULY 28, 1998

A t last. After six months — later rather than sooner — the chief figures in the Lewinsky scandal are going to have to cooperate with the investigation. One of them may even tell the truth — maybe Monica Lewinsky herself.

The head spins from six months of White House spinning. Only days after it was revealed that a young White House intern had bragged about her Oval Office antics with the president of the United States, the first lady went on the warpath. She blamed the scandal on a "vast right-wing conspiracy" spearheaded by special prosecutor Kenneth Starr and urged the nation to wait until all the facts came out. The president himself promised the public the facts. And for six months, the White House has been doing everything in its power to prevent those facts from coming out.

Shocked in January, ho-hum in July

During that time, a series of constitutional questions has arisen, largely because William Jefferson Clinton was beyond the imaginations of the Framers of the Constitution.

In January 1998, Americans were stunned by the report that their president had been having sex with a young intern in his office. By July 1998, they had gotten used to the idea. Thanks to Bill Clinton, the phrase "White House intern" has acquired new connotations, like "Arkansas state trooper."

After dozens of other major and minor scandals, this scandal looked like the one that would bring the Clinton administration down in flames — sooner rather than later. And yet the White House ingeniously exploited the sex angle to stave off the end, relying on the argument that it was "only" sex, that whatever happened in the Oval Office was "private," that Kenneth Starr was "obsessed" with sex.

The Clinton circle brilliantly hid other issues — of perjury and obstruction of justice — behind the very thing that had produced the initial shock. It used one scandal to upstage others. It used perversion to distract attention from crime, while arguing that the perversion was nobody's business.

Clinton himself denied everything, promised to tell the truth, delayed and evaded, and delegated the hatchet work to his subordinates. They, for their part, insisted they knew nothing and proceeded to frustrate the inquiry, attacking not only the special prosecutor but the press as well.

This hastily improvised strategy succeeded for a long time because the Clinton scandals were as dizzying as the Omaha Beach sequence in the movie *Saving Private Ryan*. The public couldn't get its bearings. The Republicans couldn't decide how to respond.

The most partisan administration in memory has never ceased accusing the Republicans of being "partisan." The truth is that while the Democrats were swinging meat axes, the Republicans had nobody with the nerve to squeeze the trigger. For them, Clinton's degeneracy became an almost taboo subject.

The survival of so supremely vulnerable a president tells a lot about both parties. The Democrats, even when threatened by lethal scandal, remain fiercely aggressive; the Republicans, enjoying advantages few parties have ever had, remain hopelessly timid.

So Starr has had to work without much support. Some Republicans, like Senate majority leader Trent Lott and Arlen Specter of Pennsylvania, have even taken potshots at him for taking so long, though the White House itself was systematically frustrating his quest for the long-promised facts.

The Republicans wouldn't have had to attack on the Carville level. They could simply have kept pressing Clinton to tell the truth, as he had pledged to do. "We're still waiting, Mr. President" would have been the appropriate tone — dignified, but firm and insistent.

But it looks as if Starr is going to win anyway. If Miss Lewinsky talks, there may not be much reason for the White House to delay further; it will have to counteract her testimony.

When this is over, we may look up and realize how gravely Bill Clinton has wounded our public life. He and his cronies and supporters are nothing less than a national degradation. And we are only just beginning to get the facts they have been hiding.

Monica was in a position to blackmail Clinton, and there are hints of this in his efforts to placate her with gifts, jobs, and sweet talk and to expunge or falsify records of her visits to the White House. This alone — exposing the presidency to threats from a silly tramp — is ample reason to impeach him.

"Ich Bin ein Arkansan"

AUGUST 13, 1998

T ime is running out for President Bill ("That allegation is false") Clinton. His chief defender, first lady Hillary ("Don't forget the Rodham") Rodham ("Thanks") Clinton, is reduced to blaming his and her troubles on "prejudice against our state."

I hadn't stopped to realize that there is so much bias against Arkanso-Americans. But I guess there is. And some of it, regrettably, is fomented by Arkanso-Americans themselves.

Pity the Arkanso-American!

Only a couple of years ago, a former governor of the state recalled on national TV that when he was a youth, in 1964, dozens of black churches had been burned down in Arkansas.

As it turned out, that allegation was false. Someone checked and found that no black churches had been burned down in Arkansas that year.

Incredibly, a former governor of Arkansas had invented the story! He had turned a stereotype of the South against his home state! No wonder so many Americans have a false image of Arkansas, with such politicians prevaricating like that.

That former governor's name was ... Bill Clinton. And now you know the rest of the story.

Well, the Clintons, in their hour of need, have changed their tune about Arkansas. It used to be "Don't confuse me with the rest of them hicks." Today it's "Ich bin ein Arkansan."

Hillary's latest twist on the first couple's victimhood is one more illustration of the constantly shifting grounds of Bill's defense. First it was a right-wing conspiracy, now it's geographical bigotry.

Less than five years ago the Clinton defenders were saying you couldn't trust those disgruntled Arkansas state troopers who were telling stories about procuring bimbos for their former boss. Besides, the stories appeared in a right-wing — ergo unreliable — magazine. That line of defense has been pretty much abandoned. Nobody now says the troopers were lying.

And behold, the state trooper stories begat the Paula Jones lawsuit. The Clinton defenders said you couldn't trust Paula Jones, because she was trailer trash with big hair who was just in it for the money.

Now they say you can't hold Clinton's perjury in the Jones suit against him, because the suit has been dismissed on technical grounds. But if you'll notice, they've stopped arguing that Mrs. Jones is less believable than the president of the United States. Thanks to Clinton's general and well-attested conduct, nobody now says Paula Jones was lying.

Today, as the Clintons pray that the stain on Monica Lewinsky's dress will turn out to be Brylcreem ("A little dab'll do ya"), nobody believes the guy. The premise of all sides in the raging debate is that he lies. It's his form of respiration: inhale, lie, inhale, lie... In comes the good air, out goes the Clinton version.

So now his allies are helpfully advising him on how to lie or even, if need be, tell the truth. In fact, some of them are openly suggesting that he tell the truth, not because it's the right thing to do, but because renouncing perjury for a change just might save his skin. What's more, telling the truth could even give the president the element of surprise.

You know you're in trouble when your only character witness is Geraldo Rivera. The biggest beef the Clinton defenders have left is that "Kenneth Starr has wasted $40 million of the taxpayers' money." These are people who aren't normally solicitous about the taxpayers' money.

Congress spends at the rate of $4 billion a day. That comes to $40 million of the taxpayers' money every few minutes. Starr has spent that amount over four years, costing each taxpayer about a dime a year. It's less than Clinton's pal Steven Spielberg spends making a movie. But to hear the Clinton rooters talk about it, it's the most staggering expenditure since King Tut. Even so, it might have been a little less if Clinton had cooperated a little more.

But Arkansas is in real trouble. When all this is over, the state will have to deal with what's left of its reputation, after having given us the Clintons. It might consider changing its name. And, if possible, moving.

Barney Frank complains that the Republicans on the House Judiciary Committee were "partisan" in voting to release the videotape of Clinton's grand jury testimony. If so, it's about time. The Democrats have shown they'll do anything to win, beginning with feigning belief in Clinton's denials, covering up his more serious crimes, and joining the smear campaign against Kenneth Starr. It's fitting that the chief congressional defender of a perverted president should be a militant pervert like Frank.

The word "surreal" keeps occurring to those who try to step back and assess the whole situation Clinton has created. It's impossible to imagine such a crisis under any other president; this one is an extension of Clinton's unique personality.

A Far, Far Better Thing

SEPTEMBER 1, 1998

W hen I hear people blaming Linda Tripp for secretly taping her conversations with Monica Lewinsky, I only wish Paula Jones and Kathleen Willey had been wired too. When you're dealing with Bill Clinton and his circle, you'd better make sure you're covered.

In their desperation, the attacks on Linda Tripp are like the attacks on special prosecutor Kenneth Starr. Both of them have done their best to get the facts against a president who is deter-

Nixon-haters, Clinton-lovers

mined to conceal the facts. If they manage to get evidence that can't be denied, they have to be accused of playing dirty.

The columnist Garry Wills, a friend of the Clintons and one of their most ardent defenders in the press, admits that it's time for this president to resign. He calls Clinton's enemies "dishonorable" — but doesn't apply that word to Clinton himself, for whom he feels "liking and admiration." Wills has now managed to write two articles calling on Clinton to quit without using the word "lies," which is like writing about Mark McGwire without mentioning home runs.

What is the strange power Clinton has to make otherwise shrewd people blind to his mendacity? Wills made his career as a critic of Richard Nixon, who never fooled him. But he writes about the squalid Clinton as if he were discussing a sort of tragic giant: Clinton has tried to "bring the social concerns of a whole new generation into the White House. On issue after issue, he has done just that — women's rights, gay rights, minority rights. With his emollient personal skills, he was able to speak to and for the baby boomers, overcoming the resistance and resentment felt for the whole world of the Sixties."

Wills pleads, rather pathetically, that a "principled resignation could be the one act of leadership that could save his own projects.... With resignation, he would grow. He would be saying that the goals he fought for are more important than personal pride or prerogatives." Maybe so. But I hope Wills isn't betting a lot of money on its happening.

The other day Clinton spoke to a black group, joining in a chorus of "We Shall Overcome" and recalling that he'd wept "uncontrollably" when he heard Martin Luther King's "I have a dream" speech as a boy. It was a virtual replay of his "vivid and painful memory" of black church burnings in Arkansas, which turned out never to have happened. But never mind: his audience was moved to tears. This guy is the champ.

Clinton's model isn't Kennedy or King; it's Johnnie Cochran. He's emblematic not of the Sixties, but of the Nineties. He belongs in the company of everything that is tackiest about American culture today: Larry Flynt, Al Sharpton, Howard Stern, and Jerry Springer. The cultural blight has moved right into the White House. It's even embarrassing to hear this con man called "the president."

"However we may doubt the sincerity of those who speak to us," La Rochefoucauld observed, "we think they are more candid with us than with others." That's the problem liberals have with this character. They know he's a liar, but they can't bear to think he's taken them in along with the soccer moms. They think he has to lie to Starr and the "right-wing conspiracy," but it's all in a good cause: the "social concerns" of the Sixties, which they still believe he sincerely espouses.

But Clinton has never fooled conservatives. His chief dupes have been liberals, feminists, minorities — the whole Rainbow Coalition for whom he has feigned sympathy, and whom he has seduced into defending him. They no longer dare to mention "sexual harassment," which until January was one of their burning "issues."

Now they are constructing the fantasy of a "principled resignation," in which Clinton does the dignified and decorous thing for the good of "the goals he fought for." They're confusing Bill Clinton with Sydney Carton. I can't predict how Clinton will leave the stage, but I think we can assume he has ruled out hara-kiri.

On the Contrition Trail

SEPTEMBER 10, 1998

D uring his contrition swing through Orlando, Bill Clinton told an audience of Democrats that he'd shaken hands with a schoolboy who told him: "Mr. President, I want to grow up to be president. I want to be a president like you." Clinton said that "this kid ... reminded me a lot of myself when I was that young."

Talk about warning signals! Let's hope the school counselors can reach the boy in time.

A kid who needs help

"I've tried to do a good job taking care of this country even when I haven't taken such good care of myself, and my family, and my obligations," Clinton said. He should give himself a little credit. He has taken very good care of himself. He's still doing it.

Even when apologizing and repenting, Clinton speaks in his unique style, fusing emotional histrionics with careful semantics. At every step he reduces the charges against himself from damning deeds to vague errors.

He didn't commit adultery with an intern; he had "a relationship that was not appropriate." He didn't commit perjury and try to deceive the nation; he "misled people" (albeit his statements were "legally accurate"). He didn't commit sins; he made "mistakes." He didn't betray you with cynical lies; he "let you down." He didn't do evil; he "let it happen."

"I have no one to blame but myself for my" — sins? crimes? deceits? betrayals? — "for my self-inflicted wounds." Wounds! How pathetic! Well, if they're self-inflicted, it's redundant to say he can't blame anyone else for inflicting them.

But never mind; it's not the thought that counts, it's the ooze. Lots of talk of God, family, friends, and getting back to the "issues." Lots of homiletic words like "redeem," "trust," "understanding," "forgiveness," "reconciliation," "healing." And of course "journey," as in "this journey we're on." This whole mess is a pilgrimage we're making together. As he said on August 17, it's time to "repair the fabric of our national discourse."

You have to hand it to him. Only Bill Clinton could stand in the pillory and pretend it's a pulpit.

There will be further profuse presidential apologies, but none to Paula Jones, Kathleen Willey, or Linda Tripp, who were clearly telling the truth while Clinton lied and his flunkeys trashed them, such being this administration's contribution to the fabric of our national discourse.

Nor will Clinton's high-minded quest for reconciliation extend to asking pardon of the special prosecutor, of whom he has reportedly told his friends: "That man is evil." According to James Carville, Starr is also "sex-obsessed." This administration seems to lack a sense of irony.

But then, to paraphrase Joe Stalin, how many divisions do the ironists have? In the Clintonian calculus, those who listen to public utterances with skepticism are demographically insignificant. P. T. Barnum wasn't talking about logicians when he observed that there's one born every minute.

Now that Congress has the special prosecutor's report, everything has changed. Clinton's coverup is passé. Ad hominem attacks on Starr and the witnesses are useless. Eight months of lies, denials, evasions, equivocations, diversions, and smears will be judged against the evidence. It will be the word of a proven and chronic liar against many witnesses and one dress.

Imagine the fate of a Republican president — an apostle of "family values" — who had acted as Clinton has done. Imagine the explosive mockery he would ignite if he dared to excuse his lies as attempts to protect the wife and daughter he'd betrayed with his insatiate lust.

But Clinton keeps professing his tender concern for his family, and nobody laughs! Must we now accept pro-family hypocrisy as the norm for Democrats?

Apparently so. Feminists excuse Clinton's abuse of individual women because he pursues their agenda. And liberals excuse his betrayal and exploitation of his own family because they approve of his policies. After all, it's not as if he were a conservative Republican.

Clinton may be a sign that the "New Morality" is aging badly. The idea that a man should be judged by his own principles sounds fine, until you meet the man who doesn't have any.

Poor Monica Lewinsky actually thought she might become the next Mrs. Clinton. Clinton himself encouraged her to think so by suggesting that his marriage might not long outlive his presidency. This is the real Clinton: his biographer Roger Morris reports that in Arkansas during the 1970s, another girl, the daughter of a local politician, was telling people she was engaged to Clinton — while he was already (unbeknownst to her) living with, and planning to marry, Hillary.

He never fails: "I regret that what began as a friendship came to include this conduct." Really? According to Monica's testimony, she exposed her underwear at their first meeting, and he still couldn't remember her name after she'd shown her good heart by servicing him on two separate occasions. (The women who rebuffed him obviously don't have good hearts.)

Operation Candor

AUGUST 18, 1998

H e never lets you down, does he? Speaking to the nation like a man, Bill Clinton said he was "completely responsible" for a "relationship" with Monica Lewinsky that was, he admits, "not appropriate." He'd also created a "false impression" and "misled people." However, everything he said back in January was "legally accurate."

And what did he testify in January? When asked under oath whether he'd had "sexual relations" with Miss Lewinsky, he said: "No." How that could be "legally accurate" he didn't explain Monday night. To a non-lawyer it sounds rather like a lie.

Clinton's reverse character defense

Having thus cleared the air, Clinton blamed Kenneth Starr (without mentioning Starr by name, of course) for the vexatious seven months we've just endured. It's all Starr's fault. He's guilty of "prying into private lives" in the Oval Office. And, Clinton says, "I intend to reclaim my family life for my family."

Get a load of that. By asking Clinton about that "relationship" with a young White House employee on the Oval Office couch (and whether Clinton had taken illegal measures to conceal it), Starr was ripping the veil from the intimate recesses of Clinton's "family life." And Clinton, on behalf of Hillary and Chelsea, resents it. He misled people in large part because he was "protecting my family."

Husband, father, gallant protector of womenfolk! His statement was peppered with the words "love," "wife," "daughter," "family," and "God." Was he using these terms in a legal or ambiguous sense? Who knows? Coming from Clinton, even common language turns out to be full of unsuspected homonyms.

Before the speech, everyone agreed on one thing. This time

Clinton couldn't afford to play word games with the public.

Which is exactly what he did. As usual. As always. This is a lawyer's idea of "coming clean" — a committee-crafted confession. The pundits were laboriously parsing his statement into the wee hours. It was pure, distilled Clinton.

He "confessed" less than we already knew and no more than the FBI lab is about to confirm. Yet he wants credit for candor. As his lawyer David Kendall said, he testified to the grand jury "truthfully" and "voluntarily." Well, sort of. Truthfully when trapped, and voluntarily when under duress.

It wasn't a confession; it was a concession — a tactical retreat in his war on Starr. He was counting on the public to read contrition into his nebulous formulations. But he admitted only what had become undeniable, then immediately tried to turn it to his advantage by using the buzzwords that work in the polls — "the pursuit of personal destruction," "prying into private lives," "nobody's business but ours." (This from the man who illegally gathered the raw FBI files of suspected opponents!)

During the Watergate scandal, the Nixon White House launched what it ludicrously called "Operation Candor" — an attempt to persuade the public of its honesty by admitting a few damaging facts that couldn't be concealed anyway. This is Clinton's version of Operation Candor. He says he "misled" us in January in order to mislead us in another way in August.

Among those he "misled," he says, was his wife. Why should he stress this point? Well, Mrs. Clinton reportedly opposed any admission of his adultery because she has been flatly denying it too. By saying she was "misled," the president gave her deniability: she can now pretend she wasn't lying along with him.

When the Lewinsky story broke, everyone seemed to agree that if Clinton had committed adultery with a White House intern he would have to resign, just as a general who had sex with a private in his Pentagon office would be finished. Clinton's aggressive denials reinforced that reaction.

Since then, though, Clinton has waged a seven-month war of attrition on our standards of public conduct. Much of the punditry and the citizenry have begun to accept the "it's only" argument: it's only sex, it's only lying about sex, it's only perjury about sex. Et cetera.

Clinton's strategy comes down to this: he wants his character to be defined as his "private life." That way he can mount a weird reverse character defense in which he hides his crimes behind his shabby little sins.

The Clinton defense has been audacious to the point of insulting our intelligence. It has accused Starr of being "sex-obsessed," of making "salacious" and "pornographic" charges, of conducting a "hit-and-run smear campaign." This is a verbal self-portrait of the accusers. Wilt thou whip thine own faults in other men?

Acts of contrition: Now that Bill Clinton has apologized to Africa for sins he didn't commit, I'd like to apologize, in the same spirit, to all the women who have been molested, all the witnesses who have been bullied, and all the special prosecutors who have been smeared by American presidents and Arkansas governors.

The Culture of Candor

SEPTEMBER 22, 1998

Tragically, our nation has now, for the second time in a few years, seen a president afflicted with Alzheimer's. Bill Clinton's fabled memory has broken down. During his August 17 grand jury testimony, it failed him dozens of times.

It's a shame, because he really needs his memory now. He's been the victim of so many lying and designing women: Gennifer Flowers, Paula Jones, Kathleen Willey, Linda Tripp, and Monica Lewinsky. He has disputed their accounts of his behavior with as much vigor as a memory-impaired person can, but it's tough.

Presidential memory loss

On the other hand, one advantage of having Alzheimer's is that you keep meeting new women.

There's one woman Clinton has never accused of lying: Hillary Clinton. She's the one who told us we could trust him.

Clinton is the consummate hypocrite of the generation that has rejected hypocrisy. He speaks for the Culture of Candor that has afflicted us since the Sixties. Be up front. Tell it like it is. Get in touch with your feelings. Do your own thing. Question authority.

The Culture of Candor was especially stern about Richard Nixon, the original uptight white male who Lied to the American People. Bill and Hillary were Watergate children; as a rookie politician in 1974 he called for Nixon's resignation for lying, while she served on the staff of the House Judiciary Committee that drew up the articles of impeachment.

When Nixon quit, deception was definitely Out. Long hair, sexual freedom, and raw honesty were In. Old standards of decency were equated with hypocrisy. It was no longer necessary to lie about sex, like the Puritans and Victorians; unmarried young couples lost any shame about shacking up. In the sacred name of candor, nudity became a standard feature of movies (though for some reason there was an unnatural ratio of naked young women to, say, naked old fat guys).

At the same time, those who upheld traditional standards were maliciously diagnosed. They were unhealthy — "repressed" — and had buried obsessions with sex because they weren't in touch with their real feelings.

Hypocrisy on your own side is always hard to recognize, especially when you're young and riding the wave of the future. Everyone who agreed with the New Morality was honest by definition; hypocrisy was a trait of the old reactionaries who led lives of public virtue and private vice.

But this view overlooked the subtle persistence of hypocrisy, which takes a thousand forms. The Culture of Candor eventually found its own Elmer Gantry in Bill Clinton, who found his own uses for the new shibboleths. He was "good on women's issues," with a feminist wife, while secretly behaving like a prelapsarian male chauvinist pig. The feminists still can't believe their eyes: even now they consider him their friend and ally.

And who, in the eyes of the Culture of Candor, is the villain of the story? Why, the special prosecutor, of course! Kenneth Starr is an old-fashioned Baptist who won't even put a cigar in his own mouth, but this only certifies his villainy. He is "evil," "sick," and "sex-obsessed." His report, which merely describes Clinton's hypocrisy (perjury being the most formal kind of hypocrisy) in clinical detail, is being called "salacious" and "pornographic."

Dig the irony here. For the first time, the Culture of Candor is condemning something as pornographic. And after preaching all these years that we don't have to lie about sex anymore, it excuses Clinton on grounds that "everyone lies about sex."

Starr, an old-fashioned Christian gentleman whose honor is attested by everyone who knows him, hasn't even replied to the White House smear campaign that has impugned his integrity with outrageous lies. Nor has the Republican Party defended him against this bald attempt to slander him for the purpose of subverting the investigation. He has had to fight a ruthless criminal operation with little help from those who should be supporting his efforts.

When this whole business has ended, Starr ought to take a leaf from Gary Cooper in *High Noon*. He should throw his badge in the dust and leave this town in contempt.

The unusual word "salacious" has occurred to an amazing number of people at the same time. Do you ever get the feeling you're debating with parrots?

Alas, the usually shrewd Maureen Dowd of the *New York Times* has joined the parrot chorus, accusing Starr of preoccupation with lewd detail. A decade ago this same Miss Dowd wrote a titillating front-page story in the Good Grey *Times* relating the contents of Kitty Kelley's gossipy book about Nancy Reagan, focusing on rumors about Mrs. Reagan's sex life. No sources were identified; no crime, impeachable offense, or "issue" was at stake; the interest was purely prurient, with a malicious edge. Today Miss Dowd makes equally baseless charges about Starr's motives, imputing to him the kind of lubricious curiosity she herself has exhibited.

Otherwise Honorable?

OCTOBER 8, 1998

B ill Clinton's defenders admit that he lied to the public, lied under oath in a civil suit, and even lied to a grand jury. But though he may have committed perjury, it was "only about sex," and doesn't "rise to the level of an impeachable offense."

This overworked defense dodges the question of Clinton's honor. Are we supposed to believe that he's an otherwise honorable man who lied and perjured himself only about his affair with Monica Lewinsky?

Would an otherwise honorable man have lied the way Clinton lied? Would an otherwise honorable man have engaged his wife,

> *Clinton has shown life-long habits of betrayal.*

his friends, his cabinet, his allies in Congress, and his secretary to repeat his lies?

Of course not. An otherwise honorable man, in a moment of weakness under great stress, may fib. But he doesn't lie with gusto. He doesn't set his lie to music. He doesn't compromise others, especially innocent people who trust him. He doesn't jab his finger at the public, impugning those who doubt him.

Clinton only partially retracted his lies about Miss Lewinsky, and even then only because physical evidence was about to expose those lies anyway. But the fact that they are now known to be lies casts doubt on his other sworn statements, many of which are also "only about sex."

He continues to stand by his denials of the charges of Paula Jones, Kathleen Willey, and Gennifer Flowers. He repeated those denials under oath before the grand jury on August 17. He also stands by numerous other denials, some of them sworn, about nonsexual questions. He has never acknowledged perjuring himself.

The question is whether Clinton's perjury and orchestrated lying in the Lewinsky case render his word on other matters worthless. The answer is obvious. As impeachment looms, Clinton has defined himself as the least reliable witness in the whole sweeping inquiry.

To hear Clinton's defenders, you'd think he told an isolated lie, then repented and confessed. But he vigorously reinforced the lie for seven months until he was forced to abandon it. That makes the lie a revelation of his character, his inner self, the habitual and consistent part of him that makes daily moral decisions.

Abandoning the one lie he could no longer sustain doesn't mean Clinton has become honorable — especially when he continues to maintain other denials that are incongruous with his reluctant forced admission. If Mrs. Willey had secretly recorded her interview with Clinton, does anyone doubt whose version of that incident would be upheld?

Consider another question. Would kidnapping a cat and slashing tires be impeachable offenses? Hardly — other things being equal.

But Mrs. Willey has said her cat disappeared and her tires were slashed around the time she testified that Clinton had pawed her in the Oval Office. A few months later a stranger approached her and made ominous references to said cat and tires, warning her to watch her step. If all this could be tied to Clinton, it might look more serious than routine catnapping and tire slashing. It might look like part of a pattern of tampering with witnesses — the same pattern his own inner circle refers to under the heading of "bimbo eruptions."

Character means a lifelong pattern of behavior. We already know two patterns in Clinton's life: adultery and deceit. Both are habits of betrayal. He lies not only to his enemies, but to his family and friends. Is there any area in his life where he has shown a consistent pattern of honor? On the contrary. He is suspect on many counts, some of them criminal.

When a man is accused of indecent or illegal conduct, his first line of defense should be his honor, in word and deed. But no matter what the charge, Clinton's defenders can't argue that he isn't the sort of man who would ever do such a thing. In fact, Clinton himself can't say this. After six years, the inner man — the man who lies because his own conduct would make it fatal to tell the truth — is all too visible.

That inner man is a moral void. And it has consumed his public self. What can we possibly trust him to tell the truth about?

CLINTON AND THE REPUBLICANS

Blackmail in Politics

APRIL 2, 1998

N early all discussion of politics overlooks a constant but hidden factor: blackmail. We can never know the extent to which our rulers are secretly ruled by others who know their dark secrets. And Washington, like most cities, is full of dark secrets.

Since the 1996 election, for example, it has transpired that Bob Dole was afraid to make an issue of Bill Clinton's character because he was afraid that his own extramarital affair, many years earlier, might be revealed. I first read about it in the New York weekly *The Village Voice* at the very end of the campaign.

I have no reason to believe that the Clinton team ever threatened Dole. That might not even have been necessary. Dole's anxiety might have been enough to intimidate him: "The guilty flee when no man pursueth."

Suppose, though, that the Clinton campaign had wanted to scare Dole away from "the character issue." It could have been done without an overt threat, just by letting him know, even indirectly, that the Democrats knew the name of Dole's former mistress.

Few things are more unnerving than learning that your enemy has learned things you don't want your own family to know. One reason the two parties seem so friendly to each other is that each is afraid of what the other might do in an all-out fight. Both have a lot to hide. And since keeping secrets is harder in the media age than ever before, the problem is likely to keep getting worse.

"Opposition research," as it's tactfully called, is an integral part of the Clinton modus operandi. It includes hiring investigators to gather dirt on potential adverse witnesses. It includes illegally requisitioning FBI files on prominent Republicans. It has reportedly included putting a political enemy's credit card receipts on the front page of an Arkansas newspaper.

Once you possess damaging information about your adversary, you can do several things with it. You can save it for a crucial moment. You can discreetly let him know you have it. You can leak it to the press. Or you can publicize it yourself, as both a punishment to him and a warning to others not to cross you.

The Clinton trash team has made examples of several women, thereby discouraging others from telling their stories. If you say you know something about Bill Clinton, you can bet he's going to know something about you.

These techniques aren't new. A certain Senate majority leader a generation ago was known for his ability to collect the guilty secrets of his colleagues. When he needed their votes, he made sure they were keenly aware of what he knew about their private lives. He didn't have to bully them; he could simply needle them with a rough joke that told them he'd somehow heard about that weekend in Las Vegas. They got the point as surely as if they'd awakened that morning to find a horse's head between the sheets.

We know that several presidents have used the FBI and IRS against their opposition. But we don't know how many times this has happened without coming to light even many years after the fact. Such things may remain permanently hidden from the most diligent historians. Just as we have no way of calculating how many crimes go undetected and unpunished, we can only guess how large a part blackmail plays in politics.

As long as there is sin, there will be blackmail. No reform can get rid of it. It can take many forms, not all of them illegal or provable in court. And it will always remain a hidden factor. This means that we can never completely know who controls our nominal rulers.

There is no real solution, but there is a corrective. The weaker the government, the less impact crime, corruption, and blackmail within the government can have on the rest of us.

Men in power are more criminal than people in general, not only because power corrupts but also because most people who seek power are already corrupt. This being so, the danger of blackmail is one more reason to limit the power of government.

The Clinton White House has given "spin" a new dimension, making it a kind of short-term tactical propaganda — a series of ferocious blitzkriegs against enemies and critics. Like most modern propaganda since Lenin, it's utterly, dizzyingly shameless: the Clintonites denounce "the politics of personal destruction" even as they practice it. The phrase adroitly implies that investigating Clinton's crimes is an invasion of his private life, while violating the privacy of his foes is merely an appropriate exposure of their hypocrisy. It also suggests, without meaning to, that Clinton still has a lot to hide: enough to destroy him, if it were known.

Conservatives for Clinton

APRIL 7, 1998

Most of the pundits seem to take it for granted that a popular president can't be impeached — and perhaps shouldn't be. This is also the view of Republicans in Congress, who are afraid to move ahead with an impeachment inquiry as long as opinion polls show that Bill Clinton has a high job-approval rating.

In other words, the Republicans are afraid of doing their duty if it might mean losing their jobs. They believe, or strongly suspect, that the White House is inhabited

Dark secrets in Washington

by a criminal. They have a moral obligation to insist on the "facts" Clinton himself has promised and to take appropriate action, even at risk of their seats.

But they won't do this. Career politicians don't want to jeopardize their careers, and the Republicans don't want to look "partisan."

They already look partisan. Do they imagine they look principled? Worse yet, they also look cowardly. If a president deserves to be removed from office, Congress should remove him even if some congressmen lose their seats in the next election. There are times when even a career politician should put his country first.

How easily we move from recognizing low motives as a fact of life to accepting them as justifications. "I wish I could afford to do my duty, but I might lose my job." We might accept that from a poor man supporting a family — but from a prosperous man, aspiring to lead us, who has taken an oath to defend the Constitution?

It's no wonder that grassroots conservatives are upset with the Republicans. The real wonder is that it hasn't happened sooner.

People often ask why Hillary Clinton has stayed with her fla-
grantly unfaithful husband. Well, it's not as if she gets nothing
out of it. If you stand by your philandering man long enough,
you may get to be First Lady. That's simple enough. Mrs. Clinton's
patience has been richly rewarded, in terms of the things that
matter most to her.

But why do conservatives stand by the Republican Party?
That's a much deeper mystery than the Hillary question. If it
weren't for Ronald Reagan, they would surely have bolted to a
third party long ago. In terms of the things that matter most to
them, what have they received from Jerry Ford, George Bush,
Bob Dole, and Newt Gingrich?

Ford, in retirement, still sabotages conservative candidates.
Bush swore never to raise taxes and raised taxes. Dole irritably
thinks of conservatives as "those people." Gingrich regards
Franklin Roosevelt, enemy of the Constitution and friend of Joseph Stalin, as "the greatest president of the twentieth century";
so much for the Reagan Revolution.

These are but a few eloquent details. The Republican Congress is spending far more than the Democratic Congress ever
did, while blaming Clinton (who can't spend a dime that Congress doesn't appropriate) for its own extravagance. It has done
nothing whatsoever to restore the limited government it promised; so much for the Republican Revolution.

It's fitting that the party that gave up even on the symbolic
fight over funding the National Endowment for the Arts should
claim, as its chief triumph, renaming Washington National Airport in honor of Reagan.

But don't worry: conservatives will keep voting Republican
per omnia saecula saeculorum. Why? Because, they say, going
to a third party would be "unrealistic." This is a beautiful illustration of the way conservatives understand realism. Why squan-
der your vote on the U.S. Taxpayers Party, when you can invest it
wisely in George Bush or Bob Dole and get a real return on it?

The two parties in Washington are like an unhappy family that
is always bickering about little things while implicitly agreeing

on the fundamental things that keep them together. If you listen only to the bickering, you won't understand how the political system actually coheres. You have to be aware of all the things the two parties don't argue about.

Republicans grumble about Clinton, but they cooperate with him. Conservatives grumble about Republicans, but they vote for them. So what it comes to is that Clinton still has the virtual support of the conservatives who loathe him.

Oh, no: Elizabeth Dole wants to be president! Truly, the Republicans are the party of tired blood. How many more Bushes and Doles must we endure? And why?

The Heyday
of Burtonism

C ongressman Dan Burton reminds me of Senator Joe
McCarthy. Like McCarthy, he has given liberal Democrats a welcome opportunity to change the subject.

What hath Burton wrought? He released edited tapes of jail-
house conversations between two Clinton cronies — Mr. and Mrs.
Webster Hubbell — and suddenly Demo-
crats, afflicted for months by moral laryn- *They support*
gitis over their president's ethics, morals,
and criminality, were hitting high C. Dan *him in spite of*
Burton had committed an atrocity worthy *themselves.*
of Ivan the Terrible, Tamerlane the Great,
or Jimmy the Greek.

Never mind what those taped conversations, in their entirety,
seemed to suggest about the Clintons and the Hubbells' reasons
for accommodating them. The subject of the wailing and gnash-
ing of Democratic teeth was strictly Dan Burton's malefaction.
Nothing else was worth talking about.

In McCarthy's case, the subject was Communism. But by
making charges he couldn't back up, McCarthy allowed liberals
to talk about his "methods" rather than their own love affair with
the Soviet Union. Liberals who had seen Joe Stalin as a great
humanitarian saw McCarthy as the ultimate affront to human
decency and a terrifying threat to constitutional rights.

If you think I exaggerate liberal affection for Stalin, catch the
1943 movie *Mission to Moscow* on cable TV sometime. The
bloodiest tyrant in European history is shown as an avuncular,
pipe-smoking philosopher who cares only for the welfare of the
Russian people, who are threatened by "fascism."

The movie was made by Warner Brothers at the suggestion of

Franklin D. Roosevelt, who fully endorsed this cuddly image of his Soviet friend. To underline its authenticity, Roosevelt allowed himself to be portrayed in the film.

Naturally, by 1950, liberals didn't want to talk about all that. But a lot of other people did, so liberals jumped at the chance to discuss McCarthy's crude manners rather than their own complicity in Marxist tyranny.

It worked. To this day, charges of Communist sympathies, however accurate, are all but taboo, while charges of "McCarthyism" (never defined, of course) are still routine.

Few people asked the obvious question: Why did liberalism, unlike conservatism, lend itself to Communist subversion? What was the secret affinity between the two ideologies that allowed Communist officials to serve, for example, on the national board of the American Civil Liberties Union?

Even now the standard liberal account of America in the early 1950s is that it was in the grip of "McCarthyite hysteria." The real hysteria was the liberal hysteria over McCarthy himself. It was a hysterical distraction from the Democrats' role in helping make the Soviet Union a nuclear-armed superpower.

Dan Burton is likewise serving as a hysterical distraction from far worse deeds than any he has committed. A loose cannon at the head of a congressional committee can hardly rival a president who sells military high technology to Communist China in return for discreet campaign donations, to cite just one possibility that has failed to fire the Democrats' imaginations.

In his most recent press conference, Clinton not only evaded factual questions, but declined to answer directly the more general question of whether a president should set a good moral example for the country. It was as if he had angrily denied kidnapping a child, then, when asked whether this meant that he abhorred kidnapping, replied that his lawyers had advised him not to comment on that.

Clinton clearly doesn't want to say anything that can be thrown back at him when the full truth about his conduct finally emerges. When this most loquacious of politicians goes Delphic, you know something's up.

With a little luck, the Democrats and their friends in the press may see to it that the 1990s are remembered in history as the Burtonite Era, when innocent husbands and wives were in constant danger of having their private conversations monitored and broadcast by snooping politicians. In such an account the deeds of Bill Clinton may be pushed quietly into the background, even as the wet smacking smooches between Roosevelt and Stalin tend to fade out of hearing in the great Gothic horror story of the McCarthyite Era.

Follow these events carefully now, because you won't recognize them when the liberals retell them later.

Duty, honor, pollsters: The Democrats don't want Clinton impeached; but with elections looming, the Republicans are afraid to do it as long as his approval ratings are high. So what if it's their duty? They too think in terms of options rather than obligations. Moral: A two-party system isn't a democracy; it's a dilemma.

Raising McCain

JULY 1998

I f you wonder why Bill Clinton manages to survive, consider Senator John McCain, the Arizona Republican who has learned how to earn applause from the liberal press. A former prisoner of war in Vietnam, McCain has "evolved," as they say, from a fairly reliable conservative into a champion of campaign-finance limits and, of course, federal anti-smoking legislation.

When his baby, the humongous tobacco deal, died in the Senate, McCain wrote bitterly in the *Wall Street Journal* that the conservative agenda lay "in ashes" because of the bill's defeat. What conservative agenda? Well, the bill included various

Indignation, oddly distributed

amendments for school vouchers, the war on drugs, block grants to state governments, and other fads, most of which would have further increased federal spending, taxes, and power.

As his bill was dying — other Republicans having caught on that it was a disaster in every way — McCain also disgraced himself by telling a foul joke about Chelsea Clinton, for which he had to make groveling amends to her father. It's a cinch that if he hadn't been leading the charge for liberal causes, the media would have used the joke to ruin his career. (When I quoted the joke to an old friend of McCain's, he was silent for a moment, then commented: "I've heard him tell worse.")

As a POW, McCain once refused an offer of an early release because the offer wasn't also made to his fellow prisoners. He is not without a sense of honor. He is merely without a lick of sense.

That is what makes it so remarkable that his tobacco bill, designed to raise $500 billion in new taxes, should have gone as far as it did. The Republican Party rallied against it in the nick of time. But how could such a monstrosity have been proposed at all? Didn't we just have a Republican Revolution? Hasn't the era of big government ended? Didn't someone tear down the Berlin Wall?

As long as there is a single Republican in Washington, nobody can say with any assurance that socialism is dead. Neither McCain nor his party has any conception of limited government. Until the Republicans realized that the tobacco bill was a political loser they were quite willing to support it. Finally it sank in that the bill was enraging grassroots conservatives, while all the political profits were accruing to Clinton and the Democrats. Even then, the Republicans merely managed to cut their losses, while further eroding whatever respect they still enjoyed.

Thus the allegedly conservative majority party accepts the moral leadership of a discredited liberal minority and a disgraced and weakened scoundrel of a president — the abortionists who demand new powers in the name of "protecting our children." Perish the thought that smokers and even tobacco companies have rights.

And by the way, did anyone raise the question of just which constitutional provision authorizes Congress to make such laws?

♦ ♦ ♦

Post-impeachment blues: Conservatives are understandably discouraged by Clinton's escape from justice. Meanwhile, the welfare-warfare state keeps growing, taxes remain outrageous, the Constitution is still in the deep freeze, and both parties seem to like it this way. Hopeless? Let's cheer up. Today's evils are no more entrenched than slavery was in 1860.

Where Did the Left Go?

JULY 1998

T he Clinton scandals remind me more and more of the Alger Hiss case. The charges against Bill Clinton have no logical connection to other issues, and yet the division of opinion is heavily ideological. As with Hiss, a striking number of those who strain to deny or minimize Clinton's guilt belong to the political and cultural Left. Those who want to believe it are generally on the Right.

Collectivism by other means

This is not to equate the two sides; the Right has the evidence in its favor, which is, after all, why Clinton is going to extreme lengths to conceal it.

The attacks on Linda Tripp, the key witness, are as vicious as the attacks on Whittaker Chambers were. Just as Hiss's partisans ridiculed the critical "Pumpkin Papers," the pro-Clinton forces sneer furiously at Mrs. Tripp's tapes. Just as Chambers was called a "confessed liar" because he had once been a Communist, Mrs. Tripp is being painted as a traitor who betrayed the trust of her innocent friend Monica Lewinsky. Just as Chambers was vilified as a homosexual (this was before the progressive set had discovered gay rights, of course), Mrs. Tripp is eligible for every sort of personal abuse, not excluding gibes about her looks. In a similar way, Kenneth Starr is being treated as the Nixon of the case.

Once again we see a concerted effort to discredit the whole inquiry, to marginalize and cast doubt on the central facts of the case. But it goes beyond coordinated attacks. There is an instinctive hysteria driving Clinton's partisans, who sense that everything they have fought for is at stake. And in that respect, they are right.

I've also been struck by what may seem a minor coincidence. The people who defend Clinton are often the same people who were recently calling Congress's hearings on IRS abuses "show trials." Just as they portray Clinton as a victim whose rights and privacy are being violated, they regard IRS agents as victims of demagogy. They aren't concerned about abuses of power either by Clinton, the most powerful man in America, or by the most feared agency of the federal government.

This is the latest permutation in the American version of what the great Russian dissident Igor Shafarevich has called "the socialist phenomenon." Shafarevich argues that socialism is best understood not as a modern ideology, but as a perennial tendency that periodically erupts in observable patterns. It existed long before Marx and would have broken out in the modern world if Marx had never been born.

"Socialism" is a somewhat inadequate and misleading name for the phenomenon, but it will have to do. In the twentieth century it has taken an economic guise — nationalizing the means of production, five-year plans, and so forth — but its deepest concern isn't merely economic. It ultimately seeks to remake man. It's essentially totalitarian.

Shafarevich notes that socialism's chief targets for destruction are family, property, and religion. These are the great bases of independence and freedom. They provide rival loyalties, material protection, and moral authority against the all-powerful state. The Marxist version of socialism directly attacked family, property, and religion. The liberal version, confined by narrower options in America, tries to undermine them in piecemeal fashion, but the same pattern of hostility is clear, however liberals deny it (or are simply unaware of it).

As Shafarevich also notes, socialism always waves the banner of "equality" — but an equality that diminishes and debases man, making him dependent on the state, as opposed to the Jeffersonian equality that insists that no man is by nature another's subject. Socialist "equality" is the opposite of liberty; Jeffersonian equality is its synonym, putting limits on the state.

With the fall of Marxism, wholesale socialism has been discredited as an economic system. But its driving impulse remains active in the liberals, feminists, and assorted "progressives" who still want to maximize and centralize state power under the rubrics of "social justice," "separation of church and state," and "sexual freedom." This agenda might be called "retail" social-ism. Its options are narrow; no violent revolution will create a socialist utopia all at once; but freedom and religion will be gradu-ally eaten away all the same. Most of the "issues" of today's poli-tics are offshoots of the agenda.

Clinton, who pays lip service to the family-property-religion triad, is now the carrier of progressive hope. He has proven him-self an expert at all the techniques of piecemeal socialism, cun-ning enough to maneuver the Republicans into supporting or yield-ing to his agenda, economic and sexual.

Needless to say, the "progressives" wouldn't describe their goals and techniques in these terms. Few of them would even call themselves socialists. But the words don't matter. The pat-tern matters. And the pattern discloses the instincts that animate them. I repeat: if there had been no Marx, no Stalin, no Franklin Roosevelt, no Gloria Steinem, the instincts shared by so many people would have produced much the same pattern anyway. The sort of people who would have favored Roosevelt or Stalin in an earlier generation today favor Clinton.

At bottom socialism is the rejection of God and nature, com-bined with a positive desire to create a godlike power over the human race, endowing it with a new nature (as in "New Soviet Man"). The Marxist version of utopia now seems naive as well as tainted by history, so we have to look for the socialist assertion under new forms, which change frequently.

Nearly every new liberal cause or fad can be grouped around the triad. The tobacco deal, for instance, was part of the continu-ing assault on property. "Gay rights" (and male sodomy is a far worse threat to health than tobacco) belongs to the assault on the family. Liberal theology, which is nearly always associated with liberal politics, is part of the assault on religion. If revolution is no longer feasible, the progressive forces can content themselves with taking a small left turn at every fork in the road, denying or disguising the overall pattern.

The unity of the progressive forces is like the instinctive cooperation of an insect colony. Each specialist does its job, like the many bees in a hive. None has to know the whole design. Clinton never thinks of himself as part of a revolution, but what the individual insect "thinks" is beside the point, as long as it performs its function. Just as bees communicate without words, the progressives do their stuff through their own mutual signals, indifferent to how they may appear to an observer.

In fact this account of their conduct would strike them as strange. They are apt to call any critical description a "conspiracy theory." But though they do conspire somewhat, this is second-ary to their most basic activity of instinctive hive-formation. The existence of the pattern doesn't require an overall conspiracy, and the absence of conspiracy doesn't mean that there is no pat-tern. A beehive needs no central direction; it takes shape from the spontaneous cooperation of multitudes of bees who, in a sense, don't know what they're doing.

But the bees do recognize an enemy. This is why the progres-sives all swarm, stingers poised, against such annoyances as Whittaker Chambers and Linda Tripp, to name only two of the countless targets of liberal wrath.

They also swarm in defense of such institutions as the IRS, on which their power and prosperity depend. And little as they like or trust Clinton, they know he has to be defended too.

Socialism produces nothing. It's parasitical. The fatal mistake of the Communists was to take responsibility for production, and the inevitable result was economic collapse; the Soviet Union lasted as long as it did only because it permitted the black market to flourish and allowed farmers to make modest profits. The lib-erals have learned to leave property in private hands, making its titular owners responsible for maintaining it, while taxing and regulating it as much as possible. The nominal owners can be handily blamed for any failure.

A key part of the liberal strategy is to keep the general popula-tion unaware of the ideological conflict underlying American poli-tics. To identify that conflict is to be accused of "paranoia" and, ironically enough, "ideology" ("right-wing," of course). But there is "ideology," or principle, on both sides. The "progressive" principle is still the all-powerful godless state.

Liberalism has been extremely successful at making American politics seem merely "pragmatic," with no organizing principles at stake. It likes to describe the development of centralized power in vague, mystic terms, as when it speaks of the "living" or "evolving" Constitution — which somehow always turns out to mandate more centralized power, as if there has been no protracted effort by specific human agents to twist the document in predictably socialist directions.

The idea that the U.S. Supreme Court's major rulings since the New Deal have been "unpredictable" is an absurd fiction: the Court's liberals, for many years, simply imposed their will on the country, using slender pretexts in selected phrases from the constitutional text — phrases that Douglas, Black, Warren, Brennan, and Blackmun endowed with new and wholly unwarranted meanings. Each bee does its job.

The Court's audacious mandate for legal abortion as a constitutional right had nothing whatever to do with the Constitution's meaning. It had everything to do with the progressive agenda. It was one more assertion — though an especially bold one — of the federal government's right to strip the states of their traditional powers, as well as a great leap forward for the sexual revolution.

I confess I was once deluded enough to think that the election of Ronald Reagan or the fall of the Soviet Union would put an end to the power of the progressive forces in this country. I gravely underestimated that power and the tenacity of the liberalizing forces.

What astounds me now is the optimism of conservatives who think they have "won" or "taken back the country" because the Republicans have won a few elections. The Republicans, who oppose a piecemeal but principled revolution in a piecemeal and unprincipled fashion, are just the kind of opposition the progressives want. That is, they are hardly an opposition at all.

Drawing Lines

SEPTEMBER 3, 1998

S hould the sex lives of Republicans be fair game? That's the latest ethical problem tormenting the collective conscience of the media.

The question arises in part because of an upcoming *Vanity Fair* article about some rumored infidelities of Congressman Dan Burton during his thirty-eight-year marriage. Burton, the Republican chairman of the House committee investigating President Clinton's campaign finances, has been outspoken in his belief that Clinton is a "scumbag," inter alia. He's also outspoken in his belief that Clinton is behind the *Vanity Fair* article; the magazine denies it.

Paving the way for Clinton

Burton admits that his marriage has had its rough patches, and he doesn't deny the allegations he expects the article to make. But he charges that the magazine is cooperating in Clinton's "scorched-earth" policy of digging up dirt on political opponents.

It's a charge that would be hard to prove. Besides, plenty of journalists are willing to help the Clinton cause without being asked.

On the face of it, there's a big difference between "mere" adultery in one's private life and using young interns in one's office while foreign dignitaries wait in the next room. The Clinton loyalists want to erase such little nuances. Their position is that if you've ever peeped at a copy of *Playboy,* you forfeit any moral right to judge a serial rapist. The president must be tried by a jury of virgins.

It's been said that the defense of virtue can't be left to the virtuous. Sinners aren't necessarily hypocrites when they defend public standards of conduct, and it's mischievous to threaten them with reprisals for doing so. Clinton has crossed all kinds of lines, using the presidency not only to take advantage of White House interns (at least one, probably several), but to orchestrate a huge coverup.

The question isn't whether Dan Burton deserves to have his sins exposed. It's whether the purpose of exposing Dan Burton's sins is to deter other Republicans from exposing Bill Clinton's crimes.

The timidity of the Republicans during the Lewinsky scandals suggests that the Clintonites' blackmail threats have worked. The president's possession of hundreds of raw FBI files on Republicans hasn't been lost on them. If and when Clinton is removed from office, we will still need a thorough investigation of the use of the FBI, the IRS, and the Pentagon against the Clintons' opponents.

We simply have to know how people in power have abused that power in ways that injure not only individuals, but the integrity of the political system. Clinton's claims of "privacy" and "family life" to cover his sexual relations with interns are only part of the mania for concealment marking his presidency.

When the dust has settled, we will still have to make up our minds about where to draw the line between politicians' public and private lives. The sexual revolution has caused great confusion by trying to divorce sex from honor. It can't be done.

A crooked politician may be faithful to his wife; but a man who deceives his own wife can't be relied on to deal honestly with the public. We have been getting this backwards lately. We've been assuming that you can have public virtue without private virtue.

The Democratic Party has been heading for the Clinton debacle for many years, thanks in large part to the Kennedy brothers. It winked at John Kennedy's lechery. Even after Chappaquiddick, it allowed Teddy Kennedy to become its leader and conscience.

It's no accident that Teddy veered to the left after Chappaquiddick. Having drunkenly left a young woman to drown after a wild party, he was in no position to espouse conservative morality. But the liberal press, which would have killed his career with lethal irony if he had dared to speak of "family values," received him warmly when he became an advocate of liberal causes, including abortion. (No irony there!)

It's hard to know just where to draw the line on sexual conduct. But the Democrats, by drawing no lines at all, set the stage for Bill Clinton.

The Party of Bad Faith

SEPTEMBER 29, 1998

B efore Muhammad Ali came along, you could almost predict the outcome of a heavyweight fight by looking at
the "tale of the tape": the boxer who was taller and heavier
and had the longer reach was the natural favorite.

But Ali changed everything by adding one element: speed. No
heavyweight had ever danced, ducked, and jabbed as he did. He
made his hulking opponents fight his fight, and they couldn't do
it. They stood flat-footed, swinging at the air, while he floated
like a butterfly and stung like a bee until they were exhausted.

Most of them hit much harder than he did; the problem was
that they couldn't hit him. They were prepared for toe-to-toe
slugfests, but with Ali they found themselves as out of place in
the ring as a rhinoceros in a ballet.

Bill Clinton has changed politics the way Ali changed boxing.
He speeds it up, running rings around the flat-footed Republicans by changing the subject to whatever he wants it to be — or
to no subject at all. In the midst of scandal, he appears on TV
with his dog. What's Newt Gingrich supposed to do? Get a kit-
ten?

Clinton has even taken advantage of scandal saturation. Just
what are we arguing about? Sex? Perjury? Privacy? Kenneth
Starr's tactics? Lying to the public? Linda Tripp's perfidy? Henry
Hyde's past? What ever happened to Paula Jones and Kathleen
Willey? Do their charges count for anything now that we know
Clinton "misled people" with his hand on the Bible? What about
the polls showing that "the American people" want the whole
business dropped?

Clinton's rapid-response team is always on the job, pouncing
on any chance to redefine the terms of the controversy. They fan
out, shouting the theme du jour in unison. They don't have to
clarify; their function is to add to the confusion, personalize and

embitter the debate, keep the Republicans on the defensive, distract the public. All with dizzying speed and disarming ferocity.

There is no effective Republican response. The Republicans, like Ali's old opponents, simply haven't learned to counter the Clinton style. They can't fight his fight.

Moreover, the Republicans are handicapped by a sense of honor. There isn't a Carville among them. When their enemies catch them having violated their own standards, as with Henry Hyde's adultery, they can only confess the truth. They expect to be judged by a morality they didn't invent to serve their interests, and this leaves them vulnerable to embarrassment when they fall short. How do you embarrass Barney Frank?

Then there's the semantic gap. A Democrat can pretend he doesn't know what "sex" or "alone" or "is" means when he wants to weasel out of a sexual harassment charge, just as he can pretend he doesn't know when life begins when he wants to promote abortion. (He can accept even the killing of a child by extracting its brain on the verge of birth — you may think it's murder, but "abortion" is, as it were, the "legally accurate" term.)

The Republicans, by contrast, are hopelessly literal-minded. Most of them still have the habit of using words in their common acceptations, without pulling cute tricks on the public. They just plod along, while the Democrats sneer at their stupidity.

Since January, the Democrats have shown themselves to be the party of bad faith. They have supported Clinton in all his lies and evasions. They pretend to believe him when they know he's lying, and they pretend to believe him when he pretends to repent. They professed to believe his denials in the Monica affair, then they instantly "forgave" him on grounds that "everyone lies about sex."

If they already knew everyone lies about sex, why didn't they suspect Clinton was lying before he "confessed"? Or did they think, until August 17, that William Jefferson Clinton was the only man on earth who wouldn't lie about sex?

The Democrats, taking H. L. Mencken to heart, have adopted a policy of insulting the intelligence of the American people. If they can't convince us that their president is honest, they can at least wear us down with aggressive sophistry, while Clinton coos of "healing," "reconciliation," and "repairing the fabric of our national discourse."

Liberals used to deride conservatives for objecting to federal subsidies of obscene and blasphemous art. Who, they asked, is to say what is "obscene"? Well, now they know: anything that describes Clinton's behavior in clinical detail.

Come to think of it, Starr could have avoided liberal censure by labeling his report "art" and applying for an NEA grant.

Why Censure Won't Do

DECEMBER 1, 1998

E ven if Bill Clinton is impeached by the House, the Senate will have to decide whether he should be tried as an adult. The Framers of the Constitution decreed that a president must be at least 35 years old, in the naive belief that this would guarantee that he'd be a grownup. No such luck.

Up to his old tricks, Clinton has weaseled out of giving straight answers to the eighty-one questions posed by the House Judiciary Committee. Unless his fabled memory has suffered a sudden blowout, he's still lying like the clever adolescent he is.

Is the Oval Office private?

This poses an embarrassment for those Clinton defenders who are still capable of shame. Since August 17 they've been assuring us that Clinton has confessed, come clean, repented, and apologized. And now he has made them look like fools again.

Not that Clinton's defenders themselves have set a high mark for honor. They chant that his perjury was "only about sex" and doesn't "rise to the level of an impeachable offense."

But lying about sex, in a sexual harassment case, is not just lying about your personal life in the bedroom. It's lying about your conduct in the office, which liberal and feminist Democrats have insisted (until Paula Jones, Monica Lewinsky, and Kathleen Willey came on stage) is a public matter, not a private one. But now we're told that even the Oval Office is private space!

Shifting arguments are the mark of a bad cause. At first Clinton's defenders pretended to believe his denials (as they later pretended to believe he was sorry). Now they deny that his denials, even under oath, are serious. Hey, it's only perjury!

As if perjury weren't serious. If the Constitution had mentioned as grounds for impeachment "treason, bribery, perjury, and other high crimes and misdemeanors," nobody would have asked why perjury was on the short list. There would be nothing incongruous about the juxtaposition of lying in court with taking bribes; they are kindred crimes, both corrupting the rule of law. Before Clinton, we always took the gravity of perjury for granted.

But if the Constitution had mentioned treason and perjury, omitting bribery, and Clinton had been charged with bribery, his apologists would no doubt be arguing: "Bribery doesn't rise to the level of an impeachable offense. After all, it's not as if it were perjury!"

Why has Clinton replied to the Judiciary Committee's queries with more lies and evasions? Partly because he fears criminal prosecution when he leaves office. Some of his defenders use this explanation as an excuse: they say he shouldn't be forced to incriminate himself.

But impeachment isn't a criminal proceeding. It's more like a civil suit, in which the defendant has no privilege against giving self-damaging testimony. If he refuses to answer questions, we are entitled to draw adverse conclusions about him.

The trouble is that the Democrats in Congress won't vote to either impeach or convict Clinton. They prefer the pseudo-penalty of censure.

Is censure constitutional? Some Republicans think not, but there's no evident reason why Congress, or either house of Congress, can't censure anyone, at any time, for any reason, by mere majority vote. The House and Senate could even censure Clinton separately, each expressing its disapproval in its own way.

But that's why censure would be an empty gesture. Impeachment is an exercise of power, and a real remedy for the abuse of power. Censure is a mere expression of opinion. Clinton could easily spin it into a virtual vindication, while his partisans could gloat that he had escaped impeachment and removal from office.

Censure would soften the infamy not only of Clinton's behavior, but of the Democrats' willingness to tolerate remorseless lawbreaking by the man who is charged, by the Constitution itself, with seeing that the laws are faithfully executed.

The Democrats' cynicism is a worse scandal than Clinton's crimes and misdemeanors. Their eagerness for bipartisan censure shows only that they want to cloak that cynicism in hypocrisy, with Republican assistance. Clinton himself wants to be censured (mildly, of course) lest it be too obvious that he's getting off easy.

Clinton's escape from justice would be an outrage. Nothing should be allowed to disguise it.

Even the impeachment of a president was not supposed to create a general disturbance. But the centralization of power in the Union (no longer truly "federal"), and especially in the executive, has made impeachment seem an earthshaking decision.

Good Losers

FEBRUARY 16, 1999

Well, the knaves have extended their long victory streak over the fools. The Republicans have lost another hand in which they were dealt four aces. And they seem determined to make their defeat worse.

After Bill Clinton's acquittal, the GOP is "moving on," worrying about reshaping its "image," sheepish about having impeached a president. It hopes the public will forgive — and forget — its virtues.

The Republicans acted honorably, if not always adroitly, in trying to remove a criminal from the highest law-enforcement office in the country. For their own sake, as well as for the country's, they should firmly insist that their defeat was also a defeat for justice. To be good sports about this defeat is to play into the Democrats' propaganda line that the whole fight was "partisan" — meaning partisan on the Republicans' side.

The truth is intimated in the letter Senator Dianne Feinstein, the California Democrat, read into the Congressional Record, acknowledging awkwardly that Clinton "gave false or misleading testimony and his actions have had the effect of impeding discovery of evidence in judicial proceedings." This letter was signed by twenty-nine of the Senate's Democrats, while the other sixteen chose not to sign it.

This statement should be treated as the virtual confession it is. It basically, though evasively, concedes the essential truth of the two charges — perjury and obstruction — Clinton was being tried on. Those twenty-nine Democrats would have been enough to convict him on both counts. And they give the lie to the sixteen Democrats who deny the obvious.

The Senate Democrats' real verdict was "guilty, but acquitted anyway." This gross miscarriage of justice will be a bone in the throat of American history. Most Americans will form their final judgment of it according to the subsequent conduct of the two parties. The Democrats, of course, won't apologize. If the Republicans seem apologetic, it will only confirm the impression that they were in the wrong.

Instead of acting as if Clinton has been exonerated, the Republicans should say frankly:

"The president was guilty as charged, and both parties know it. He was rescued by his own party's partisanship. So we are forced, for the next two years, to do business with a perjurer and a suborner of perjury. The responsibility for this situation, unfortunately, lies at the feet of the Democratic Party. We can't ascribe all our differences to honest disagreement.

"Yes, someone in this story is 'sex-obsessed,' but it's not our party or the special prosecutor. This whole horror began because the President defiled the Oval Office and resorted to lies, perjury, and slander to cover it up. He might have indulged himself in some private place, with someone other than a young White House employee. If he'd been even ordinarily discreet, any problem would have been between him and his wife, and it might not have complicated a lawsuit brought on by his earlier abuse of another office.

"The president's sexual vices, repellent as they are, wouldn't in themselves be grounds for impeachment. But he has shown a disturbing habit of using his office, his lawyers, and his subordinates to put out slanders of the women who cross him.

"Such 'politics of personal destruction' are entirely in keeping with his and his supporters' vendettas against the special prosecutor's team and members of the House Judiciary Committee. His attempt to smear Monica Lewinsky as a 'stalker' can't be excused as an effort to protect his 'family life.' It shows a vicious streak he has usually managed to conceal from the public. It shows the real Bill Clinton.

"How can we assume that Mr. Clinton will behave any differently in the future? Some of his people have already announced his, and their, intention to take revenge on members of our party in the next election. In our dealings with him we have long since learned that he can't be trusted.

"So we have no choice but to proceed on the assumption that we have in the White House a treacherous man, devoid of honor. If our impeachment effort accomplished nothing else, it established that, for all time. His acquittal doesn't require us to be blind to facts we ignore at our peril."

DEMOCRATS,
FRIENDS AND ENEMIES

No Adult Supervision

AUGUST 4, 1998

W hy does Bill Clinton carry a Bible with him wherever he goes? Probably in case he feels a sudden need to commit perjury.

It's universally recognized that the prospect of testifying under oath on August 17 presents Clinton with a dilemma. Why? Because everyone assumes he's been lying audaciously to the public, on top of committing perjury.

Wanted:

A Dutch uncle

Yet Clinton's dilemma is discussed in terms of options, not obligations. How, the pundits ask, can he still save his presidency? By implication, telling the truth is merely a possible survival tactic, not an absolute duty. Never mind whether his presidency should be saved, or whether honor requires that he tell the truth and resign.

Clinton the man is not beyond redemption, but his presidency is. And his disgrace extends to his fellow Democrats. Nobody in his party has had the integrity to repudiate him.

Unfortunately, Clinton typifies this generation of Democrats. In the old days it might have been different. The question is not what Clinton should say now, but what other Democrats should have said to him when he arrived in Washington. A Tip O'Neill, a Tom Foley, or even a Jim Wright might have taken him aside and told him something like this:

"Look, pal, we've heard all about the way you carried on in Arkansas — the women, the drugs, the funny deals. We don't know how much is true and we don't care. We're not saints either. But if you pull that stuff here, you'll be playing with fire, and we're not going to let you take us down with you. If you behave, you'll find we're loyal Democrats. But we expect loyalty in return. If we ever hear about you messing around in a way that jeopardizes us, we're not going to wait for the Republicans to nail you. We'll do it ourselves."

Clinton would probably have swallowed hard and gotten the message. At least the guidelines would have been clear, and his own party would have imposed some discipline.

Why hasn't this happened? Well, the elder statesman of today's Democratic Party is Ted Kennedy. Can you imagine him giving a speech like that? How about Barney Frank?

As these selfless public servants illustrate, much of the Democratic leadership today has openly adopted "lifestyles" that would once have exposed them to blackmail and even now might get them classified as security risks. Like Clinton himself, they had to be elected, because they couldn't have been appointed.

That's why they're in no position to control Clinton or even to admonish him. So for nearly six years he has played president without adult supervision.

During the Watergate scandals the Democrats ceaselessly and solemnly intoned that Richard Nixon was "lying to the American people." Today lying to the American people is accepted as legitimate "spin." The last remaining inhibition is that the president mustn't tell a lie that can be refuted by hard evidence or by a witness who has more "credibility" than he does — though even a perjured young floozy may have more credibility than he does.

Today's Democrats roared against Clarence Thomas for a single charge of obscene speech. During Thomas's confirmation hearings the Democrats didn't say it was "only about sex," that "everyone lies about sex," that what he did in his office was his "private life," or that it was "irrelevant to his performance of his job." They wanted him destroyed.

As the Good Book says, to everything there is a season. There is a time for opportunism, and a time for principle. And even the opportunists are recognizing that the time for principle is at hand. The Democrats are finally beginning to edge away from Clinton. Soon they'll all be swearing that they never knew the man, that he was a weird anomaly who somehow fooled them and sneaked into the system.

But if Clinton were an anomaly, he'd never have had so much fervent support from his party. He'd have long since been denounced, disowned, isolated — and out.

Like many delinquents, Clinton had nobody to save him from himself before he got into serious trouble. Conspicuously missing from the Democrats' inclusive ethnic tapestry is a Dutch uncle.

The Democrats' plight recalls Fritz Lang's classic movie *M,* in which Peter Lorre plays a serial killer of children. His crimes so terrify Berlin that the police crack down on the criminal classes, with whom they have previously had easy relations. The criminal classes, in turn, stage their own manhunt, capture the killer, and hold an eerie trial to decide how to dispose of him — not to protect children, of course, but to get the cops off their back. You might say that, well, it's the economy, stupid. The Democrats likewise don't like Clinton, who is pretty awful even by their standards, but they don't know what to do with him for getting them all in the soup.

Giving Thanks
to Clinton

JULY 7, 1998

A salacious article in the current issue of *Mirabella,* a frothy women's magazine, has caused a flurry in the normally sober press.

Nina Burleigh, a former White House correspondent for *Time,* admits she had the hots for Bill Clinton. Once, after he "ogled" her legs, she was "quite willing to let myself be ravished" by him. She was thrilled: "He found me attractive.... I probably wore the mesmerized look I have seen again and again in women after they have met him."

Miss Burleigh goes further: "I'd be happy to give him [oral sex] just to thank him for keeping abortion legal." We've come a long way from the "adversary press," haven't we?

Journalists didn't use to talk that way. One thinks of Walter Lippmann. Or, for that matter, Hunter S. Thompson. In the old days, if one was a reporter, one was expected to keep a critical distance from the people one covered, or one might find oneself out on one's keister.

True, some journalists got into bed, in a strictly figurative sense, with their subjects: in the 1950s Arthur Krock of the *New York Times* was secretly on the payroll of Joseph Kennedy, an arrangement that advanced the political careers of Kennedy's boys. And less compromising alliances between journalists and politicians who have shared goals are fairly common even today.

But Miss Burleigh insists that erotic feelings about Mr. Clinton didn't affect her detachment as a reporter in 1993 and 1994, when she was assigned to cover the Whitewater scandals. They seized her later, during a flight on Air Force One.

At any rate, she doesn't mind making her feelings clear now. And the most interesting of her feelings isn't lust: it's gratitude

— gratitude for Clinton's efforts to keep abortion legal.

What's even more interesting is that she's willing to express that gratitude in the most flamboyantly obscene terms. She doesn't expect her colleagues to disagree with her sentiments or to reproach her for couching them in vile and debasing language.

Not only is Miss Burleigh the first journalist to profess willingness to sodomize a president; she assumes that, with this president, everyone will recognize sodomy as an appropriate tribute. Would she have paid these peculiar compliments to a man she perceived as a good husband?

That speaks volumes about what the liberal journalistic community thinks, not only about Clinton's character but about his relations with Monica Lewinsky. It assumes that he did indeed have sex with her, as Miss Lewinsky privately alleged and as she and he have both denied under oath. And it disapproves of neither the sex nor the lying.

Here is the subtext of the whole Lewinsky scandal. Clinton's partisans in the press don't believe him, but they don't blame him. They blame Linda Tripp for "betraying" Miss Lewinsky by taping and revealing her confessions; they blame special prosecutor Kenneth Starr for making use of the tapes.

Did Clinton betray anyone — his wife, his daughter, the public? His partisans don't care. But they show wildly disproportionate indignation toward Linda Tripp. Even if we stipulate that she treated Miss Lewinsky contemptibly, this has no bearing on the value of her evidence. Journalists often accuse their critics of "shooting the messenger," but that's exactly what a lot of journalists are now doing to Mrs. Tripp. Other potential witnesses, take note.

What we are watching is the Hiss case of the sexual revolution. Like Alger Hiss, Clinton has ferocious defenders who realize that their cause will suffer heavily if he is convicted. They don't really believe he's innocent, so they change the issue to the conduct of the key witness and the chief investigator. Old-timers will recall the vilification of Whittaker Chambers, Richard Nixon, and the "Pumpkin Papers."

As with Alger Hiss, the legal question may come down to per-jury. The deeper question is whether the American public itself has been betrayed.

And just as some liberals didn't feel outraged by Hiss's secret allegiance to the Soviet Union, some liberals don't feel outraged by Clinton's "private" conduct — in the Oval Office. "I don't believe he did it" often means "I don't care if he did."

I don't want to add to the lewd merriment, but I can't help thinking that Clinton was skating on thin ice by trying to deny that his preferred form of recreation was "sex." He risked alienating Barney Frank.

False Prophets

SEPTEMBER 8, 1998

B y now it's pretty clear that no airports are going to be named after Bill Clinton, except perhaps at Mena. You'd have been better informed about his character in 1992 by reading the far-out radical right-wing press than by listening to respectable journalists.

To the radical right, Clinton was sinister and criminal. To the mainstream press, he was a brilliant baby boomer whose marriage to an equally brilliant woman had survived a few rocky patches.

The extremists were right — as usual.

If it weren't for David Brock's shattering 1993 article on Clinton's use of Arkansas state troopers to procure women, Clinton might still be riding high. When the article appeared, it was denounced as unreliable because it appeared in the "right-wing" *American Spectator* and Brock wasn't a "true" journalist.

Brock himself has tried to go respectable by repudiating the piece, but he'll certainly never again write anything with the impact of that one. Though he and the *Spectator* have gone their separate ways, they have made history. Brock's article led to the Paula Jones suit, which led to the Lewinsky scandal, which has unraveled countless other Clinton secrets.

Apart from confirming rumors that Clinton was a horny devil, Brock showed that as governor of Arkansas he'd used the perks of office for his own gratification and advantage, virtually turning a public trust into his private property. That's basically what Clinton has done in the Lewinsky scandal — first exploiting a White House intern, then using his connections to get her a job and keep her quiet, and finally using the entire presidential staff to sustain his lies.

When three Senate Democrats denounced Clinton's adultery the other day, you'd have thought three Old Testament prophets had hit town together. Joseph Lieberman of Connecticut, Daniel Patrick Moynihan of New York, and Robert Kerrey of Nebraska have been hailed as moral giants for scolding their president, albeit more in sorrow than in anger.

The truth is that they revealed nothing; they merely made a very belated partial admission, more or less as Clinton had done in his disastrous August 17 TV speech. Their speeches would have been praiseworthy in February; coming in September, they were tardy acknowledgments of the obvious.

We already knew that committing adultery in the Oval Office was immoral and that lying about it compounded the offense. Did it take these three senators seven months to figure that out? And why did they say nothing about Clinton's use of public servants not only to propagate his lies, but to smear the inquiry? How many millions of the taxpayers' money has this president spent, during those seven months, evading personal responsibility for his misdemeanors?

Lieberman said it would be "premature" to call for Clinton's resignation or impeachment. He praised Clinton's presidency as a whole and defined his offenses narrowly. He blamed Kenneth Starr and Linda Tripp for Clinton's seven-month ordeal. And when asked by NBC's Tim Russert whether he still thinks Clinton has the "morality and integrity" to continue as president, Lieberman said: "I do."

Lieberman's friendship with Clinton goes back more than twenty years. That should have been time enough for him to assess a character that seemed transparent enough to others who hadn't known him so closely or so long.

Or are Lieberman, Moynihan, and Kerrey playing dumb? It appears that the three Democrats coordinated their speeches and purposely chose to deliver them while Clinton was out of the country. Why might they do this? Well, maybe they anticipated the slime job any one of them, speaking alone, might have received from the White House, via, say, Geraldo Rivera.

If so, they know what they're dealing with, just as the Republicans do. It would be comical, if it weren't so dispiriting, to see so many people in Washington professing shock at the revelation that Clinton is a liar, an adulterer, and a perjurer.

Kenneth Starr's report will no doubt give the Democrats an opportunity to act shocked at further revelations of their president's criminality. But the thing that really shocks them is that conservatives have been proved absolutely right about this miserable man.

Clinton has made the world safe for Teddy Kennedy, who for obvious reasons prudently kept a low profile during the Clarence Thomas hearings. Teddy has now assumed a posture of moral indignation at the impeachment proceedings. It's often said that we are becoming more like France; personally, I'd say Massachusetts.

Explains a lot: When the Democrats controlled Congress in the early 1980s, they gave us a preview of their gentle treatment of Bill Clinton: they refused to expel Congressman Gerry Studds of Massachusetts, a militant homosexual who had sodomized a juvenile page — and who was defiant about his offense. Studds stayed until 1997, one of the boys, helping define his party's moral standards.

Clinton's Prudes

SEPTEMBER 24, 1998

Since nobody now can plausibly say: "I believe the president," the only way to save Bill Clinton is to equate him with his enemies. *Cui bono?*

Sure, Clinton is bad, his defenders admit, but special prosecutor Kenneth Starr is just as bad — or worse. Maureen Dowd of the *New York Times* says Starr's report has given us a "legacy of lust." Mary McGrory of the *Washington Post* decries "Starr's pornography press." Richard Cohen of the *Post* calls Starr a "menace to society" (in contrast to Clinton, who "has behaved abominably, but not in a way that threatens us all"). Other pundits in other papers are joining the chorus.

Look who's blushing!

Yet none of these champions of decency is proposing what would seem the obvious solution: Clinton should fire Starr.

As Ann Coulter points out in her lively book *High Crimes and Misdemeanors* (just published by Regnery), one purpose of having an impeachable executive, as opposed to an unremovable monarch, was, as the Framers explained, to enable us to hold the ruler responsible for the misdeeds of his subordinates. Clinton, ironically, is responsible for Starr, who is part of the executive branch.

If Starr "threatens us all," it's Clinton's duty to get rid of him, just as it was his duty to get rid of those who'd illegally acquired hundreds of raw FBI files of Clinton's suspected enemies. Which raises a question.

Why are these pundits so much more upset about Starr than they were about Craig Livingstone and Anthony Marceca? Doesn't building a blackmail data bank "threaten us all"? Does anyone now doubt that Clinton would have used any dirt he could have found on Starr?

Trouble is, there's no dirt to be found on Starr. As far as we know, he's been faithful to his wife. No woman in his employ has accused of him making a lewd pass at her. He hasn't lied to the public. He's never been charged with anything illegal (except by Clinton's spokesmen).

Starr seems to keep good company, too: his friends, unlike so many of Clinton's, manage to stay out of jail.

The liberals have come to prudery rather late in life. They used to ridicule Christians who objected to the federal funding of vile art. Miss Dowd, who speculates (without proof) that Starr enjoys dishing lubricity, wrote a famous lip-smacking piece retailing Kitty Kelley's gossip (also unproved) about Nancy Reagan's sex life. How prim we've become!

Cohen has actually applauded militant homosexuals who outed the son of a prominent conservative, Phyllis Schlafly. In fact blackmailing homosexuals is fine, if done in a good cause: Congressman Barney Frank, the Massachusetts Democrat, once threatened to expose homosexual colleagues who voted the wrong way. Liberals didn't seem to mind.

A new play off Broadway portrays Jesus Christ as a sodomite. But this is apparently less outrageous than presenting the abundant evidence that Bill Clinton has brought sexual perversion to the room where Lincoln signed the Emancipation Proclamation.

After Clinton's seven months of emphatic denial, Starr had to produce emphatic proof. At the last minute, Clinton, knowing he was trapped, tried to upstage the proof with a partial admission that was no more honest than his denial. Now we're told that Starr has given us too much proof.

"Too much" is a judgment call. What would the right amount be, when Clinton has lied and perjured himself, and when he continues to lie even as he pretends to be sorry?

If Clinton believed his own charges against Starr, he'd have fired him long ago. But he knows the same evidence would remain even without Starr. That evidence isn't the product of Starr's diseased imagination; it's the rotten fruit of Clinton's behavior.

Clinton also benefits from a remarkable vein of Smart Set snobbery. His defenders, who include the glittering stars and moguls of Hollywood, harp derisively on the lack of glamour of the Baptist Starr, the frumpish Linda Tripp, the "trailer trash" Paula Jones.

Despite their current prudish poses, Clinton's defenders despise the morality he has flouted. That's why he's their favorite church-going hypocrite: they know he's really on their side against the squares. They don't so much forgive his sins as approve them, and they hate Starr for exposing them.

Seriously: Did Starr really have to spell it out so graphically? Yes, he did. It would be one thing if Clinton had made a single pro forma denial of sexual relations with Monica and left it at that. But he stabbed his finger at us, lied repeatedly, and waged an aggressively mendacious campaign for the better part of a year. Every detail we now know dramatizes the extent of his perfidy. If he'd been accused of financial misconduct, similar lies would have required an equally detailed survey of the ledgers.

If Clinton's relations with Monica weren't "sexual," how can Starr's account of them be pornographic?

Left and Right

OCTOBER 22, 1998

B ill Clinton's defenders, whatever their reservations about his character, can always be rallied around the idea that his enemies are "right-wing." This incantation has a magical power to convince them that Clinton's sins and crimes are too trivial to prosecute, as if Abe Lincoln were being distracted by a nuisance suit in the middle of the Civil War.

The Clinton troops never explain why the "right wing" is bad. They never even define what it is. It's merely a devil-term. In the minds of liberals, anything from a libertarian (who favors severely limited government) to a fascist (who favors total government, though not the kind liberals favor) is "right-wing."

Attila the Hun: the first liberal?

You might think that the right wing, whatever it may be, would be in some measure vindicated by events in its early assessment of Clinton as a cynical and mendacious man. But in the minds of liberals, truth itself is discredited if uttered by the right wing. The right wing is all the more dangerous when it's proven correct!

A standard liberal witticism is to say a given conservative, especially a Christian, is "to the right of Attila the Hun." We're never told what was "right-wing" about Attila. He was a formidable enemy of Christendom and not particularly devoted to limited, constitutional government.

It's somewhat easier to imagine the marauding Attila assisting Joseph Stalin, or even serving in the Bureau of Alcohol, Tobacco, and Firearms, than arguing against the encroachments and usurpations of the federal government. Nor was he likely to have had delicate scruples about abortion, even in the last hours of pregnancy. His alternative lifestyle included mass murder, mass rape, mass torture of hostages, and he was barely deterred from sacking Rome by a bold visit from a right-wing Pope, Leo the Great, who risked his life to plead to Attila in his tent.

If words mean anything, any civilized person is "to the right of Attila the Hun." But the phrase is meant to imply that savagery is on the right, while humanity is to be found on the left, a view that flatters liberals but is somewhat at odds with the history of the twentieth century.

This is no doubt why liberals are coy about admitting that they are "left-wing." The left-leaning news media insist that they are ideologically neutral, but they constantly identify conservatives invidiously as "right-wing," while they seldom refer to liberals as "left-wing." It's this sort of loaded language and verbal camouflage that makes conservatives so suspicious of media claims to impartial reporting.

All of which raises an obvious question. Should our conventional labels be abandoned? Are they nothing more than partisan cusswords? Or is there a way of using the terms "right" and "left" that makes sense in American politics, identifying two broad sides without insulting either?

Throughout American history, the country has been polarized by two opposite tendencies. One, usually prevalent, has been the tendency to centralize power; to increase the powers of the federal government against state and local government; and to amend and construe the Constitution in ways that favor federal power. On this side we may place (somewhat arbitrarily) Alexander Hamilton, Daniel Webster, Lincoln, Theodore and Franklin Roosevelt, Woodrow Wilson, Earl Warren, William Brennan, Lyndon Johnson, the Clintons, and nearly all recent liberals. This side may be fairly called "the left."

The other side has resisted the growth of federal power and has favored a "strict" construction of the Constitution. Most presidents before Lincoln were on this side, notably Jefferson; so were John Calhoun, Grover Cleveland, Calvin Coolidge, Ronald Reagan, and most recent conservatives and libertarians. This side may be fairly called "the right."

We can debate which tradition has the balance of truth, justice, and wisdom. We can argue that neither tradition has a monopoly of political virtue, that both have something to say, that opposing principles may have more or less pertinence at different times.

That's the point. We should be discussing principles, not making wholesale accusations with tendentious nicknames. Rational discussion is impossible if "left" and "right" are reduced to synonyms for good and evil. The essence of civility is the acknowledgment that even your enemy may have something to teach you.

AFTERMATH

Chelsea's Father

AUGUST 6, 1998

One lesson of the Clinton debacle may be that the sexual revolution devours its children. No other president has used his office to promote the sexual revolution — the overthrow of the West's moral code. Clinton has and does. He aggressively favors such causes as "gay rights" and grisly late-term abortions. He has also used his office, as governor and president, to participate actively in the revolution, whose principle is that sex should have no consequences.

The girl comes in handy.

But he's now facing frightful consequences. Never mind whether he's impeached; his place in the annals is already fixed. He's the great dirty joke of American history. Worse yet (if it matters to him as much as it should), he has done terrible things to his family.

Clinton's defenders argue that "it's only sex, and everyone lies about sex." In the first place, sex isn't trivial, and not everyone lies about it. Sexual behavior is an important test of honor. That's the whole point of pledging fidelity in a marriage vow. People lie about sex when they've done something dishonorable.

But the sexual revolution was supposed to do away with sexual hypocrisy by doing away with the need for it. Has it done so? Not if Clinton is any index. Not only has he cheated on his wife throughout their marriage, but he still takes regular Sunday morning photo ops on the church steps, clutching his Bible. Talk about church-going hypocrites.

Clinton has been joined in his duplicity by the feminists who ignore and excuse him, after having impaled Senator Bob Packwood for wet kisses going back twenty years.

The real beneficiaries of the sexual revolution are irresponsible men — men who won't accept marriage and children as the condition of sexual pleasure. Most men feel the price is well worth it. If they had to choose between their children and sex, they wouldn't hesitate. (They might wince, but they wouldn't hesitate.)

Having a child usually changes a man. It changes the whole relation of the self to the world. The ego learns to say "we." A decent man can't bear to hurt his child by doing anything disloyal or disgraceful.

That's the point. It's "only sex"? It's only betrayal and bitter shame for Clinton's only child, the one person in the world he should want to shelter from such things. Maybe he and his wife have an understanding. Besides, Hillary Clinton is herself a public figure, as well as an adult. She can take care of herself. But Chelsea Clinton is different.

Clinton makes a point of being photographed with Chelsea, talks about her in public, and uses her to create the image of a loving family man. So we're entitled to draw some conclusions about his treatment of her. And apparently she's only a prop, like that Bible and Buddy the dog.

Now Clinton is being urged to make a public apology, saying he lied about his amour with Monica Lewinsky to protect Chelsea! Yes, Chelsea certainly comes in handy.

Jay Leno, in a serious mood, remarked the other day that Clinton has never left high school. Exactly. He's the eternally precocious, clever, impressive, but immature class president, outwardly polite to the grownups, secretly cynical about them, in the conviction that he can get away with anything. He can "read" people shrewdly to get what he wants — he's a master of feigned sympathy, full of formulaic liberal "compassion" — but nobody else is quite real to him. He has little enough compassion for the Betty Curries who have to cover for him; in his mind they exist only for his sake.

Even his adulteries display arrested development. The Mitter-and model — a stable relationship with a sort of second family — is not for him. He likes the daring quickie, the new conquest, the young stuff. The risk of doing it in a forbidden place adds to the thrill. He flirts with external consequences because there are no internal ones.

Not even parenthood has taken Clinton outside his self-absorption. When he looks in a mirror, he may see a handsome, dashing lover. What he doesn't see is the only man who might have saved him from himself: Chelsea's father.

Endgame

FEBRUARY 25, 1999

T o my amazement, Bill Clinton has been acquitted. My earnest hope that the Democrats' consciences would make an eleventh-hour stampede has proven vain.

Henry Hyde made some mournful remarks about the polls, but the real problem is what shaped those polls: the Clinton War Room. Only the most aggressive defense could have saved this criminal, and it did. James Carville, the Cajun Goebbels, led the shameless daily propaganda barrage that overwhelmed the relevant facts. And Carville was only one of many Clinton spokesmen who turned on a dime when the fatal dress proved they had been promulgating a pack of lies; after pausing to say they forgave their now-contrite friend, they quickly began promulgating a new pack of lies.

It was ball control. The Republicans play politics the way white men used to play basketball, back when the game was slow and deliberate, and most of the action was dribbling and set shots; lying aside, the Democrats play politics the way blacks play basketball, with speed, steals, leaping, rebounding, and slam dunks. It's a rougher game, but it's also a faster game. You have to grab the ball; you can't wait for it to come to you. The Republicans were outplayed at every turn, and nobody was calling fouls. The white guys lost.

Consider the way the Democrats were able to create new clichés — for example, the line that "the Framers of the Constitution meant for impeachment to be used only against crimes that seriously threaten our democratic form of government." The truth is that the Framers expected impeachment to be a regular part of the process of governing, a way of getting rid of corrupt officials, including corrupt presidents. "High crimes and misdemeanors" don't have to be revolutionary acts. There isn't a syllable of evidence — in the Constitution or the ratification debates — to support the cliché.

But the Republicans never effectively replied to such constitutional ad libs. They were up against a combination of cynicism and velocity, and they couldn't counter it. They never set up their own War Room.

I don't mean to slight the role of dirty tricks. But even these might have backfired if the Republicans had put pressure on the White House and the Democrats to repudiate Carville, Larry Flynt, and blackmailing tactics. Republicans kept wondering why the public wasn't more outraged by their enemies' foul play. Well, public opinion in the media age is notoriously fluid. If the Republicans had themselves expressed more outrage, they might have elicited more of it from ordinary people.

The Democrats did a superb job of manipulating the polls; it wasn't the pollsters' fault. Moral indignation actually worked in favor of a president who had committed sexual perversions in the Oval Office, lied about it for seven months, and committed several felonies, because the Democrats themselves acted far more outraged than the Republicans did. Carville actually called Kenneth Starr "sex-obsessed" and got away with it.

If the Republicans had had their wits about them, they could have made a terrific joke of nonsense like that. Starr isn't the guy who plays with interns and cigars, uses his underlings to procure women, gets sued for sexual harassment, and attracts defenders like Flynt. But they were afraid of their own mission — so afraid that they were speechless when the Democrats accused them of the very things Clinton and the Democrats were guilty of. They couldn't even find irony in the charge of "partisanship"; they earnestly tried to defend themselves against it, without turning it against their accusers. I was often reminded of the late phase of the O. J. Simpson murder trial, when the hapless Marcia Clark was forced to distance herself from Mark Fuhrman instead of discussing whether the defendant had slashed two throats. "It's not the size of the dog in the fight," the old saying goes; "it's the size of the fight in the dog."

Even before Clinton's acquittal, the Republicans were starting to slink away in shame from their own impeachment effort, thereby reinforcing the Democrats' claim that the whole thing was an illegitimate partisan "coup." The House managers did a fine job, as far as it went, but they were undermined by Senate Republican "moderates." Nobody seems to have noticed, by the way, that most of the Senate Republicans who crossed over to vote for acquittal were pro-abortion — a clue to what the larger controversy over Clinton is really about.

Take Arlen Specter — please. The Pennsylvania Republican "moderate" exemplifies what's wrong with the party. At every crucial moment, he betrays the conservatives, and he did it again by voting for acquittal. He tried to straddle the fence by calling the Senate trial a "sham" and denouncing Clinton's behavior, but this only made his Democratic colleagues as angry as his fellow Republicans.

The White House quickly put out the word that it would punish the House managers by seeking their defeat in the 2000 elections, then — this being a time for healing and reconciliation — denied any such intention. If these worthy gentlemen lose their seats, they can thank Republicans like Specter for undermining their efforts.

Well, no good deed goes unpunished. For further confirmation of this adage, behold the career of Christopher Hitchens, the left-wing Brit journalist. Liberals have readily forgiven his bitter invectives against Mother Teresa, but they are ganging up on him, viciously, for revealing that Sidney Blumenthal lied under oath when he denied having called Monica Lewinsky a "stalker." Hitchens says Blumenthal relayed this lie to him and other reporters last year while Clinton was still denying everything. He says his purpose in disclosing it was not to embarrass Blumenthal, but to help undo Clinton, whom he loathes. It was clear to him, he says, that Clinton was the source of the lie.

Washington's liberal set doesn't mind Blumenthal's role as a Clinton flunky; it minds Hitchens's "betrayal" of Blumenthal. Never mind that Blumenthal was betraying (or helping Clinton betray) the press and public by trying to destroy the young woman whom Clinton had only recently been leading on, even encouraging her to think he might eventually marry her; what matters is that Hitchens has proved he isn't a reliable member of the team. Among the charges levelled against him are that he's a "Judas," a drunk, and a Holocaust denier.

Meanwhile, it appears that Hillary Clinton, who joined her husband in lying to the public for most of 1998, will run for the New York Senate seat that Patrick Moynihan is retiring from next year. And in Arkansas, Judge Susan Webber Wright may hold Bill in contempt for perjuring himself in the Paula Jones suit. Which may help Kenneth Starr if he is still considering indicting this scoundrel.

The Moral Mafia

MARCH 11, 1999

O ne of the best things written about Bill Clinton's acquittal was "Parliament of Wimps" by George Kendall, in
the February 25 issue of *The Wanderer,* arguing that
abortion is the thread that runs from *Roe v. Wade* through the
Senate's rejection of Robert Bork to that same Senate's acquittal
of Clinton. Never mind character. Never mind crimes. Bork was
"unfit" for the Supreme Court because he was anti-abortion.
Clinton is "fit" for the presidency because he is pro-abortion. It's
just that simple. Even most of the Republicans who voted to acquit Clinton were pro-abortion.

Paul Weyrich has acknowledged that a "moral majority" no
longer exists in this country. But we do have a sort of moral mafia
— a vast left-wing nonconspiracy, if you will, which comprises a
power elite and its popular following, united in their alienation
from Christianity.

I've nicknamed this social formation "the Hive," because it
operates like bees and other cooperative insects. The specialists
perform their various functions spontaneously, without secret
central direction; but their free actions as individuals harmonize
to produce a certain social order.

The Hive distrusted Jimmy Carter because of his Christian
sincerity; by the same token, it trusts Bill Clinton because of his
Christian hypocrisy. It has to love a guy who can carry a Bible
while cheating on his wife and promoting Hive morality (which
is inseparable from the Hive economy). He can't keep faith with
anyone, but his own interests and appetites make him a pretty
reliable bee.

Those interests and appetites, along with his hypocrisy, also
make his endless scandals inevitable. His supporters are open
advocates of practices he can't fully espouse, even though he
engages in them too.

Now it appears that Clinton has taken sexual freedom all the way, by taking the ultimate liberty: rape. Juanita Broaddrick's accusation is totally plausible, and Clinton's denial isn't. And there have been reports of other rapes, going all the way back to Oxford University in 1969.

According to a new rumor, Clinton is telling his aides that he did have sex with Juanita Broaddrick in 1978, but that it was "consensual." His statement, made through his lawyer, denied only that he "assaulted" her. He won't release records of where he was on the day of the alleged rape, which suggests that the records would show he was at the Little Rock hotel where Mrs. Broaddrick says it happened. So "consensual" may be the only fallback defense left to him if the story won't go away.

And it won't go away. The pundits are fascinated by it. The networks are ignoring it the way they ignored Paula Jones for several years, but close observers of Clinton believe it. They will keep it in reserve until more evidence emerges or other women make charges.

Since Mrs. Broaddrick hasn't been destroyed, other women may now be emboldened to tell their stories. Rape victims may not want to go public, but victims of hotel-room flashings and other less traumatic Clintonian amatory maneuvers can probably come forward safely. Clinton told Monica Lewinsky that if he settled the Paula Jones suit, "hundreds" of other women might be encouraged to take legal action against him.

Meanwhile, a new book called *Gideon's Spies: The Secret History of the Mossad,* by Gordon Thomas (published by St. Martin's Press), says the Israelis bugged Clinton's phone sex calls to Monica and used them to blackmail him. Is it true? Clinton himself told Monica that a foreign embassy was tapping her apartment phones. But even if not, the story is a reminder of Clinton's fantastic recklessness and his willingness to put the country's safety at risk for a sexual thrill.

If the story is true, it's also another reminder of Israel's treachery toward its chief benefactor. The unspoken fear of Jewish power in this country can be measured by the fact that to this day, no high U.S. official, elected or otherwise, dares to refer publicly to the Pollard spy case, let alone discuss what it implies.

Israel is said to have a mole in the White House, whom the Justice Department and FBI have been unable to identify; but the Israelis deny it, saying they stopped such operations after Pollard was caught. But why should they stop? The chief lesson of the Pollard case is that the U.S. Government lacks the spine to make them pay for any betrayal. They have never returned a single document Pollard stole, and they have never lost a single dollar of U.S. aid.

Blackmailing an American president would be in character for the Israelis, and Clinton is eminently eligible. The president who gets away with everything is made to order for the country that gets away with everything.

Clinton the Klutz

SEPTEMBER 9, 1999

B ill Clinton is a genius at all the low arts of politics. He has tested the few remaining limits on presidential power by raising campaign funds from foreign donors, citing executive privilege to frustrate a criminal investigation, waging undeclared war, issuing unwarranted executive orders, renting out the Lincoln Bedroom, etc. What will he think of next?

The failure of Congress to remove Clinton from office last winter only removed his restraints. He now figures he can get away with anything, even what might otherwise be impeachable offenses. He isn't embarrassed to tell outright lies that nobody really believes. The Republicans feel that if they really take him on, he will win.

But for that reason, he may also have a hubris problem. After all, he has also committed some terrific blunders. He began his first term by trying to legitimate sodomy in the armed forces. His national health care plan took a nosedive. He got his famous runway haircut at Los Angeles International Airport (though a persistent rumor says he wasn't actually having his hair cut). He failed to drum up support for war on Iraq. And there was the Lewinsky business: though he escaped justice, he paid heavily for his lechery, perjury, lying to the public, and recklessness.

Now he has committed another faux pas. Once more abusing his presidential power, he has offered pardons to sixteen convicted Puerto Rican terrorists (members of the Armed Forces for National Liberation, or FALN, and an offshoot group) for the purpose of helping his wife's Senate campaign in New York, where nearly a million Puerto Ricans live. It's all the more remarkable in that Clinton has rarely exercised his power to pardon before, as either governor or president, and in that he has been willing to bomb even *suspected* terrorist bases across the globe. (The Sudanese pill factory, bombed a year ago as a terrorist chemical plant, turned out to be nothing of the sort, but it was time for urgent measures: Clinton was about to be cross-examined by Kenneth Starr's team. Even as everyone compared it to the film *Wag the Dog,* Clinton got away with wagging the dog.)

This move, approved and probably inspired by Hillary, has backfired badly. In the first place, it was too transparently cynical to work. Second, it could hardly attract enough Puerto Rican voters to justify the cost. Third, New York, with its heavily Jewish electorate, is the worst place to be seen as coddling terrorists of any description.

Daniel Patrick Moynihan, whose Senate seat Hillary is seeking, has blasted the proposed pardons. So has most of the press, citing FALN bombings that have killed, maimed, and blinded several policemen. The FBI and other concerned federal officials solidly opposed the idea, but Clinton ignored their objections.

The proffered pardons have conditions attached, chiefly that the recipients must renounce violence and the FALN. But they appear unwilling to do this. Since 1993, when a petition for pardon was submitted to the White House on their behalf, none of them has expressed the slightest remorse, repudiated their comrades, or asked for mercy. They prefer to serve their prison sentences, which run up to seventy years. They may be fanatics, but they are more principled than Clinton — who for six years took no interest in the case, until his wife was running for office.

The Clintons don't try very hard to be subtle, even when they're using the powers of the presidency for sheer personal advantage. Once again Bill has blundered because of his own inability to anticipate the reactions of people who actually believe in something. He is incredibly crass, with a conscience as impenetrable as a tortoise shell.

Dick Morris, Clinton's former advisor and now his fierce critic, says Mayor Rudy Giuliani, Hillary's likely opponent, could probably win the election on the pardon issue alone. It would take only a few TV campaign spots featuring the policemen who were left blind and legless by FALN bombs. If only Giuliani weren't pro-abortion! It's very hard not to root for him in this contest, but of course we mustn't.

An Alternative to Impeachment

NOVEMBER 19, 1998

The Democrats say Bill Clinton shouldn't be impeached because his offenses aren't that serious. The Republicans say censure would be too mild a punishment. Is there a third alternative?

Happily, there is. This reporter hit upon it after giving up on the weary haggling of the CNBC talk shows and yielding the TV to his eleven-year-old grandson, who switched the channel to professional wrestling. A few moments later, an idea was born.

It is simply this. The lengthy impeachment process should be abandoned, and the president should be put into the ring with Minnesota's Governor-elect Jesse Ventura, who could body-slam him a few times. No choking or kicking or banging his head into those corner things; just a little airplane spinning and a few good bounces off the canvas, punctuated by apposite shouts. ("That's for obstructing justice!" "That's for lying to the American people!" "That's for Kathleen Willey!")

It goes without saying (in case the Secret Service is reading this) that no serious injury would be inflicted. Governor Ventura would be instructed to desist when the president's body had turned red all over, but before any bones were broken. Before raising the obvious objection that such an encounter would be "violent," consider that this is the same president who once said he'd like to punch an aging columnist for calling his wife a liar. What goes around, comes around.

Except for a few right-wing extremists, most people would find this a sufficient penalty, including many Democrats and White House aides who have had to defend this president. So, probably, would Mrs. Clinton, who could both take some satisfaction and continue as first lady. Maybe a Supreme Court justice could serve as referee.

That way a chastened Clinton could still serve out his term, though Vice President Gore might have to fill in for a few days, during which parents of White House interns might enjoy some peace of mind. Granted, this solution wouldn't do much for the dignity of the presidency, but that's pretty much shot by now anyway.

Governor Ventura (who was not consulted before this article was written) might not be willing to do this without some assurances that Clinton won't pull some dirty tricks in the ring. After all, he is used to dealing with a relatively honorable class of people. Come to think of it, the event might demean the dignity of wrestling. But that is a risk the nation must be willing to take.

A further possible result might be that Governor Ventura would emerge from the encounter as a viable third-party presidential candidate for the year 2000. In fact he might be the first third-party candidate to run unopposed.

Uninhibited wrestling matches could replace debates as the highlight of our presidential campaigns. They would be a lot more interesting, somewhat more civilized, and less mortifying to behold. It would be difficult for the participants to lie. The public wouldn't feel that its intelligence was being insulted, and we wouldn't need a panel of pundits after the event to tell us who had won.

Such a format would probably invite a new generation of office-seeking wrestlers, but we could use some new faces, even if some of them were wearing masks. And there would be no further need for term limits and other gimmicks to dislodge incumbents. We could watch them being thrown out. Literally.

The old labels — liberal, conservative; left, right; Republican, Democrat — would become useless, and we would have to find fresh terms in which to define the issues. Most of these fresh terms would, of necessity, be words of one syllable, some of which may be unfamiliar in a political context, though not in a professional wrestling context.

Like all reforms and truly new ideas, this one would be sure to encounter reactionary opposition. Monarchists used to reject proposals for popular elections as turning government over to "the rabble," and advocates of elections would no doubt say the same thing about wrestling. But let's not waste our breath trying to reason with such people; there is nothing more powerful than an idea whose time has come.

Index

Note: The letter "n" following a page number indicates that the reference is to be found in the nuggets printed in boldface at the end of an article.

Ford, Gerald: 201.
Foreign Affairs: 81.
Foster, Vince: 17–18, 113–14, 115, 121, 175, 176.
Founding Fathers: 10, 42, 78, 144, 152–53, 156n, 218, 244–45.
Four Freedoms: 54.
Framers of the Constitution. See *Founding Fathers.*
Frank, Barney: 58, 173, 183n, 216, 226, 230n, 235.
Freemen: 43–44.
Fuhrman, Mark: 245.

Gantry, Elmer: xv, 193.
Generation X: xii.
George III, king of England: 19.
Germany: 70.
Gideon's Spies: The Secret History of the Mossad: 249.
Gingrich, Newt: xii, 38, 49, 201, 215.
Giuliani, Rudolph: 252.
Godfather, The: 99, 128, 136, 198.
Goldwater, Barry: 29.
Gore, Al, Jr.: 35, 70, 116, 121, 172, 254.
Grady, Sandy: 84.
Great Society: 29, 41.
Greenberg, Paul: 16.
Greenfield, Meg: 21.
Guinness, Sir Alec: 93.
Gulag Archipelago: 49.
Gulf War: 46, 65–66, 72.

Haiti: 40.
Hall, Gus: 2–3.
Hamilton, Alexander: 86, 152, 161–62, 238.
Hefner, Hugh: 85, 130.
Hersh, Seymour: 75.
High Crimes and Misdemeanors: xi, 152–53, 234.
High Noon: 194.
Hill, Anita: xvii, 123, 128.
Hiss, Alger: xii, 1, 4, 85, 177n, 208, 229–30.
Hitchens, Christopher: 246–47.
Hitler, Adolf: xvii, 27n, 40, 107, 135.
"Hive": 248.
Ho Chi Minh: xvii.

Homosexuality: 8, 9, 11, 14, 23, 28–29, 36, 38, 40, 53, 129, 210, 233n, 235, 241.
Hot Springs (Arkansas): 43.
House Judiciary Committee: xix, 183n, 192, 218, 219, 222.
Huang, John: 18.
Hubbell, Webster: 148, 203.
Hussein, Saddam: 40, 66.
Hustler: xi, 60–61.
Hyde, Henry: 58, 59n, 215, 216, 244.

Imus, Don: 12, 159.
Independent Counsel Law: xiii.
Invasion of the Body Snatchers: 51n.
Iran: 66.
Iraq: 44n, 65–66, 77, 78, 80–81, 251.
Isikoff, Michael: 125.
Israel: 70, 249–50.

Jackson, Jesse: 61.
Japan: 70.
Jefferson, Thomas: 13, 52, 54, 238.
John Birch Society: 29.
Johnson, Andrew: 144–45, 173.
Johnson, Lyndon: xvii, 9, 41, 48, 65, 72, 89, 95, 101, 107, 146, 238.
Johnson, Paul: 17.
Johnson, Samuel: 18.
Jones, Paula: xii, xiii, xvii, xviii, 11, 13–14, 18, 55n, 59n, 81, 104, 123–24, 125–26, 127, 129, 132, 136, 138, 140, 145, 148–51, 154, 164, 176, 182, 184, 187, 192, 195, 215, 218, 231, 236, 247, 249.
Jordan, Vernon: 105, 148, 170, 177.

Kelley, Kitty: 194n, 235.
Kelley, Virginia (Bill Clinton's mother): 63, 120.
Kendall, David: 141, 190.
Kendall, George: 248.
Kennedy, Edward: xi, 214, 226, 233n.
Kennedy, John F.: 9, 11, 13, 14, 31, 103n, 185, 214.
Kennedy, Joseph: 4, 228.
Kenya: 67.
King, Martin Luther, Jr.: 14, 68, 185.
Kerrey, Robert: 232.
Kinsey, Alfred: 15–16.

O'Brien, Conan: 12.

Packwood, Robert: 242.
Pakistan: 69.
Panama: 44n.
Partial-birth abortion. See *abortion.*
Pearl Harbor: 69–70.
Peguy, Charles: 46.
Peron, Juan: xvii.
Perot, Ross: 9, 36.
Pincus, Walter: 86.
Pity of War, The: 82.
Playboy: 213.
Pol Pot: xvii, 136.
Pollard, Leon: 249–50.
Powell, Colin: 9.
Presley, Elvis: 31.
Primary Colors: 133.
Psycho: 61.
"Pumpkin Papers": 208, 229.

Quayle, Dan: 34, 35.
Quinn, Jack: 135.

Rainbow Coalition: 185.
Rather, Dan: 78.
Reagan, Nancy: 194n, 235.
Reagan, Ronald: 23, 31, 78–79, 100, 145, 146, 201, 212, 238.
Reno, Janet: 86, 99, 173.
Richard III: 7, 90.
Richardson, Bill: 84.
Ripken, Cal: 136.
Rivera, Geraldo: xi, xvi, 182, 232.
Robertson, Pat: xii.
Roche, Sir Boyle: 92.
Rockefeller Foundation: 15.
Rockwell, Norman: 45.
Roe v. Wade: 248.
Roosevelt, Eleanor: 93.
Roosevelt, Franklin Delano: xvii, 4, 8, 9, 23, 38, 40, 48, 49, 54, 70, 84–85, 93, 101–102, 144, 145, 201, 204, 205, 210, 238.
Rosenberg, Julius and Ethel: 1.
Rostenkowsky, Dan: 37.
Rushmore, Mount: 13.
Russert, Tim: 12, 232.
Russia: 81.
Russian Revolution: 49.

Ruth, George Herman (Babe): 21.

Salon: 59n.
Sandel, Michael: 101.
Satan: 56–59.
Saving Private Ryan: 179.
Sawyer, Diane: 131.
Schlafly, Phyllis: 235.
Senate Whitewater Committee: 113, 114.
Serbia (see also *Yugoslavia*): 74.
Shafarevich, Igor: 209.
Shakespeare, William: xi, 5–7, 20, 53, 57, 90, 159–60, 164.
Sharpton, Al: 185.
Shays, Christopher: 141.
Sheen, Bishop Fulton J.: 45.
Sidwell Friends School: 25–27, 37.
Simpson, O. J.: 17, 97–98, 104, 134, 167, 169, 177n, 245.
  Bruno Magli shoes: 98, 141.
60 Minutes: 11.
Smeal, Eleanor: xvi.
Social Security: xv, 48, 49.
Somalia: 40, 44n.
South Africa: 69.
South America: 11.
Soviet Union: 4, 46, 69.
Specter, Arlen: 179, 246.
Spence, Jerry: xvi.
Spielberg, Steven: 182.
Spin Cycle: 128.
Spotlight, The: 70.
Springer, Jerry: 133, 185.
Stalin, Joseph: xvii, 3, 4, 8, 19n, 20, 26, 27n, 48, 55, 75, 84–85, 97, 111n, 187, 201, 203, 205, 210, 237.
Starr, Kenneth: 59n, 104, 131–32, 134, 135, 138, 150, 154, 160, 166, 167, 169–71, 173, 174n, 175, 176, 178–79, 182, 183n, 184, 185, 187, 189, 190, 191n, 193, 194n, 208, 215, 217n, 229, 232, 233, 234–36, 236n, 245, 247, 252.
Steffens, Lincoln: 85.
Steinem, Gloria: 32, 130, 164, 210.
Stephanopolous, George: 25, 92.
Stephens, Alexander: 42–43.
Stern, Howard: 185.
Stevenson, Adlai: 37.

Joe Sobran

Joe Sobran has been a nationally syndicated columnist since 1979. He was a senior editor of *National Review* for 18 years and a regular commentator on CBS Radio's *Spectrum* series from 1979 to 1991.

Sobran's path-breaking book on the Shakespeare authorship question, *Alias Shakespeare* (The Free Press), appeared in 1997. He is also the author of *Single Issues: Essays on the Crucial Social Questions,* published in 1983. He is currently writing a book on the abandonment of the Constitution. Sobran is a lecturer and speaker who appears frequently on major talk shows and at conferences around the world.

In 1994, he founded his monthly newsletter, *SOBRAN'S,* which is available in print and electronically. His twice-weekly column, distributed by Griffin Internet Syndicate, is available by e-mail subscription. Archived columns and other material are stored at the *SOBRAN'S* website at www.sobran.com.

Joe Sobran lives in Burke, Virginia, a suburb of Washington, D.C.

This book was made possible through the generosity of many
SOBRAN'S supporters including the following:

Mr. Jeffrey Arnold
Mrs. Ute Bailey
Mr. and Mrs. Jack Barrett
Mr. William Borst
Mr. John G. Breen
Mr. Philip Brumder
Mr. and Mrs. Robert Buzard
Mr. William J. Casagranda
Mr. and Mrs. John Cianflone
Mr. Duncan Clark
Mr. Christopher Condon
Mr. John C. Cooke
Mr. J. Douglas Cooper
Mr. and Mrs. Dale Crowley
Sir John and Lady Dalhoff
Mr. and Mrs. John Deardeuff
Mr. Robert W. Demers
Mr. and Mrs. Tom DiJulia
Dr. William Campbell Douglass
Mr. Brendan Eich
Mrs. Zadalee Furlano
Mr. Victor Gerhard
Mr. and Mrs. James Gimpel
Mr. and Mrs. Robert Hale
Mr. Parker Harvey
Dr. Michael R. Heaphy
Mr. Frank Hegarty
Mr. Michael Humphrey
Dr. and Mrs. George D. Jacobs
Mr. and Mrs. J. B. Jamieson
Mr. Bill Jasper
Mr. Franklin Lee Johnson
Mr. G. E. Johnson
Dr. Peter Jost
Dr. Eleanor Kelly

Mr. Andrew I. Killgore
Dr. Richard J. Kossmann
Rev. Edward Krause
Dr. and Mrs. Steven J. Lantier
Mr. Dominic Lemma
Prof. Leonard P. Liggio
Ms. Susan Claire Loeffel
Lois O. Conkle Revocable Trust
Mrs. Patricia Lynch
Dr. and Mrs. Francis Macaulay
Mr. Carl Mansfield
Mr. Thomas McCarthy
Mr. J. Laurence McCarty
Mrs. A. Ruth McFarland
Mr. Steve J. Medve
Rev. Matthew Mitas
Mr. Paul D. Molineaux
Mrs. Joan Naylor
Dr. and Mrs. David L. Nelson
Mr. Steven A. Nemeth
Mr. Robert E. Nye
Mr. Eugene Owens
Dr. and Mrs. Leon Podles
Mr. and Mrs. James Raines
Col. and Mrs. John G. Schmitz
Mr. and Mrs. Lester B. Searer
Major Reginald Shinn
Mr. Norman Singleton
Mr. and Mrs. Frank Sklaris
Mrs. Jerome C. Slad
Mr. and Mrs. Bennett Smith
Mr. Edward C. Smith
Dr. G. Keith Smith
Mr. and Mrs. Howard Walsh
Mr. Jon Basil Utley